If Only It Were Fiction

THE AZRIELI SERIES OF HOLOCAUST SURVIVOR MEMOIRS:
PREVIOUSLY PUBLISHED TITLES

ENGLISH TITLES

Album of My Life by Ann Szedlecki
Bits and Pieces by Henia Reinhartz
A Drastic Turn of Destiny by Fred Mann
E/96: Fate Undecided by Paul-Henri Rips
Fleeing from the Hunter by Marian Domanski
From Generation to Generation by Agnes Tomasov
Gatehouse to Hell by Felix Opatowski
Getting Out Alive by Tommy Dick
If Home Is Not Here by Max Bornstein
Knocking on Every Door by Anka Voticky
Little Girl Lost by Betty Rich
Memories from the Abyss by William Tannenzapf / *But I Had a Happy Childhood* by
  Renate Krakauer
The Shadows Behind Me by Willie Sterner
Spring's End by John Freund
Survival Kit by Zuzana Sermer
Tenuous Threads by Judy Abrams / *One of the Lucky Ones*
  by Eva Felsenburg Marx
Under the Yellow and Red Stars by Alex Levin
The Violin by Rachel Shtibel / *A Child's Testimony* by Adam Shtibel

TITRES FRANÇAIS

L'Album de ma vie par Ann Szedlecki
Cachée par Marguerite Elias Quddus
Étoile jaune, étoile rouge par Alex Levin
La Fin du printemps par John Freund
Fragments de ma vie par Henia Reinhartz
Frapper à toutes les portes par Anka Voticky
De génération en génération par Agnes Tomasov
Matricule E/96 par Paul-Henri Rips
Objectif : survivre par Tommy Dick
Souvenirs de l'abîme par William Tannenzapf / *Le Bonheur de l'innocence* par
  Renate Krakauer
Un terrible revers de fortune par Fred Mann
Traqué par Marian Domanski
Le Violon par Rachel Shtibel / *Témoignage d'un enfant* par Adam Shtibel

If Only It Were Fiction

Elsa Thon

FIRST EDITION
Copyright © 2013 The Azrieli Foundation and others

THE AZRIELI FOUNDATION
www.azrielifoundation.org

Cover and book design by Mark Goldstein
Endpaper maps by Martin Gilbert
Map on page xxv by François Blanc
Photo 3 on page 245 courtesy of Elwina Pokrywka

LIBRARY AND ARCHIVES CANADA CATALOGUING IN PUBLICATION

Thon, Elsa, 1923–, author
    If only it were fiction/ Elsa Thon.

(Azrieli series of Holocaust survivor memoirs. Series 5)
Includes bibliographical references and index.
ISBN 978-1-897470-33-6 (pbk.)

1. Thon, Elsa, 1923–. 2. Holocaust, Jewish (1939–1945) – Poland – Personal narratives. 3. World War, 1939–1945 – Underground movements – Poland. 4. Jews – Poland – Biography. 5. Polish Canadians – Biography. I. Azrieli Foundation II. Title. III. Series: Azrieli series of Holocaust survivor memoirs. Series; v

DS135.P63T46 2013   940.53'18092   C2013-902772-6

PRINTED IN CANADA

The Azrieli Series of Holocaust Survivor Memoirs

INTERNATIONAL ADVISORY COUNCIL

Doris Bergen, Chancellor Rose and Ray Wolfe Chair in Holocaust
 Studies, University of Toronto
Sara R. Horowitz, Director of the Israel and Golda Koschitzky
 Centre for Jewish Studies, York University
Nechama Tec, Professor Emerita of Sociology, University of
 Connecticut
Avner Shalev, Chairman of the Yad Vashem Directorate, Jerusalem

Naomi Azrieli, Publisher

Andrea Knight, Managing Editor
Jody Spiegel, Program Director
Arielle Berger, Editor
Elizabeth Lasserre, Senior Editor, French-Language Editions
Aurélien Bonin, Assistant Editor / Researcher, French-Language Editions
Elin Beaumont, Educational Outreach and Communications
Tim MacKay, Social Media and Marketing
Susan Roitman, Executive Coordinator (Toronto)
Mary Mellas, Executive Coordinator (Montreal)
Michaela Ryan, Program Assistant

Mark Goldstein, Art Director
Nicolas Côté, Layout, French-Language Editions
François Blanc, Cartographer

Contents

Series Preface:
In their own words...

In telling these stories, the writers have liberated themselves. For so many years we did not speak about it, even when we became free people living in a free society. Now, when at last we are writing about what happened to us in this dark period of history, knowing that our stories will be read and live on, it is possible for us to feel truly free. These unique historical documents put a face on what was lost, and allow readers to grasp the enormity of what happened to six million Jews – one story at a time.

David J. Azrieli, C.M., C.Q., M.Arch
Holocaust survivor and founder, The Azrieli Foundation

Since the end of World War II, over 30,000 Jewish Holocaust survivors have immigrated to Canada. Who they are, where they came from, what they experienced and how they built new lives for themselves and their families are important parts of our Canadian heritage. The Azrieli Foundation's Holocaust Survivor Memoirs Program was established to preserve and share the memoirs written by those who survived the twentieth-century Nazi genocide of the Jews of Europe and later made their way to Canada. The program is guided by the conviction that each survivor of the Holocaust has a remarkable story to tell, and that such stories play an important role in education about tolerance and diversity.

Millions of individual stories are lost to us forever. By preserving the stories written by survivors and making them widely available to a broad audience, the Azrieli Foundation's Holocaust Survivor Memoirs Program seeks to sustain the memory of all those who perished at the hands of hatred, abetted by indifference and apathy. The personal accounts of those who survived against all odds are as different as the people who wrote them, but all demonstrate the courage, strength, wit and luck that it took to prevail and survive in such terrible adversity. The memoirs are also moving tributes to people – strangers and friends – who risked their lives to help others, and who, through acts of kindness and decency in the darkest of moments, frequently helped the persecuted maintain faith in humanity and courage to endure. These accounts offer inspiration to all, as does the survivors' desire to share their experiences so that new generations can learn from them.

The Holocaust Survivor Memoirs Program collects, archives and publishes these distinctive records and the print editions are available free of charge to libraries, educational institutions and Holocaust-education programs across Canada, and at Azrieli Foundation educational events. They are also available for sale to the general public at bookstores.

The Azrieli Foundation would like to express appreciation to the following people for their invaluable efforts in producing this book: Sherry Dodson (Maracle Press), Sir Martin Gilbert, Farla Klaiman, Elwina Pokrywka, Mia Spiro, and Margie Wolfe and Emma Rodgers of Second Story Press.

About the Glossary

The following memoir contains a number of terms, concepts and historical references that may be unfamiliar to the reader. For information on major organizations; significant historical events and people; geographical locations; religious and cultural terms; and foreign-language words and expressions that will help give context and background to the events described in the text, please see the glossary beginning on page 225.

Introduction

The two recurring threads that weave together Elsa Thon's beautifully written, clear-sighted and poignant memoir are her love of family and her deep belief in destiny. How else but fate to explain that she is the lone survivor of her close-knit family? Thoughts of her parents and her older sister, Regina, radiate from nearly every page. Even her thoughts of family before she was born – as in the imaginary excerpt from her paternal grandmother's diary based on stories told to her by her mother – are full of love, loss, regret and a mother's imprecations against war.

It took Elsa half a century to be able to write about what she experienced during the five years of the Holocaust, the "adventures, entanglements and terrible blows – a life in hiding, forged documents, the privations of labour camps and the rigours of a forced march." Although the process of writing about her parents and her sister was painful, she also felt the urgency of the task. "I am in a hurry," she writes in her preface. "It is getting late, and my memory is not quite as efficient as it used to be.... I am the only one left to tell their story."

⌒

Elsa Thon was born Balbinka Synalewicz on January 10, 1923, in Pruszków, Poland, and her childhood was blessed by her parents' love story. When the family sat around the kitchen table – before the advent of television, she reminds us – she and her sister, Regina, couldn't get enough of hearing about how her parents had stayed true to each other at a time – World War I – when letters were few, and Elsa's mother, Sonia Samoilovna Pishnow, was not without other suitors.

Her Polish father, Nachman Synalewicz, had been recruited into the Russian army and met her mother in her home town near St. Petersburg before he was sent to the front, where he spent years before he was captured, placed in a prisoner of war camp, escaped and was re-captured. By the time he made a second successful escape and arrived at Sonia's sister Masha's home in the Ukraine near the Polish border, Sonia had waited nine long years. But the couple had no peace – falsely accused of treason by a jilted suitor of Sonia's, a judge ordered Nachman, along with his wife, Sonia, and their daughter, Regina, to return to Poland.

These were the stories that flowed across the kitchen table. Ever dramatic, ever a testament to their love. After they had settled and started a new life in Pruszków, another daughter was born, Elsa.

Next to her family, Elsa's other great love was "her" Poland, the Poland before World War II, the Poland that "had the shape of a heart." She inherited her patriotic feeling for Poland from her father and tells us: "It was true love that we felt for our country." This love for Poland was also reinforced by Elsa's school and she writes with great pride of the Polish artists and scientists – both Jews and non-Jews – who made contributions to world music, the arts and scientific discovery.

Jews had lived in Poland for close to one thousand years, protected by such Polish rulers as Bolesław the Pious, whose 1264 General Charter of Jewish Liberties granted Jews the freedom of worship, trade and travel, and King Casimir the Great, whose 1332 Wiślicki Statute freed Jews from paying additional taxes and lifted restrictions as to where they could live. As a result of this history of tolerance, Poland had the largest Jewish population of any European nation at the time. Pogroms were not unknown – in 1648, for example, 200,000 Jews were murdered in a peasant uprising – and there was an active policy of Polonization, but the country was still one of the safest places for Jews in Europe until the late nineteenth century. Beginning in 1881, however, increasing antisemitism and a violent new wave of pogroms triggered a surge in emigration, especially immigration to the United States.

By the end of World War I, the Jewish population in Poland was mostly urban, compared to the primarily rural Polish Catholic population, and practiced a spectrum of professions in the towns and cities where they lived. Between World War I and II, 10 per cent of the population of Poland was Jewish and about 30 per cent of that population lived in Warsaw. They mainly engaged in industry and commerce, and included numerous independent craftsmen and shopkeepers. Many were Polonized, having become to different degrees assimilated, but many held to their religious observances and created schools and robust synagogues. The Polish capital of Warsaw was home to a vibrant and thriving Jewish quarter.

Elsa's family was observant, but she and her sister attended state schools. Education was important to them – when Elsa dreamed of becoming an acrobat or a street singer, her disapproving father nagged her to study math. The family spoke three languages at home – Russian, Polish and Yiddish – and Elsa's passion was writing. Her father was very proud of the poetry she began writing at the age of eleven. That too ended when the Nazis invaded: "When the war broke out," Elsa writes, "I lost both five years of my writing and my hopes – they turned into ashes, to oblivion."

Indeed, just before the invasion of Poland, Elsa's life was full of promise. Having finished one level of schooling and contemplating what to do next, she had taken a job as a photograph retoucher. She had done so well that her employer had persuaded a photography school in Warsaw to take her as a student, even though ordinarily the school was only open to Warsaw residents. The future couldn't have looked brighter.

Then Germany invaded Poland on September 1, 1939. When the Soviet Red Army invaded on the eastern front on September 17, the Polish army recognized defeat and by October 6, Germany and the Soviet Union had divided Poland between them. In their western portion of the country, the German occupying forces quickly established Jewish ghettos, transit and forced labour camps. The "Final Solution," the explicitly planned murder of Jews, was not formalized until 1941, but the occupying army put the ghettos in place in order to concretize well-established Nazi racial policies. In December 1941, the occupying German forces opened the first killing centre in Chełmno to deal with Poland's Jewish population.

One of the underpinnings of Nazi propaganda was to blame much of what was happening in the larger society, from unemployment to Bolshevism, on Jews. The first two Nuremberg Laws passed in Germany in 1935 established an understanding of who was a Jew and forbid marriage between Jews and "Aryans" – the Nazi term for Germanic peoples. These policies were developed from an elementary understanding of evolution that the Nazis developed into a theory of the division of the human race into higher and lower forms of order. Jews, and later Roma and Negroes, were considered lower forms, and therefore the so-called Aryan race had to protect itself from contamination by them. These theories were adopted by the Nazis in an extreme form to lead to a belief that all lower forms of humanity should be exterminated, starting with the Jews.

The Germans began by moving as many Jews as possible from villages and towns to larger cities and specific Jewish neighbourhoods. Then they isolated those neighbourhoods and began deportations to labour and death camps, as well as organizing groups of workers for factories. Those groups would move in and out of the ghetto, but the ghetto itself was isolated. Housing was crammed, food was scarce, and medical care was severely limited.

When the persecutions started, Elsa's family was first sent to the ghetto in Pruszków. As Pruszków had a large Jewish population, the camp was overcrowded and without the necessary basics. The family was then transported by truck to the Warsaw ghetto.

The Warsaw ghetto was first established by decree on October 2, 1940, and by April 1941 contained about 460,000 inhabitants. The whole process of ghettoization was central to Nazi plans implemented immediately after the invasion. First, Jews were forced from their jobs or had to sell their businesses (usually at a considerable loss). Extraordinary taxes were applied to all Jewish activities. All Jews over the age of eleven were required to wear white armbands with the Star of David. Random attacks, thefts and humiliations were perpetrated by German soldiers and the non-Jewish population without repercussion.

When all Jews were ordered to move to the ghetto, entire families carried what they could from their homes to this restricted area. Two, three or four families often had to occupy housing meant for one. In the first few weeks the boundaries of the ghetto were quite fluid, based in the core of the Jewish district, and arguments about who should be inside or outside the ghetto borders would be presented by occupants, street by street. Some streets were exempt because, for example, a Christian church was located on the corner.

During this period, occupants managed to move in and out of the Warsaw ghetto; to some extent, Polish and Jewish police turned a blind eye to the smuggling of goods in exchange for food. With German occupation, the Polish population in general had been issued food coupons, but Jews received so little in coupons that the food allocated – even if it could be found – was not enough to live on. Bartering became a way of life. Women and children were often the best conduits of material in and out of the ghetto, the children because they could squeeze through fences and between narrow buildings to the outside world. That became much more difficult when the ghetto was sealed off with a wall and barbed wire on November 16, 1940. At that time, about 30 per cent of the population was crowded into less than 3 per cent of the city. That population increased with the enforced removal of Jews from the villages and towns surrounding Warsaw; as was the case in most ghettos, the Nazis were transporting Jews from all towns and villages to larger urban centres or camps.

Soon after the Synalewicz family had established themselves in the Warsaw ghetto in January 1941, Elsa's sister, Regina, joined one of the many Zionist youth movements that flourished in Poland during the interwar period. The organizations varied in the radicalism of their politics, their degree of religious observance, the language used – Yiddish or Hebrew – and how the group thought they should achieve their objectives, but, in the end, the goal was the same for all: preparing their members to become *chalutzim* (pioneers) in British Mandate Palestine and help establish a new state of Israel. Two of the best known among these organizations were left-wing Hashomer Hatzair and Dror, and Elsa, following Regina, joined the latter, which was particularly active in the Warsaw ghetto. In pursuit of their ideal of a Jewish state the movements directed their energies toward educating young Jews for life in pre-state Israel – teaching them everything from Jewish literature to agricultural methods – and establishing *kibbutzim* (collective farms) to train kibbutz members. These *kibbutzim* were eventually dismantled during the occupation (sometimes disbanded outright; sometimes by turning them over to non-Jews), but in the early days after the invasion, some Jewish youth went to the farms to escape the ghettos.

It was hard for Elsa to leave her mother to join her sister in the Dror commune, but harder still when she was separated from Regina and sent to a collective farm in Czerniaków, ten kilometres from Warsaw. Nonetheless, Elsa prospered there in her own way, her cheerfulness inspiring her sister to accuse her in a letter of suffering from a kind of madness. For Elsa, though, ignoring the sadness was the only alternative to despair and living in the moment became her mantra. Time became inconsequential.

There can be no doubt that, whatever her pain at being separated from her family, living on the farm saved Elsa from the fate of most of the Jews in the Warsaw ghetto. Between 1940 and mid-1942, an estimated 83,000 Jews in the ghetto died of starvation and disease. In the summer of 1942, about 250,000 children, women and men were transported to the killing centre at Treblinka and approximately 35,000 Jews inside the ghetto were murdered. On January 18, 1943, when Nazi troops moved to conduct a mass roundup for transportation, it triggered the beginning of the widely known Warsaw Ghetto Uprising. The Jewish Fighting Organization (Żydowska Organizacja Bojowa or ŻOB), an armed self-defense unit that included a strong core of Zionist youth from both Hashomer Hatzair and Dror, responded to the threat with street-by-street combat. More German troops were brought in and implemented a levelling policy that demolished the buildings occupied by the ghetto fighters. The final battle was lost on April 19 and by May the entire ghetto had been liquidated.

Six months before these events, however, in the summer of 1942, Elsa was recruited along with others from the kibbutz to join the Jewish underground resistance. This was not an anomaly – many members of the pre-war Zionist youth organizations became part of the larger Jewish resistance movement, establishing underground cells inside and outside the ghettos, transporting everything from food to weapons, organizing the distribution of goods, undertaking the education of younger people and setting up communication networks.

Supplied with false papers that would allow her to pass as a Catholic, the underground sent Elsa to Krakow where she was able to draw on her pre-war experience to quickly find a job as a retoucher in the Bielec photography studio. Living this life was complicated for Elsa – she wanted to survive and wanted to help in the resistance, but was uncomfortable lying to people she grew fond of. In particular, she felt disloyal to Jozef and Victoria Starowicz, the Polish couple who gave her room and board, people whom she called Grandma and Grandpa and who came to be a surrogate family. "I was a fraud," she writes. "I carried forged documents. I lied all the time. I robbed decent people of their trust. I wasn't who I said I was." Remembering the prayers of the Catholics with whom she had attended school saved her more than once, but the dishonesty and fear of being found out weighed on her. At Easter, when she went to confession with the Starowicz family, the temptation to confess her real identity was almost more than she could bear: "Walking to the church, I was thinking of what the priest would say if I told him I was Jewish. Silly thoughts! I was becoming obsessed with the idea of telling someone my secret. Each day, the pressure seemed harder to bear."

Elsa was betrayed to the Polish police in early summer 1943, and two Polish agents came to the studio to take her in for questioning. When the Germans occupied Poland, they had co-opted the Polish police force into a collaborative organization to investigate criminal activities, patrol the ghettos and serve as undercover agents. There was a brisk business in turning in and blackmailing Jews. Both home-grown and imported antisemitism was rife in Poland and, although some Poles did risk their lives to help Jews, they were very few and far between.

Fearful of a vicious interrogation, Elsa readily confessed to being Jewish. She was transported to Płaszów, or Kraków-Płaszów, a Nazi forced labour and concentration camp built near Krakow by the SS. One of the most infamous camps in Poland, Płaszów was run by SS commander Amon Göth, whose name became synonymous with brutal crimes against Jews who were interned there. In mid-November 1943, Elsa was herded into a cattle car and moved to the Skarżysko-Kamienna forced labour camp, set up in 1942 in part to take advantage of the munitions factories and Skarżysko-Kamienna's important railway juncture.

These Nazi forced labour camps were run by the SS, but in order to save costs and "divide and conquer" their prisoner populations, they relied on what was known as kapos or "prisoner self-administrators" (*Funktionshäftlinge*). These kapos, who answered to the SS, were given privileges such as exemption from harsh work details, better food and improved living quarters. In camps with mixed prison populations – comprised of non-Jewish criminals and political, racial and religious prisoners as well as Jews – the kapos were drawn primarily from the ranks of ethnic German criminals who viciously competed for favour from the SS. In camps with exclusively Jewish populations, however, the work gangs were overseen by Jewish guards who were often recruited with the understanding that refusal meant death.

Some Jewish kapos, not surprisingly, took on the work to protect themselves from the brutality meted to their fellow prisoners and some went so far as to internalize the mentality of their SS overseers and became as ruthless as their recruiters. Some, as Elsa describes, followed the lead of the SS in sexually exploiting the Jewish women prisoners. Others risked their lives to help where they could, using what limited power they had to make life for other Jews easier. The discussion around the complicity of police and guards in the ghettos and camps is fraught with controversy. Although they might have held a fair amount of power within the camp or ghetto, they were still Jews and few ultimately escaped the fate of other Jewish prisoners. Nonetheless, some, like the ones that Elsa encountered at Skarżysko-Kamienna, were just cruel.

Conditions in the camps were horrific and Elsa, working in a munitions factory on rations that barely sustained life, contracted typhus. In Skarżysko-Kamienna and in the long march after, time became fluid. Prisoners had no watches, no way of knowing one day from the next, only an awareness of the seasons. But these traumas live on in the tale of Elsa's imprisonment and final release, and she remembers the details if not the days on which events occurred. Details rather than time become the more important aspect of remembering. And even today, Elsa speaks of the dress she gave up reluctantly after being free. It was the only thing she owned and each piece – a pocket or a seam – contained important and indelible memories.

After liberation, Elsa's ordeal was not over as she discovered that

Jews were not welcome in their homeland. Many were killed after having survived the war when they attempted to reclaim property. Post-liberation Poland did not even want to acknowledge what had happed to their Jewish neighbours and compatriots. "Before the war, Jews in Poland were always simply labelled as 'the Jews.' After the war," she notes bitterly, "we entered the statistics as 'Polish citizens who perished in the war.'" When the time came to leave Poland, Elsa and her new husband, Soviet tank-driver Mayer Thon, moved to Israel, then to Argentina and finally to Canada. Each place they triumphed. They had survived.

Elsa had suffered through some of the worst transit, labour and death camps in Poland. She had lost her parents and only sister, as well as other much-beloved relatives. She had assumed a false identity, lived in constant fear. But Elsa Thon's "destiny" was to survive. She could find no better way to understand why she and not so many others had lived – from 1939 to 1945, 90 per cent of Polish Jews were killed. It is striking, though, that despite Elsa's deep belief in fate, despite her assertion that "In the end, I didn't solve my problems by myself... It was destiny that guided me," she never once gave in. On the contrary – she seized opportunities where she found them, used her wits to extricate herself from dangerous situations.

Elsa's recollections contain joy and fear, honesty and betrayal, the exuberance of youth and the reflections of maturity. Her poems, which are included in her memoir, commemorate her family, her homeland, her adopted countries and events such as the Warsaw Ghetto Uprising. She tells her tale as one of fortitude, luck and stamina, and it must have taken all of those things for her to endure. Throughout her memoir, however, it is evident that she was always emboldened and sustained by the cherished story of her parents' love.

Sylvia Vance
DPhil (Oxford)

SOURCES

Clendinnen, Inga. *Reading the Holocaust*. Cambridge, England: Cambridge University Press, 1999.

Gutman, Yisrael. *The Jews of Warsay, 1939–1943: Ghetto, Underground, Revolt*. Trans. Ina Friedman. Bloomington, IN: Indiana University Press, 1982.

Herman, Judith. *Trauma and Recovery*. 1998. London, England: Pandora, 2001.

Kapralski, Slawomir, ed. *The Jews in Poland*, vol. 2. Cracow, Poland: The Judaica Foundation, 1999.

Kremer, L. Lillian. *Women's Holocaust Writing: Memory and Imagination*. Lincoln, NB: University of Nebraska Press, 1999.

Langer, Lawrence L. *The Holocaust and the Literary Imagination*. New Haven, CT: Yale University Press, 1975.

Mendelsohn, Ezra. *Zionism in Poland: The Formative Years, 1915–1926*. New Haven, CT, and London, England: Yale University Press, 1981.

Pakula, Zbigniew. *The Jews of Poznan*. Trans. William Brand. London, England, and Portland, OR: Vallentine Mitchell, 2003.

Plaszow Camp. www.jewishgen.org/forgottenCamps/Camps/PlaszEng.html. March, 31, 2012.

Tucker, Erica L. *Remembering Occupied Warsaw: Polish Narratives of World War II*. DeKalb, IL: Northern Illinois University Press, 2011.

Vinecour, Earl, and Chuck Fishman. *Polish Jews: The Final Chapter*. New York, NY: New York University Press, 1977.

Zuckerman, Yitzhak. *A Surplus of Memory: Chronicle of the Warsaw Ghetto Uprising*. Translated and edited by Barbara Harshav. Berkeley, Los Angeles, Oxford: University of California Press, 1993.

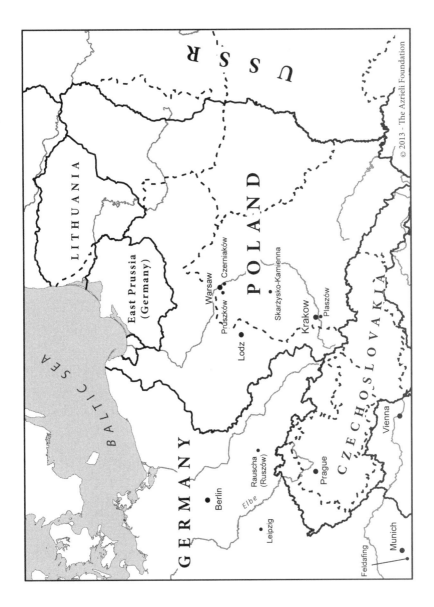

BALTIC SEA

LITHUANIA

East Prussia
(Germany)

USSR

POLAND

Warsaw
Pruszków
Czerniaków
Łódź
Skarżysko-Kamienna
Kraków
Płaszów

GERMANY

Berlin
Elbe
Rauscha
(Ruszów)
Leipzig

CZECHOSLOVAKIA

Prague
Vienna
Munich
Feldafing

The ugly and the stupid have the best of it in this world. They can sit at their ease and gape at the play. If they know nothing of victory, they are at least spared the knowledge of defeat.

– *Oscar Wilde*, The Picture of Dorian Gray

How sharp the point of this remembrance is!

– *William Shakespeare*, The Tempest

I'm thankful to my children, Sonia and Nathan, for their support and for encouraging me to continue writing after I first started this book.

Many thanks, too, to my daughter-in-law, Lucia, for teaching me how to use a computer to make this work easier, and to my grandchildren, Naomi, Jonathan and Joshua, for their love.

I'm thankful to my husband, Mayer, for the time I took away from him to spend on writing.

Thank you all. I love you.

In memory of my father's mother, Ita-Baila Litman Synalewicz

An imaginary excerpt from my grandmother's diary. The facts, as mentioned many times by my mother, are true.

August 1921
Oh Almighty! You have not heard my prayers. Four sons killed in the line of duty, defending Poland! I feel pain inside my body – it hurts. Oh God! Four boys, good and healthy. Each time I begin to write, I think of them. What a punishment! I watch their widows and their children growing without their fathers. It opens my wounds. I would not mind if my daughters-in-law remarried – they are still young. I have seen them crying. But they remain loyal to their vows.

August 1922
Today, I visited my daughter-in-law Sonia, the wife of my youngest son Nachman. He returned from the war with a wife and their baby girl. I like her; she is well-educated and wise. A good wife for my son. Now she is pregnant with her second child. Sonia misses her people back in Russia. It has been two years since she last saw them. She named their first child Regina, after her mother, Ita-Rifka. Now she is concerned about choosing a name for the second child. I tell her not to worry. She will have a name when the child arrives. I know that I will keep my promise. She will remember me through her child. I'm tired of suffering. I'm feeble with age. Oh God! Why are there wars?

On Remembrance Day

In memory of all those who perished before
reaching the places where they could be remembered.

The rooms are silenced, the nests blown apart,
The cradles are empty, covered with dust.
The righteous, the young – there are no shadows of them.
Forgotten faces, not named on this day …
Where are they?

The air is heavy, the sun not in sight,
The laughter is gone, their laments unheard,
Their tears, their fears, no glory for them.
They shared in the horror, but are not named on this day …
Where are they?

Shame in their eyes, their journey in pain,
Helpless, abandoned, their souls flown away.
It's hard to accept that so many are gone,
They are not named, erased from the scroll …
Where are they?

Love is a myth, the names washed away
There are no signs of their lives,
They are not remembered on this day.
Memories have flown, with no graves to cry at,
Nowhere to lay flowers, nowhere to say goodbye …
Where are they?

Trembling lips whisper their names,
They are not remembered,
Forgotten this day.
Still, in our hearts they forever remain,
We are still grieving in pain …
Where are they?

Author's Preface

I kept my past to myself for a half-century until I suddenly reached the point where I could no longer contain the compressed weight of pain inside me and I poured out the facts of those five years onto paper. In my memoir, I describe adventures, entanglements and terrible blows – a life in hiding, forged documents, the privations of labour camps and the rigours of a forced march.

As I wrote, it hurt to relive the cruelties of war, to again experience such awful emotions, which are as heartbreaking now as they were then. I am a witness to and a victim of the degradation of humanity. I know that nothing can change or heal my wounds. Still, this is my story, which I hope in some way may serve as a lesson to all who read it.

As this is, in a way, a history of this period, I have tried to present facts in chronological order. I have recounted events as accurately as I could, though inevitably, there will be some errors in fifty-year-old memories. Because I rarely read a newspaper or saw calendars or clocks, I often had to rely on my memory of the season or whether it was day or night when something happened.

Throughout writing this work, the memory of my parents and my sister was foremost in my mind. I also remember, with great respect, every soul I knew who perished or survived. I was compelled to write about their lives and describe their legacy of honour and rectitude, of love and respect. I owe them this.

I'm filled with memories of my parents and my sister. I want to keep their image alive forever, to describe their many adventures and misadventures. Perhaps I will be able to give my children and grand-children a visual portrait of them, so that they will be remembered by future generations. I am in a hurry ... it is getting late, and my memory is not as efficient as it used to be. Perhaps some episodes fade but, in spite of that, I will try the best I can. I am the only one left to tell their story.

It is curious how memory works; I wonder how after so many years and from such a distance I can visualize my father sitting at the table, my mother coming from the kitchen, serving supper, my sister and I sitting at opposite sides of the table. I memorized the room I was born in and all the furniture, even though it was not of great value. Now, I realize that anything material is dispensable – only my family was a treasure.

I can still also see Pruszków, the city I grew up in, alive with peo-ple walking in the streets, the stores, the buildings, the schools, the alley where I used to stroll. The pictures roll in front of me as if they were on a movie screen. I can walk through the city anywhere by only wishing it, remembering people and their dwellings. It is my duty to remember and describe the city where I was born and narrate as many episodes as I can recollect.

I keep asking myself why I am so obsessed with the past, but I know the answer – I feel nostalgic. No one around me knows any-thing about me from those days, which makes me want to hold on to the scenery in order to retrieve my lost past.

While visiting Israel once, a friend and I played a game to remem-ber Pruszków. In our imagination, we walked through the streets and named the people who once lived along them. It was quite an adven-ture. At the end, however, we were in tears. Still, after all, I think it is good to remember. The past is a guide for the future, and the values I learned as a child stayed with me as proof of my roots and an affirma-tion of who I am.

As I wrote out the first part of my memories, very slowly and carefully, I touched fragile contents that I have treasured for so many years. In spite of time, I am still carrying the heavy load of remembrance. I resist erasing those pictures from my brain. It is all that is left from my past, and I have kept it with love and respect. Finally, after half a century, the loneliness that has been my true company for many years in my life compelled me to write this memoir.

I suppose it was pure luck that I survived – or perhaps a chain of miracles. I have no other way of explaining it. Was it my destiny that I should be left alone, with no trace of my family? The scars are painful, the damage incurable.

Elsa Thon
2006

Oral History

When we were very young, when television didn't exist, stories were told, not read. My sister, Regina, and I used to sit at the table, eager to listen to Father's stories. My father's nature was jovial and he told us stories cheerfully. He was a world of information, both personal and historical. As we grew older and the stories were more detailed, we understood more of their political and historical context and the questions we asked were more meaningful. Both our parents enthusiastically related their experiences whenever we asked them to tell us a new story. Since we were fascinated, sometimes the story was told again, with my parents adding new episodes each time. My parents loved us and, although my father wanted a boy instead of a girl for their second child, I didn't disappoint him. Now, I think that he would have been proud of his second girl.

Mother's stories were as astonishing as Father's. From their narratives, we got to know who our parents were and at the same time learned about our roots, which began with an old-fashioned romance entangled in politics and history. Throughout betrayal and struggle, their desire stayed alive and they overcame many desperate situations in order to be reunited. It is common for young people to fall in love. What is uncommon in my parents' love story is that they were separated for many years, waiting and hoping to be together. It is a true love story.

When we asked our father why he married our mother, he answered, "Because she was beautiful." When asked the same question, our mother said, "Because I loved him."

~

In the late eighteenth century, Russia and the neighbouring countries of Austria and Prussia divided the territory of Poland, virtually wiping Poland off of the map. Russia took advantage of the territory it occupied, recruiting young men for military service to prepare them for combat and in 1910, at the age of twenty-one, my father was called up for his compulsory military service near Ekaterinoslav, which is now called Dnepropetrovsk. My father, Nachman Synalewicz, was born in Grodzisk, Poland in 1889. He was taller than average, with an oval face, perfect features, dark hair and brown eyes. Physically, he was always in good shape.

He was taught discipline, war tactics and how to use weapons, and he also learned the Russian language. At home, he would sing soldiers' songs in Russian. Sometimes we understood the words but did not get the meaning. One song I remember was "Madeline." It was very popular during World War I and was later translated into Polish. When we asked our father if he had shot enemy soldiers in the war he answered, "Never." He never shot anyone. He pointed his rifle up and fired into the air. "Right up into the sky?" we asked. "Yes," he said. He didn't like life in the barracks. He couldn't change his clothes often, he spent hours in the trenches in bad weather, the shooting was constant and there were lineups for meagre food. But he was young then, and could overcome the discomfort of war.

The Russian military allowed the young Jewish soldiers to pray during the high holidays, Rosh Hashanah and Yom Kippur, in a synagogue in Kharkov, close to where they were stationed at the time.[1] It

---

1   For information on Rosh Hashanah and Yom Kippur, as well as on other religious and cultural terms; major organizations; significant historical events and people; geographical locations; and foreign-language words and expressions contained in the text, please see the glossary.

was there that my parents met for the first time. Both remembered their encounter and, separately, related exactly the same story – it was love at first sight. They prayed for the coming year to bring health and happiness, as was the custom. History followed its course, and their story unfolded.

My mother, Sonia Samoilovna Pishnow, was born in Russia in a small town on the outskirts of St. Petersburg in 1886. Her father was a grain dealer and the family owned both a house and land. At the time, there were terrible pogroms against the Jews. In the late nineteenth century, Tsar Alexander III increased the previous restrictions on where Jews could live by expelling Jews from the cities of St. Petersburg and Moscow to parts of Byelorussia, Lithuania, and Ukraine. They were barred from holding land or engaging in agriculture, which resulted in their search for other ways of survival. They became merchants, artisans and craftsmen. But not even this way of life prevented them from being expelled. These episodes forced much of the Jewish population to emigrate to other countries.

Although my maternal grandfather, Samuel Pishnow, was a businessman and had the privilege to stay, the insecurity was impossible to bear and the Pishnow family moved to the border of the Ukraine. My mother and her older sister, Masha, both attended a Hebrew school for girls, Beth Jacob. When they were still young, their mother, Rifka, died. Their father mourned her for only one year and then married a woman who, although she might have been right for him, mistreated his children.

This part of my mother's story was sad, and I remember that we cried when it came up. We loved our mother and knew she wouldn't do to us what her stepmother did to her. She and her sister grew closer as they defended themselves against their stepmother, but their unhappiness grew. The situation at home didn't change until they became older and their stepmother didn't dare to confront them any longer. Masha met a young man with the last name of Milichan and they married. The young couple moved to Kharkov, now the Ukrainian city of Kharkiv, where Jews were allowed to live. Masha soon invited Sonia to stay with them and her life changed considerably – living with her sister gave her a sense of purpose. She worked and audited courses at the university, which made her happy, satisfying her curiosity for learning.

When she met my father at the synagogue, my mother's life changed once again. They fell in love, knowing that my father could be sent to the front line at any time. In 1913, when his departure was imminent, I presume that our parents swore faithfulness, hoping that some day he would return from the war and they would marry. They allowed themselves to dream in spite of the dangers of war. When he was called to the front line, they relied only on their youth, hope and the strong love that brought them together.

Although all this happened before I was born, the story was told and repeated so many times that it became engraved in my memory. I suppose that my mother prepared herself for a long separation. She was happy attending her literature classes and working as a handicraft teacher, although her wages weren't great. She used to skip meals to go to the theatre whenever she could afford it. My mother worked as a handicraft teacher for almost three years but lost her job because of the economic situation. Soon, she found work as a seamstress in the theatre. She loved to attend theatre performances and was proud to tell us how many plays she had seen. However, after working there three years as well, the theatre had to close – there wasn't enough money to pay the artists or the staff. She next found a live-in job in a private home for the wealthy Niemetz family, making dresses for the lady of the house and her daughter. They were kind to her and she was treated as a friend.

Unfortunately, the country was in turmoil; the population had been divided between Bolsheviks, Mensheviks and other factions long before the revolution in 1917. The revolution succeeded, but the turmoil continued, and the family where my mother worked lost their wealth. She still worked there, but her wages dropped and she had to move into her sister's home again. Masha had two children at the time, a girl named Ronia and a boy named Shura.

My mother was beautiful and wise, and all the neighbours knew her. "How long will she wait for him?" they asked, referring to my father. "She is getting older, refusing all suitors." Some pitied her, while others admired her loyalty. Meanwhile, she worked and helped her sister, distracted from her waiting only by her books.

In her neighbourhood, my mother met a young man named Mikhail, whose intention was to marry her, although she did not give him any encouragement. She talked to him when they met in the street but otherwise tried to avoid him. She waited for my dad honestly and devotedly. Mikhail didn't give up and kept waiting for her when she returned from work. When she told him that she was engaged and was waiting for her fiancé to come back from the war, he responded maliciously, "He will never come back." She retorted, "He sent me a letter saying that he is coming." "We'll see who will win in the end," he responded.

As the years passed, my mother received few letters from my father. Just when everything felt bleak and desperate, both my paternal grandmother, Baila, in Poland, and my mother, miles away in Russia, received letters from him. In those days, the mail took a long time to get to its destination. After years on the front line, the Germans had captured my father and he was a prisoner of war. For my grandmother, the small hope of seeing her son alive was a spark in the darkness – she still grieved for her sons who had fallen in the line of duty at Port Arthur during the Russo-Japanese War of 1904. For my mother, who had waited for so long to see her beloved again, the letter gave her the strength to go on waiting until her dream came true.

After a year in prison, my father tried to escape, but he was caught and punished, forced to do heavy labour. The next year, he tried to escape again and succeeded – a strong desire works miracles. After weeks of wandering through cities, he finally reached Kharkiv.

I remember a photo of my father from when he was in the German prison. He looked twenty years older than he was. What a change in comparison to a picture of him at home nicely dressed in a suit. With all his hair, he looked like a dandy. In the prison picture, he was pensive and serious-looking in a dark grey buttoned-up jacket.

My mother was at work when my father, still in his prison clothes, approached Masha's home. Some neighbours recognized him. "Synalewicz has come back!" they exclaimed. In Russia, the surname was usually used to identify a person. Even the children Ronia and Shura recognized him from the photo that hung on the wall. "Mamushka," they cried, "Synalewicz is here." Masha welcomed him heartily. My mother worked not too far away and someone went to tell her the news. She apologized to her employers for the sudden urgency to go home. "I didn't walk, I ran," she used to tell us. Her heart beat strongly with every step she took. When she arrived, they embraced each other for the first time since his departure more than five years earlier.

~

In 1919, there was still unrest in Russia after the Russian Revolution. Rules were imposed, and anger and suspicion reigned. People took different sides and it was often dangerous to trust a neighbour or a friend. Everyone suffered from the uncertainty.

At this time, my father was staying in Masha's home. She wouldn't let him leave after what both he and her sister had gone through. Masha loved her sister and, wanting to see her happy, soon arranged a date for our parents' religious wedding. My mother made a suit for herself and gave a tailor the same material to make a suit for my father. I clearly remember them telling us that they wore the suits that she had prepared to their wedding.

A few months after the wedding, their happiness was interrupted by another disaster. My father had been reported as a counter-revolutionary activist and was arrested and sent to jail. It was a false accusation, but the police wouldn't say who the accuser was or what he said. I remember my mother telling us that she would go to the street where the jail was located every day to see my father through the bars of the window.

My mother was pregnant with my sister at the time and when she was born, at the end of December 1920, my father was still in jail. On the day of the trial, my mother sat in the courtroom with baby Regina. Masha, her husband and neighbours who knew about their love and struggle to be reunited came willingly to testify.

When one of the three judges stood up and read the opening statement of accusation and the evidence, everyone froze. Nachman Synalewicz, my father, had been accused of treason against the People's Revolution. This was a serious accusation; if he were convicted, he would be sentenced to death. The eyewitness to the transgression was listed as Mikhail Chortkow, the man who had wanted to marry my mother. This foolish, nasty man had turned their lives into a nightmare. He declared that he had seen my father gathering weapons from a field, which had supposedly been left after a battle between the Reds and the Whites, and that he gathered them in order to initiate a counterattack against the Bolsheviks. It was outrageous!

My father explained that the accusation was an act of revenge against his wife and that he had witnesses who could testify to Chortkow's intentions toward her when my father was a prisoner of war. Mikhail Chortkow, on the other hand, had no witnesses to testify to his contention that my father was gathering arms from a field.

As the judges retired to their chamber, my mother felt that, after all the years of suffering, waiting and hoping, their dreams could fall apart like a house of cards. If the judges didn't believe Chortkow's accusation, they might give my father the benefit of the doubt. Maybe they were wise enough to see that it was a false accusation. Also Poland was then free and independent – perhaps a Polish citizen would be judged differently. All my mom could think of was that the believers in the Revolution wouldn't sentence an innocent man to death. They had to be just. They were idealists, not murderers.

The judges returned to the room. One asked my father to describe the place where he was from. My father mentioned the Majewski pencil factory. The judge cleared his voice and continued, "Nachman Synalewicz, Polish citizen, you are sentenced to walk, under supervision, from one city to another until you reach the Polish border. There you will be freed and able to travel to the place where you lived before." Everyone took a deep breath of relief.

Mom celebrated this event on every Simchat Torah – a festive holiday – by cooking *gołąbki*, minced meat wrapped in cabbage leaves, and she invited neighbours and friends for dinner to share in the miracle. Although we weren't very religious, our mother kept a kosher kitchen.

Immediately after the sentence was pronounced, my mother decided to follow my father, who had been told that he would begin his journey in a few days. She wouldn't be separated from him again. The sentence was actually easier on my father because he slept in jails, where he received food rations, but my mother slept outside the jails. She walked beside him with the baby. If the guard was compassionate, he allowed my father to carry his child. In some places, a guard would let my mom sleep in the entrance hall of the jail. However, more often than not she would approach a house near the jail, asking to be allowed to bathe Regina. A lot of the people she asked for help were indifferent. The guards were often exceptionally cruel. Once, when Dad took Regina from Mom, a guard got angry, pulled out his bayonet and attempted to split my sister's head open. Instinctively, Dad had put his hand on her head and he received a deep cut on his hand. Like this, weeks passed, until they were close to the Polish border.

My parents arrived in Poland in the early spring of 1921. Dad was free. They took the train to Pruszków, not quite twenty kilometres southwest of Warsaw, where my grandmother lived close to the train station. She was thrilled to see her son and was immediately fond of my mom. This was not true of my aunt Dina, who had been married to one of my dad's brothers and widowed when he was killed at Port Arthur. My mother, in a short wide skirt and with her hair cut short, was too modern for Dina's taste. Dina always wore a long skirt and her hair was gathered behind her ears with pins.

When grandmother, who lived in Dina's home, had received the letter from her son letting her know that he was alive, Dina took it into her head that Dad would marry her. She had four children, two sons and two daughters. But when Dad came home with a wife and a child, Dina was bitter and disappointed and showed very little tolerance toward her, which lasted for as long as I can remember.

My Poland

Before World War II, Poland had the shape of a heart. Ironically, the annihilation of the Jewish population – perhaps the most shameful chapter in the annals of humanity – would take place in this heart-shaped country. I inherited my patriotic feeling for Poland from my father and, later, from school. It was true love that we felt for our country.

Poland was a pagan country until the year 966, when the ruler Mieszko I was baptized and Poland was proclaimed a Christian land. In the fourteenth century, with the increasing immigration of German Jews to Poland, King Kazimierz III Wielki (Casimir III the Great) included the protection of Jews in his enlightened economic and social policies. The Jews introduced commerce and craft into Poland and were able to practise their faith. The influence of German Jews expanded the realm of the Yiddish language – a mix of Slavic and German that became popular and was adopted as the language of the Jewish population.

In the nineteenth century, poets such as Adam Mickiewicz, Juliusz Słowacki and Zygmunt Krasiński introduced Romanticism into Polish literature and also focused on nationalistic themes. Other notable novelists were Bolesław Prus and Henryk Sienkiewicz, who received the Nobel Prize in 1905 for his many historical novels, among them the famous *Quo Vadis*. Dramatists Stanisław Wyspiański and Stefan

Żeromski produced many works, and writer Władysław Reymont won the Nobel Prize for literature in 1924. Julian Tuwim, a Polish Jew, marked a significant epoch in experimental literature. A famous painter of the time was Jan Matejko. Frédéric Chopin was recognized as a world-renowned pianist and composer. In 1903, Marie Skłodowska-Curie and Pierre Curie shared the Nobel Prize in physics with Henri Becquerel. In 1911, Skłodowska-Curie received her second Nobel Prize, in chemistry, for the discovery of radium and polonium. The world of my childhood included all these excellent models to follow and learn from.

~

My parents had to get remarried by the municipal authorities in Pruszków because their Jewish marriage certificate from Russia wasn't recognized in Poland. Pruszków, a village since the sixteenth century, was incorporated as a town in 1916. It was an important industrial city and when my parents lived there, the population was approximately 16,000, of which one thousand were Jewish.

My father's family business was delivering food supplies to private clinics. He and his brothers had all worked with their father until his death, when they took over the business. Later on, when they were called, one by one, to military service, my grandmother took it over. My grandmother was proud that her sons were healthy and fit for military duty, but after their tragic deaths, she sold the business and moved in with Aunt Dina to help her with her children. Grandmother was unhappy living with Dina, but she never complained. Dina, as the widow of a soldier, was entitled to a government licence, not generally permitted to Jews, to sell monopoly goods such as tobacco and alcohol. Grandmother helped her open a small store that sold cigarettes and matches but instead of alcohol, which she refused to sell, she added chocolate, candy, ice cream and fresh fruit. She was a heavy woman and she would sit all day while her clients helped themselves with their purchases, approaching her only to pay.

With Grandmother's help, my father was able to rent a small room with a stove behind a bakery. He bought a bed, a table, two chairs and a cradle for my sister. Grandmother couldn't help him with anything else, as the rest of her money went to help Dina and her children. But in no time, my dad went to Warsaw and found a job in a knitting factory where they produced various kinds of sweaters for men, women and children.

I suppose that my father earned good wages because my family moved to a house before I was born. They lived in one room on the first floor of a house just across the street from where they had lived before. They had to bring in water from a pump in the huge yard and the outhouse was at the end of the yard. There were a few trees where Mom hung wet clothes to dry. The landlord, his wife and their six children lived on the same floor. His room was even smaller than ours and he also worked as a shoemaker there. He was poorer than we were in the beginning.

Mom bought a sewing machine and asked around the neighbourhood for sewing jobs. At first, people who could afford to have a dress made didn't trust her with new material; they commissioned her to turn their old dresses into smaller ones for their children or to overturn the collars of men's shirts. So the jobs were mostly repairs but Mom accepted anything that people brought in. In the 1920s, the economy in Poland was disastrous. The wars and battles for independence had impoverished not only Poland but also much of Europe. Mom understood this and didn't blame anybody.

The news soon got around the city that Synalewicz had come back from the war with a wife and a child and that his wife was a seamstress. My father was a very handsome man and many girls in the city had been under the illusion that some day he would marry one of them. Even though so many years had passed and those girls were already married with children, they still somehow considered themselves my father's brides. Out of curiosity, some women wanted to meet my mother and would show up with a piece of new fabric for a skirt or a blouse. My mother travelled to Warsaw and bought a fashion magazine so that they could choose a style from it. The women were satisfied with her work and came back with new material for dresses. Her clients called her "Sonia the Russian." It did not take very long, when they got to know her better, for them to call her "Sonia the Wise."

A STORY WITHIN A STORY

In the early 1950s in Israel, I decided to gather friends together a few times a year to tell nostalgic stories about our childhood. Like a ceremony we greeted each other, taking seats for the reunion.

One Friday evening before the last meeting of the year, I was invited to a friend's house for dinner. We had just cleaned the table when a couple I didn't know arrived. After a brief greeting, the men sat down at the table to talk about work, and the woman approached me on the sofa and cheerfully introduced herself as Rose.

My friend poured us some wine and went to prepare coffee. As we sat sipping the wine, the conversation flowed more easily and we soon were better acquainted. Rose had beautiful eyes, truly cat's eyes, grey-green, with short black stripes in them. She asked me where I was from and when I answered that I was from Pruszków, her cat's eyes opened wide and she told me that her grandparents had lived there. We discovered that I had indeed known Grandma Malke and Grandpa Barl – they had lived not far from us. Malke's head was always covered with a black cloth, which matched a blouse and wide-pleated long skirt that had lost most of its colour from frequent laundering and become a very dark grey. In the winter, she wore a good quality black sweater and a woollen shawl that covered her head and shoulders. Suddenly, I remembered that Malke had the same eyes as Rose. Barl, of average height with an oval face and a short well-trimmed beard, was an artisan who replaced broken window glass. I used to see him in the street, always neatly dressed, carrying glass under his arm and his tools in his other hand.

When Rose asked me how I happened to remember them so well since I was only a child at the time, I told her that whenever I thought about my childhood, all the little details passed through my mind as if they were on a screen. I also had a particular reason to remember Malke.

One night we heard someone knocking at the door and shouting, "Nachman, wake up! You promised me you would take me out to the ballroom. Wake up! Come dance with me! Come on, I'm waiting for you!" My sister and I woke up frightened. After more knocking and calling of my father's name, I heard Mom say, "I will talk to her." She approached the closed door saying, "Malke, this is Sonia. Nachman is married. He has children. You will wake them up. Go home. Go to bed." Malke left, but in the morning my parents talked about what had happened the night before, discussing Malke's delusion that she was in love with my father.

~

My mother had always been an outsider, no matter how hard she tried to please people. I inherited this feeling of isolation from my mother; I too was a newcomer later in my life, and people often don't know how to handle newcomers. To them, our stories are strange or unbelievable. I think these kinds of reactions are shallow, but some people prefer to stay ignorant. People seldom understand what it means to be transplanted to a different place and how difficult it is to adjust to other customs. My own family and I experienced this in our moves to other countries.

Grandmother often came to visit my mom. She liked her and felt sorry that she couldn't help more. Slowly, my parents began to prosper and soon, Mom got pregnant with me. She told me later that she had mixed feelings about it. She was happy to have another child, but it bothered her that she was so far away from her family. Her loneliness often overpowered her and she found it hard to get accustomed to her surroundings.

Once, my grandmother came in and when she saw how depressed my mother was, she asked her if something had happened. Mom could talk to her because Grandma understood what she had been through and that she needed someone to trust. Mom found an excuse for her worries – she told my grandmother that she didn't know what to name her child. I presume that it wasn't the name that bothered her, but that without family or friends, she felt isolated. Grandmother told her, "Don't worry, Sonichka" (that is what both Grandmother and my father called her), "you will have a name for the child at the right time."

A few months later, Grandmother died and my parents named me Balbinka after her. My mother had loved her dearly and she paid for her tombstone with her own money. None of her other daughters-in-law made an effort to contribute. Nonetheless, Aunt Dina's jealousy of my mother grew, especially when it turned out that Grandmother had left my mother her seat at the synagogue because she knew how to pray.

On January 10, 1923, I was born at home, as was the custom at that time. When my mother was due to have me, my father brought in the midwife. While the midwife helped with my birth, the door opened and a Gypsy woman came in out of nowhere (there were many Gypsies, as we called the Roma at the time, in the neighbourhood). Dad rushed to the door and asked her to leave, but she was stubborn and wouldn't go away. Dad pushed her out, closing the door, but she had time to curse me, saying that my life would be a constant struggle, a prediction that came true.

I still remember the large room where I was born, although we moved again a few years later. My parents had a big wooden bed, a dresser and a big table with chairs. My sister and I slept together in another bed, all of us in the one room. In the kitchen stood my grandmother's chest. It was really a bedroom chest that Grandmother had used for linen, but my mom kept dishes, groceries, pots and pans in it. I remember that at the end of the day when it was getting darker, I used to be afraid to walk into the kitchen because the chest was black. I was even afraid of a feather flying from a pillow. If a feather made me tremble, how did I later endure so much suffering, loneliness and betrayal?

I was also afraid of an invalid who used to sit on the sidewalk not far from where we lived. He had dark skin and black curly hair, and he wore shabby clothes. His eyes sparkled maliciously and he smiled constantly. When I had to walk by where he sat, I crossed the street to avoid him. It didn't help. I was little and was still afraid that he would grab me at any moment. Mom explained to me that he wouldn't do me any harm, that he was only begging for some money, but no one could convince me. At night, I woke up screaming from nightmares about him.

In desperation, Mom took me to Warsaw to see Aunt Shprintza, my father's late brother's wife. She had been left widowed with three children – two girls and one boy – after my uncle had fallen in the line of duty during the Russo-Japanese War. When we got there, my aunt melted wax and when it had cooled slightly, she poured it on my head. Mom told me that the beggar's name was Ignac and that his entire body and wild hair flowed out of me through the wax on my head. I do remember that after that procedure, I wasn't afraid of him anymore and never cried again.

One year on Purim, Mom was bathing me late in the afternoon. It was already dark outside and the large room was lit with a naphtha lamp, which hung close to us. Suddenly, the door opened and my cousin Marysia, whom I always liked to see, came in. She was my aunt Dina's younger daughter. But her face was painted black and she wore such a strange outfit that I got frightened and couldn't stop crying. Mom explained the custom of masquerade during Purim to me, but I kept crying and my poor cousin had to go home. That fear of people who appear to be false or deceptive is something that has stayed with me all my life, and to this day I am still afraid of people wearing masks or who have their faces painted with makeup, as they often do at Purim and Halloween.

In spite of the awkwardness between Aunt Dina and my mother, my sister and I often visited her and her family. My mother's opinion was that children didn't need to get involved in family disputes. Dina's younger son, Benjamin, was the only one from his family who visited us frequently. He taught me how to whistle and would pick me up to take me to their store and give me an ice cream.

I remember one particular incident with Dina's oldest son, Hersh Itzhak. One night, he was stabbed by a bunch of non-Jewish hooligans who thought that his fair-haired and blue-eyed fiancée was Aryan. They taunted him, saying, "Why did you choose an Aryan girl and not a Jewish one? We will not allow a Christian to marry a Jew." When they stabbed him, he didn't feel any discomfort, but when he rushed home and took off his coat, Aunt Dina saw blood on his shirt. The doctor who examined him said that he was lucky – the knife hadn't perforated his lungs but had come very close. He was in the hospital for days. There were many such antisemitic incidents in Poland.

My aunt Gela, also a widow of another one of my father's brothers, lived with her son in Błonie, about twenty kilometres away from us. She was a religious woman and sent her son to study at a yeshiva. He graduated, but later he rebelled and left the religious life. When he got married and had a son, he again became a believer. He liked my mom and often came to visit us.

~

The Pruszków I grew up in was a beautiful small city with a population of about 20,000. The houses were neat and the sidewalks were clean. Just over one thousand Jews lived there – craftsmen and businessmen, among other professions. Because Pruszków was so close to Warsaw, many young Jews travelled there to attend the ORT technical school, the Jewish Gymnasium (high school) or one of the business schools. My sister and I often went to Warsaw to go to the theatre or fancy ice-cream parlours. Pruszków had one Jewish primary school and a synagogue, three public elementary schools, one high school, some sports clubs and two cinemas. I particularly remember Anielin

Park, which was like a small island on a river. On late Saturday afternoons in the summer, an orchestra played dance tunes and the park was filled with people. The young came to dance, the old to enjoy fresh air and socialize. There were boats people could rent to row around the island. In the winter, the water froze and it became a skating rink.

My sister was three years older than I, and Mom enrolled her in the Jewish school that was just around the corner from where we lived. The teacher and principal was Mr. Koziebrodski. Most of the students were boys, and Regina ended up staying only one year at that school; the government-run school went up to Grade 7, but that school only went to Grade 4. At the beginning of Regina's second year, Mom took her to a different school called Tadeusz Kościuszko. She had to take an examination in mathematics and reading to be accepted, which she passed – my sister was very bright and always studied diligently.

When I was three years old, Mom took me to a private kindergarten where I met my friend Halina, who was one of about five or six children there. Even now, by correspondence, we still maintain our friendship, and she and her late husband came from the US to visit us when we arrived in Canada. When I began writing my memoir, I sent Halina a few pages of my manuscript to test her reaction and to tell her that she would be in my book. She told me that she was surprised how much I remembered, and that it made her happy but also made her cry.

Halina lived around the block across the street, so we could easily walk to each other's homes, and we played together almost every day. In the backyard of her house there were wooden planks on which we ran and climbed, as well as fruit trees. Her parents, who owned a brick factory and built a lot of houses, were wealthy. When we were a little older, her mom would even send us to the bank together, which was on the same street where my aunt Dina lived, to bring money to pay their workers.

If I had an argument with Halina and stopped going over, her mother would call up to me from our front steps, "Please, Balbinka, come to play with Halinka, she is alone. I have to go out." Before the high holidays, Halina's mom felt the need to do good deeds. Once a year, she bought shoes or material from the local stores to help their businesses prosper. When she showed us the material she had bought for two dresses for Halina, one printed with tiny blue and red cornflowers, my mom went to the same store and bought the same material to make me a dress as well.

Every day, Mom took me to the kindergarten. I remember one day when Mom came rushing in to pick me up in the middle of class activities, telling the teacher that an anti-Piłsudski rally was being led by Józef Haller and his troops. She didn't even let me walk home, carrying me in her arms instead. My mother listened to the news on the radio – although she often refused to speak Polish or learn how to write it, she understood every word. She was interested in politics and knew exactly what was happening in the world. I inherited my interest in politics from her. The next day, Mom took me back to the kindergarten. Haller's troops had rallied, but had not started an uprising, as she had feared.

In early 1929, Dad decided to go into business for himself while he was still working at the knitting factory. He bought merchandise from work and then rented a stand in the market, putting Mom in charge of the sales while he was at work. The business, however, didn't turn out to be a good idea. My parents initially thought that it was just a slow beginning and that they had to be patient, but that year, the depression hit. It wasn't that people weren't interested, but the economic situation in the country was terrible. People just didn't have any money to spend.

My friend Regina Postolski's father also had a stand in the market, selling textiles for dresses. They too had to give up their business and just hope for a better future. The economy affected everyone, but those who had lived in the city for decades usually managed to go on with their businesses or trades. Their circumstances were differ-ent, but at least they had always lived in the same place. Mom used to say, "Even a rock grows if it lies on the same place." My parents had to start from scratch, expecting a new struggle every day. They had to prove their ability and intelligence because they had neither an inheritance nor a family business to fall back on. They had only themselves and their hope, but they were courageous.

During this time, Mom decided to ask a woman who had a stand at the market if she would sell housedresses that Mom would make, and she agreed. Mom was competent and imaginative, and the wom-an successfully sold the first dozen dresses and ordered more of dif-ferent sizes. But as a consequence of our financial difficulties, Mom stopped taking me to the kindergarten – we could no longer afford to pay the fee. Public kindergartens didn't exist in Poland at that time. I don't know what the teacher told the other mothers, but somehow the children became aware that I wasn't there any longer and they refused to go to the kindergarten. I didn't know, at that age, what a strike meant, but there was certainly passive resistance from the chil-dren. I am sure that they didn't know about camaraderie to support social rights, but they did it their way. Mrs. Raisberg, the teacher's mother, hurried to our place and asked my mom to let her take me to the kindergarten because otherwise her daughter would lose her business. She told my mother not to worry about the money and that she could just pay when she was able to. The kindergarten mainly catered to rich families, but I think that my sister and I were accepted everywhere because we had been brought up with excellent manners. I returned to kindergarten, and everyone was happy.

In the kindergarten, I not only learned how to read and write, but I also, at the age of four, had a "boyfriend." His name was Zdzisiek Pawlowski and he used to accompany me home from school with one of Halina's parents. His and Halina's parents were partners in some sort of business. When the neighbours saw me walking with Zdzisiek they would joke to my mother, "Mrs. Sonia, look at your daughter, she is walking with a gentile boy already at this age." He had two sisters much older than he was and, observing that his sisters' boyfriends used to walk them home, he had decided to do the same. After the war, Halina told me that she had heard from one of Zdzisiek's sisters that he had fought in the underground during the war and had disappeared without a trace.

~

My father kept trying to succeed and he continued to work for a while, but nothing turned out. After six months or so, he decided to go to Uruguay, hoping, I guess, that there he would find a better opportunity for our family. Mom was still getting orders from clients, but it wasn't enough to keep up with the household expenses. Sometimes a woman would come with fancy material and choose a dress from a fashion magazine, asking to have it ready almost immediately. Mom was patient with all these capricious clients. She was skilful and hard-working.

It was late summer 1929 when Dad left Poland. We went with him to the electric train station, from where he would first travel to Warsaw and then to Gdansk to board a ship. I was too young to know if Mom agreed with Dad's decision to make this trip, but she never said anything against him. What I do remember is that while Dad's absence had given us hope that our circumstances would change, after a few months we woke up in a cold room to a table without bread on it. In the end, he was gone for almost two years.

I was six when my father left and missed him terribly. I wrote letters to him in Uruguay and sent him drawings to share what I learned in kindergarten. Mom said that maybe reading books would distract me and told me to borrow a book from the library written by Edmondo De Amicis entitled *Heart*, which was about the life of a young boy who suffered a lot. When I talked to her about the story she said, "If you don't suffer, you don't know what life is." I don't remember if I understood it then, but I know now what she meant about life.

Mom bought beautiful fabrics and made new dresses for all of us. Ours were pink, and hers was steel-coloured. She also sewed dressing gowns for both of us from a pitch-coloured corduroy. We went to the Abramowicz studio to be photographed. I posed in one photo with my sister and the second photograph was of all three of us. My mom sent them to my father. In return, he sent Regina and me dried leaves and butterflies. For Mom, he sent money.

At the age of six, I finished the first stage of my education and became my mom's helper for the summer. She taught me how to sew buttons and hems and also to turn belts. In the morning, there was always a pile of dresses ironed and neatly folded. We got accustomed to hearing the sound of the sewing machine until we fell asleep. As more time passed, we managed to survive pretty well. Mom was finally able to save some money in case we had to travel. Twice a week, we went to the library to borrow books. It was at this age that Mom taught me the printed letters in Russian. The first book I read entirely in Russian was *Little Lord Fauntleroy*. Mom worked hard and I was her right hand, helping her with whatever I could. My sister attended school and after school she had to do her homework, so she had no time to help.

My mom soon registered me at the Józef Piłsudski school. The Tadeusz Kościuszko school, where my sister went, wouldn't accept me because, according to a new municipal order, we didn't belong to the school district. Mom asked the teacher to allow me to enter the first grade even though I was underage for the school requirement. This teacher spoke Russian and was willing to listen to my mother's explanation that I knew how to read and write and that I would have no trouble with the work. Mom stroked my head, knowing that keeping busy would be the best thing to heal my sadness from missing my father.

I was excited when I got accepted to the Józef Piłsudski school. It had a big yard to play in at recess and for gym in the summertime. Near the school was a little garden with birch trees, chrysanthemums, flowerbeds and vegetables. My teacher was in charge of it and chose me to water the chrysanthemums in the morning before the classes began. She gave me the key and every day I fulfilled my obligation, which I very much enjoyed. Some evenings, when she had spare time, she would ask me to help her weed or pick up the seeds for the next spring. I liked the school and, although I wasn't very ambitious, I learned a lot.

Once a month, a doctor came to school to check the students' health and every week a hygienist came to examine our nails. Our shoes had to be polished and our hair had to be clean. Once, I complained to the doctor that I had a pain on the right side of my body. When she couldn't find anything wrong, she just said, "Well, we aren't made of rubber." So many years have passed since this episode, yet I still remember her words.

At some point well into my father's absence, he sent us papers granting us permission to travel to Uruguay and my mother made all the arrangements. We even had the date set. Mom sold everything that we couldn't take with us, and we were ready to go. But there are some things that I can only believe are the result of destiny. Without its cruel game, my whole family might be alive.

The Friday before our intended departure, Mom, as usual, cleaned and cooked for the Sabbath. We were talking while she washed the floor and I don't remember what we were talking about, but I remember that I said, "Mom, shush, maybe Dad is standing at the door and listening to what we are saying." She had just finished the cooking and lit the candles and we were about to sit down at the table when we heard knocking at the door. A neighbour came in and said, "Sonia, what would you do if Nachman arrived just now?" "Nothing," my mother responded, "he would be welcomed." Then the neighbour told her that he had met my father at the train station and had hurried to tell us that he had arrived before my father could stop him.

At that point, Dad walked in with two suitcases. I remember that I had imagined him with a beard because he hadn't been home for so long. But he came as he went, clean-shaven, in a suit and hat. When he took me into his arms, I wasn't comfortable. I looked at him as at a stranger. Mom explained what my problem was and in the morning he showed me how he shaved every day. He even put a little foam on my nose, as he used to do before he went away. He told us that he had won money in the lottery in Uruguay and had a small knitting factory there. I don't know why he came back. Perhaps he thought that Uruguay was not a place for his daughters.

Adventures and Uncertainties

When my father returned home in 1931, we were in the middle of the depression. People had lost their jobs and students had lost their stipends. The municipality created some road reparation work to ease the students' hopelessness by giving them work a few days a week, and also helped the poor by providing them with potatoes, coal and bread. I remember this because when I walked to school in the morning, I would see the students, with their exclusive university hats, repairing the sidewalks.

At school, I met a girl in my class who lived at her grandmother's place. She never mentioned her parents. Thin and small, with olive skin, large dark eyes and very dark hair, this girl told me that she performed in a circus as an acrobat. She never took part in group activities and was usually alone, without any friends. One day she approached me and told me that I would be able do all the pirouettes that she knew how to do because my body was as flexible and thin as hers. She would often do acrobatics and dancing in the corridors at school. I was excited when she taught me all the exercises and I followed her example, improving rapidly. Eventually, I could put both legs around my neck, do the splits and dance on the headboard of my parents' bed without falling. When I put on a performance at home, my dad was astonished, but he didn't approve of my acrobatic skills.

Even so, Dad later took me to Warsaw to a circus performance.

The huge circus building was built of bricks, but inside had the shape and canvas of a traditional circus tent. The title of the show was "Circus Under Water." There were all kinds of athletic performances and clowns and also a scene about the abduction of Helen of Troy. I didn't really know anything about Helen of Troy, but I was watching what happened after Theseus abducted her. Horses galloped around the stage and Polydeuces put her on a horse and they escaped. While this was showing, the centre of the circus was in darkness. When the light shone back to the middle of the circus, I saw a pool filled with water. Girls in bathing suits jumped into the pool, swimming and performing acrobatics. The show was magnificent. I was thrilled and my father was delighted that I liked it.

After trying my hand at being an acrobat, I decided to be a street singer. I was excited by this idea and wanted to convince my father that this was what I really wanted to do. I loved to sing – I had a good voice and a good memory for songs, so I had all I needed for my career. I liked the idea of walking freely from one street to another, singing school songs and modern songs from the radio. My father, however, didn't want a singer in the family. He nagged me to study math, which I had trouble with. My father wasn't very strict, but he didn't just allow us to do anything we wanted. I knew that I could sing in the street even if I didn't know the multiplication table, but he didn't want an acrobat or a singer for a daughter; he wanted me to study. We had the same dialogue every day:

"How was school?" he would ask.

"Everything was just fine, Daddy. When the teacher gives a mathematical problem to solve, I write out the questions and my classmate does the counting. She never makes a mistake. She is good in math, and I am very good in Polish. We get high marks."

"Daughter, you will never learn this way. Tomorrow you have to solve the math exercise by yourself, including the counting."

"I can't remember all the numbers."

"I know that you remember a lot of songs and poems by heart."

"I know, but it is because they rhyme. You see, I remember six times six is thirty-six. And five times five is twenty-five. All the rest is very difficult."

"You can learn if you want," he would always reply without a smile.

My parents were different from the other parents in our community. None of my friends had one parent from Poland and the other from Russia, and none had a mother who spoke Polish with a Russian accent or mixed Russian and Polish words. We spoke three languages at home: Polish, Russian and Yiddish. When I began to write poems, Dad was proud of them and showed them to a neighbour, who told him that I had an excellent command of Polish and that the poems were very good. When the war broke out, though, I lost five years of both my writing and my hopes – they turned into ashes, to oblivion.

~

A few weeks after my father came home from Uruguay, I was asked to go to the principal's office. He greeted me nicely and invited me to sit on a chair on the opposite side of the desk. The principal was a short, hunchbacked man with a small oval face and blue eyes. His hair and moustache were completely white. He wore a three-piece suit and his glasses were attached to a thin chain. He gave me a letter for my father. The next day, Dad went to meet the principal, who welcomed him and asked him about his trip. Then he told my father that he had invited him to ask if he would carry the Polish flag to the church during an upcoming parade for a patriotic celebration. My father was grateful for the important distinction, but told him that, as a Jew, he preferred not to go into the church. The principal then told him that there was another purpose for his visit: since I was a very intelligent student, he wanted to guide my future education. Dad thanked him, without giving him any assurances. In spite of the principal's offer, Dad registered me at the Tadeusz Kościuszko school that my sister and Halina attended, where the principal knew our family. The district boundaries had changed and it was closer to home.

In 1934, at the age of fourteen, my sister graduated from elementary school. Although my parents wanted her to go to high school, Regina refused. Influenced by her friends, she wanted to work. In no time, she was hired as a salesgirl in a big retail textile store. The owners trusted her and even sent her to Warsaw to buy merchandise for the store. Once, she surprised me with a present of a navy blue raincoat, which fit me perfectly, and sporty brown shoes with a little heel from the Bata store. The store where she worked needed another person to help out before the summer holidays. I was only twelve years old, nearing thirteen, but the storeowner still asked me to come in. I didn't do much there, but sometimes they gave me money for my time. On other occasions, they gave me gloves or stockings. Once, the owner gave me the key to a drawer full of money. She asked me to make change for the larger bills. When I immediately returned the key to her and started to count the money, she watched me. From that day on, she trusted me completely.

I had my own ideas on how to make money. I asked my mom to buy batiste material and coloured thread and I crocheted it around with a nice lace pattern. It looked like a really expensive handkerchief and I sold it. Mom let me do almost anything I invented, though she didn't like when I accepted money from people who asked me to write letters for them. Once, I even wrote a petition for installing power to a family's home and they gave me fifty groszy for it. Mom kept telling me that this was a favour and I shouldn't accept money for it.

During the time I helped in the store, the owner asked me to accompany her and her two children to Morszyn-Zdrój, a resort near the Romanian border, during the summer vacation. Her son was seven and her daughter was nine, and she needed somebody to entertain them. Mom sewed a few beautiful outfits for me especially for the resort. The children were absolute savages; their behaviour was outrageously disrespectful and they didn't have basic manners. They didn't know how to sit properly at the table, they didn't pay attention and instead of walking, they ran. I tried my best to entertain them by telling them stories or reading to them, and I even invented games to make them interested in something. I tried to make them more civilized and when I couldn't succeed I was sad, frustrated and homesick. It was my first time far away from home.

~

I was still attending school when the Spanish Civil War broke out in 1936. After school, I read newspaper articles about the positions of the government forces and the civilian population who had taken up arms against the government. The losses were heavy on both sides. I could understand what a war meant because of my history lessons, but fighting against one's own brothers because of different ideologies wasn't easy for me to understand. I would need to know more about politics to truly comprehend what fighting for power meant. What especially wasn't clear to me was how there could be hate even among families. How could brothers kill one another?

When it was time for me to graduate, I was nervous. There was a party for the graduating students and I needed to know how to dance. Dad had taught us how to dance when we were quite small by having us stand on his feet as he moved along, but now I had to have more serious lessons from him. I wore my pleated navy-blue skirt and a white blouse with a sailor collar to the party. The male teachers wore their best suits and the female teachers wore the nicest dresses I had ever seen. I remember Mrs. Mazurkiewicz, the principal's wife, who taught us handicrafts, and her brown taffeta long dress with a pleated collar high around her neck, Mary Stuart–style. My Polish and social studies teacher, Mrs. Olejnikowa, who also taught carpentry to the boys, wore a sleeveless long black dress. Our geography and botany teacher, Miss Swietlinska, wore a floral printed dress and her long string of amber beads that came to her waist. She had often worn the necklace, which I loved, in class. When I described my graduation party to my daughter, she must have kept that episode in mind. So many years later, when I came to visit her in Canada, she gave me a string of amber beads that came from Russia. They are beautiful, but I seldom wear them because I am afraid to lose them.

At the graduation, the tables were covered with white tablecloths and trays filled with canapés and soft drinks. When the music began to play, Mrs. Olejnikowa opened the dance with me because I was light and she was pregnant at the time. The boys were shy, and chose to dance with girls taller than me. We were well-prepared for the event, having been shown how to behave in a ballroom and how to invite someone to dance. Mr. Ordysinski, who taught anatomy and physics, asked me to dance. I still remember my math teacher Mr. Biernacki's advice for the future: "Whatever you do, try to be the best."

The summer after I finished elementary school, I was confused and didn't know what to do next. Mom didn't want me go to the ORT technical school to learn a trade. She said that she didn't want us sewing. A few of my friends registered there, while others went on to high school. There was still time to register, but I couldn't decide. One day, as I was walking with my friends along the street, we stopped at the Abramowicz photography studio to have a look at the pictures in the showcases that hung on both sides of the entrance. I noticed a small paper in the office window that said, "Apprentice to learn photography required." None of my friends paid attention to this ad, but I started thinking perhaps it was what I wanted to do.

When I returned home, I confided in my mom. In the morning, she told me to buy new ribbons for my long braids and she combed my hair and put the new ribbons in. Then I went to the studio and asked if I could learn photography. Mrs. Helena Spiegel, the daughter of the owner, asked me my name and right away knew who I was. Smiling, she put a lectern on a small table beside the desk for me and gave me pencils and negatives. She asked me to sit on the chair and showed me how to sharpen the pencils and how to retouch the imperfections on faces. After two hours, she told me to come back after lunch. I concluded that I hadn't done too badly because at the end of the day she told me to come in the next morning at eight. I was happy, but when I told Dad about it that afternoon, he got angry because he knew the Abramowicz family from when he used to date Mrs. Helena's older sister, Mary. A big portrait of her sitting on a stone hung in the studio. She was really beautiful. When my father left for the military, she had married Dr. Handelsman, who was in charge of the psychiatric patients at the hospitals in Tworki, not far from Pruszków.

After two weeks of training, Mrs. Helena called my dad to sign a paper, since I was a minor, for benefits. It wasn't easy for him to relent, but he signed. Mom made a beautiful overdress of heavy black georgette material for me to wear to work and Mrs. Helena, with great care, taught me everything that I needed to know. She showed me how to take pictures and retouch positives. She was pregnant at the time and soon I would be able to replace her when she had her baby, which was why they had been looking for an apprentice. Apprentices usually got one złoty a week, but she gave me three. The whole Abramowicz family was very nice to me.

There was another woman who worked for the studio and retouched the negatives at her home in Warsaw. Having to bring the negatives back the next day to the studio was inconvenient for her – she was a friend and was doing it as a favour. She quit as soon as I was ready to take over all the work at the office and gallery. When there was an overflow of work, Mrs. Helena gave me negatives and a lectern to take home so I could work at home in the evening. It was piecework and I earned a lot of money. I was paid the same as the other retoucher even though she had been doing this type of work for thirty years. The custom then was to give any money earned to one's parents, and my mom kept mine for me until I needed something.

I had chosen something I liked to do, I was responsible and the work was artistic. But Mr. Henryk Spiegel soon had other plans for me. He found out that the government had opened a School of Photography and Cinematography on Nowy Świat Street in Warsaw and he made inquiries, thinking that this school would be just the right one for my future. The only problem was that the school only accepted students from Warsaw. Mr. Henryk didn't give up, though. He asked for a meeting with the city's mayor, Mr. Stefan Starzyński, who had been his comrade in the battles for Poland's independence under the command of Józef Piłsudski. I waited, anxious to find out what would happen.

Mrs. Helena gave birth to a son and I replaced her in the studio. I had to work on Sundays until she recovered and could start to work at the studio again. One Saturday, a handsome young man came in and asked if a picture he needed for his workplace identification could be ready on Sunday. I had him wait while I went up to ask Mr. Abramowicz if he could make an exception and let me do it that quickly. He said that if I retouched it on Sunday morning, he would make copies. I did and the man greeted me from outside the window every day as he passed on his bicycle on his way to work. I was flattered – he was maybe three years older than I was. The responsibility of working in the studio and making decisions about everything that happened in there made me feel important.

Another time, a woman came in with a fashionable hairdo. I didn't focus the camera properly for the shot and it came out rather blurry, but she liked it anyway. Another time, a woman came in with a plant that bloomed only every seven years. She was happy with her photo as well. I made a mistake retouching a circus artist who stuck needles into his arm. I was supposed to leave this part untouched but instead, I retouched it out. Mrs. Helena explained to me that it had to be visible. I wasn't trained for these things, but I did my best. Mrs. Helena doubled my weekly wages in addition to the negatives that I was retouching at home, so I was doing very well financially.

One day, my father told me some good news: the president of our Jewish community council, Mr. Rosenblum, had offered to rent us an apartment that had been built in the yard of his building. It had an electric light, two large rooms – a bedroom and a kitchen – and the apartment building had a cellar and an attic. Dad liked it and we moved again. He ordered a wide settee for us, covered with Gobelin, a tapestry material, and my sister and I slept on it together in the kitchen. As long as my dear sister, Regina, didn't bother me, which she sometimes did by pinching my nose, everything between us went smoothly. I had to follow my dad's philosophy and respect my older sister, even if she annoyed me, simply because she was older. In the bedroom, a white-tiled oven warmed the room. Mom made odd-looking stuffed dolls and put them on the top of the oven to decorate the room. She made beautiful drapes and Dad bought plants for her. On the walls hung embroidered tapestries that my sister and I had made. A lot of sun came in through the windows and the place was warm and cheerful, but we still had to bring in water from the yard.

I had a bright future. I felt secure, loved and appreciated. My parents gave us everything they could. Although we weren't wealthy, I don't remember feeling poor or jealous. I did not dream of living in another house or desire anything my rich friends had. When I think of my past, I think of having everything a child needed. I accepted my surroundings and did the best I could under the circumstances. Dad always said, "It is better to be a rich tenant than a poor landlord." He had an optimistic perspective. I don't think we were content, necessarily; rather, I would say that I had been brought up to be realistic, to adapt to any situation.

We may not have had a wide-open window to the world, but our imagination could flow in all directions, wherever we wanted, limitless. Everything was harmonious, an inspiration for my poetic soul. I liked the sun, the rain, the golden leaves in autumn and the glittering snow in winter.

Now, I realize that giving us a decent life had been a struggle for my parents. My father had had a hard time finding work in Pruszków when he returned and had then tried to find work in Warsaw, but the knitting factory where he worked before had gone bankrupt and he couldn't find any work. Next, he rented an orchard on a farm outside Pruszków that had various kinds of fruit trees. He was very good at estimating the profit he would obtain from it, but he had to stay there all summer to protect the fruit from thieves. He had to be there until he picked up the last fruit and sold it. He rented a basement to keep the fruit that had to ripen, such as apples and pears, and sold them in winter when fruit was more expensive. The second year, Dad took me with him for a few days. He taught me how to ride a horse and the farmer gave us fresh milk and cheese every day. He would pick a carrot right from the soil, wash it and then give it to me to eat. Dad's orchard work lasted for two years and that was it – Mom didn't like him to be away from home for so long.

When my father next went to Warsaw to look for work, he found a factory where small fish such as sprats were smoked. He bought a few cases and sold them to the grocery stores in Pruszków, taking orders for future deliveries. It was a good idea and he was able to make a decent income, but it was difficult for him to manage the business. Sometimes, when he was tired, he asked me to collect money from his clients. I did it willingly, introducing myself and asking for the money his clients owed him. His clients commented to him on how well behaved I was.

In 1937, two years before the war broke out, a young man named Mieczyslaw came by to speak to my father. My father knew his family, who, like his family, had been in Pruszków for many generations. Mieczyslaw had contacts with cattle breeders near the border with Ukraine and he made a business proposal to my father. The breeders produced all kinds of cheese and Mieczyslaw said he could order a certain quantity for distribution. He called my dad "Father," as his father had died a long time ago. Dad accepted the proposition. The first order came in, which my father sold, and more followed. When the war broke out, however, the German military forces occupied Poland and the transport trains were only used for military purposes. It was no longer possible to send the cheese by train.

I had never heard any friction between my father and Mieczyslaw, but when my father asked Mieczyslaw to return the money he had given him in advance for the next shipment, he replied that he would not give the money back because in wartime there was no obligation to continue business. My father had invested a considerable amount of money to both purchase the merchandise and transport it. He was so affected by his partner's attitude that, as I watched, he grew pale and fainted. I quickly ran to where a doctor lived and asked him for help. He came immediately and, after checking my father, asked me to come with him to his apartment to make a strong infusion of coffee for him. Mieczyslaw was still standing there when I returned with it. When my father felt better, I couldn't hold my temper and shouted at Mieczyslaw, "You see what you did to my dad! You aren't an honest man. You took money that belongs to us."

~

Just before the war, Mom suddenly began having nightmares, which were strange premonitions. She kept dreaming that someone had taken her children away, and she often cried in her sleep. The next day she would be sensitive, thinking about her dream. She looked sad. Mom had never truly felt happy in Poland, but she did the best she could. Few people understood her uneasiness, and we were too young to understand and give her the attention she needed. I recall my mother telling us about her dreams and asking us to be careful. Her plea couldn't help us when the war broke out.

I too had a dream before the war; it was about my parents and it worried me for a long time. I held back from telling anyone about it, apprehensive of being criticized and made fun of. I was also wary of not being able to capture the dimension of my experience, which felt extrasensory. One night, I went to bed at 11:30, falling asleep at once. Suddenly, my body felt light. Fearing that I would fall out of the bed, I grabbed the edge of the mattress. I felt myself rising higher and higher. Dark clouds surrounded me. I am not a fast thinker by nature, even though I wouldn't have known what to do anyway. I do remember thoughts of whether or not I was dying passing through my head.

This sensation lasted a while, until the clouds started clearing and I saw my parents appear from behind thick, dark clouds. They were standing very close to each other. I could only see them above their knees and I remember my mother's dress. It was brown with a matching jacket that had an artificial flower pinned to the lapel. It was a fall season garment. My father wore a suit with tiny brown squares over an aviation-blue background. Their clothes were muffled up in grey smoke, but their faces had their natural skin colour. They were standing there watching me. I called to them, "Mother! Father!" I didn't notice any expression on their faces, nor did they move or communicate to me in any way.

They appeared to be indifferent to my need to talk to them. I stretched my arms out to embrace them, but couldn't reach them. I started to talk again, this time desperate. "I am your daughter. I've been alone a long time. Let me stay with you. I remember you every day; I remember what you have taught me. I am well-behaved, as you wanted me to be. Let me go with you." I felt rejected, not getting any response from them. I was utterly devastated.

The cloudy image of them lasted for a while. Then, light broke through and I could see them brightly. My urge to get closer to them led nowhere. My parents moved slightly, turned around and, holding hands, they walked away. I still couldn't see their legs, so thick were the clouds around them. My mother turned her head for a last glance at me. My father walked away, not looking back. Still holding hands, their image disappeared behind the clouds. I felt a great emptiness; I was disconsolate. Then I felt myself being lowered to my bed. When I became fully awake, I was petrified, convinced that it wasn't a dream. I remained in bed until I was sure the events in my dream hadn't really happened. I fixed in my memory the feeling of levitation, the image of my parents and also the feeling of being lowered.

I was left with a lot of strange feelings and a heap of unanswered questions. Was it a privilege or a warning? Maybe it had been a premonition? I felt curious and unusual. I made up my mind that it was something I could neither explain to myself nor tell my family. The best thing was to keep it secret.

That dream has stayed with me, vivid, ever since it happened.

~

One day, my parents and Regina were sitting at the table, waiting for me to come home from work and have lunch with them. When I arrived, I was so excited that I couldn't even think of eating. I had good news to share with my family – I had been accepted to the newly opened school for photography and cinematography in Warsaw! With special permission from the mayor of Warsaw, I had been allowed to enroll. I was thrilled by the opportunity to get a higher education. Even more exciting to a girl my age was being able to wear the hat that was specially designed for the school. I would have to travel to Warsaw every day by train, but everyone was willing to help me with whatever I needed. My family talked about this event enthusiastically and wished me well. I was overwhelmed by the magnitude of the opportunity.

By this time, anxious rumours of war were swirling all around us. When Hitler became chancellor of Germany in 1933, he promised that his priority would be to reunite the territories the country had lost after World War I in the 1919 Treaty of Versailles. He broke the military clauses of the treaty by rearming and building an air force, and he prepared the population and his war machinery for territorial expansion. Germany had been economically broken by the previous war, and Hitler promised to improve the economy. His power of persuasion even convinced leaders of the socialist party to vote for him, at a time when the communists successfully held seats in many of the bigger cities. Hitler campaigned that reconstructing the country under his leadership would lead to the greatness and purity of their fatherland.

During the year before World War II, the Polish Minister of Foreign Affairs, Colonel Józef Beck, and Polish ambassador Józef

Lipski met with German Foreign Minister Joachim von Ribbentrop on a few occasions to debate territorial issues. The Treaty of Versailles had given the newly independent Poland a strip of previously German territory called the Polish Corridor, which provided Poland access to the Baltic Sea. The treaty also turned the city of Danzig, now Gdansk, into a free city, independent of both Germany and Poland. Gdynia, close to Gdansk, was soon developed as the main Polish port. Even apart from this arrangement, Poland had the right to that strip of land. Poland had some historical claim to the area, once the territory of Pomorze, which had been taken by the Germans in various battles. The population there spoke Polish and German, the Poles living side by side with the German population in harmony. Hitler's claim on the corridor was just an excuse for his plan of expansion. He precipitated the outbreak of the war by refusing further negotiations that had been on the agenda between Poland and Germany for a long time.

Before Germany invaded Poland on September 1, 1939, the mayor of Warsaw, Stefan Starzyński, made a public appeal on the radio for citizens to dig defence trenches. I volunteered to dig trenches along with other youth, supposing that it would help against air attacks. Many of us went to the train station to support the drafted soldiers travelling to their units. We sang and waved to them. Every patriotic gesture was a commitment to the greatness of our country.

Commander-in-chief Edward Rydz-Śmigły had succeeded Marshal Józef Piłsudski, the head of the Polish armed forces who had died in 1935. In Rydz-Śmigły's memorable speech, he said, "We will fight to the last button on our uniform." He lost more than his buttons; in the end, Poland would be ruined, bombed and occupied by the Germans, and there would be no escape for Poland's Jewish population.

September 1939

It was a sunny day in "golden autumn," as we called the season in Poland, when we heard the sound of heavy aircraft. The roar of engines was unusually loud and menacing. We all ran outside the house to look at the sky. Suddenly, darkness spread over us. I felt wrapped in a thick, smoky black cloud. I heard people saying, "Niemcy!" (Germans!) The darkness isolated me from my family. Although my mother and sister were near me, I felt surprisingly alone at that moment. That was the day war broke out. In Pruszków, the first bombs fell on the railway line. Then, the bombs fell all over the city.

After a few days of uncertainty, my father decided to go to Warsaw to help organize resistance. "We will fight the German forces," he said. "We won't let them occupy our capital city." He was also hoping for help from his nephews in Warsaw, who had served in the military a few years earlier.

My whole family walked the seventeen kilometres to Warsaw. When we arrived at the homes of our relatives, my father asked my cousins about joining the army, but it was already too late for volunteers to help defend our homeland. There was no army to join – Poland was defeated only a few weeks after the outbreak of war. The speed at which the Nazis invaded crushed the Polish army's resistance in a short time. Now, I can see how mistaken my father's expectations were. He didn't realize that the mechanisms of war had advanced so much since 1914. In 1939, technology replaced old-fashioned combat as the barbaric means of destroying human lives. We walked back from Warsaw to Pruszków. Along the same road, German troops, who appeared to me to be all the same height, marched triumphantly toward Warsaw, singing.

Soon, the SS Death's Head Brigade began harassing religious men in the streets of Pruszków by cutting off their beards. Those they couldn't recognize as Jews were pointed out to them by local Polish Nazi sympathizers. Now, there were collaborators within Poland. Even children in the street pointed to a Jew, shouting "Zyd" to make the Nazis' work easier. The Lithuanians and the Ukrainians in the German military beat up Jews who were pointed out by the Poles. This was just in the first weeks of the invasion.

Then, German soldiers grabbed us in the street and we were forced to do cleaning jobs all around the city, no matter how old we were. My father was assigned to the Nazi headquarters since he spoke perfect German – he had learned the language when he was a prisoner of war in World War I. My mother was sent to clean a school and my sister to clean in a factory. I was sent to clean a technical school for a short time, where the students laughed at me and told obscene jokes at my expense.

I kept working at the studio, although Mrs. Helena was careful not to let me be seen there. To avoid any contact with the German soldiers who came in to have their pictures taken, I worked in her bedroom at a table by the window. One day, Mrs. Helena's father was beaten on the street. He had lived in Pruszków all his life, was well respected and until two years earlier, he had been the only photographer in the city. Photographs for schools, police and official institutions, as well as weddings, graduations and religious events had all been taken at the Abramowicz Photo Studio. Everyone in town knew him. He still worked in the darkroom, developing negatives and printing the positives. He was a huge man, old by this time. Even he wasn't exempt from the pattern of general harassment of Jews.

In November, Jews were ordered to wear an armband with the Star of David. Jews continued to be grabbed in the streets, beaten and forced to work. Terrorized, they submitted, resigning themselves to obeying German orders.

One day, I met a former classmate at the library. He was the son of the principal of Gymnasium Zana and we had shared the same bench in the Józef Piłsudski primary school for many years. Now he turned to me and said, "What are you doing here?"

"The same as you, borrowing books," I answered innocently.

"Not any more! You are a Jew!" he retorted. I told him that I had the same right to be there as he did. The two women clerks at the checkout counter stopped working, frightened. They knew me and my family, as far back as my grandparents. It was a Saturday afternoon, the library was crowded and people began to express their opinions on the situation. I can't say it was evenly divided and, although not all of them objected to my being there, no one defended my right. I was lucky that just at this moment a neighbour, a poet whom I knew from my work at the studio, came into the library and risked his own safety to get me out of there.

Actually, this was the second time I had come up against the principal's son. Our first run-in had happened when we were schoolmates. Polska Kasa Oszczędności, the Polish Savings Bank, had organized an essay competition on the subject of the floods in the Polesie region of Poland. The prize was a small strongbox with a lock. After we wrote our essays, my teacher told me that mine was the best and that she had sent it to the principal's office with the highest possible mark, 5+. Nevertheless, the Gymnasium principal's son won the prize. During recess, the teacher told me, "You must know why that happened, but yours was the best." I recall it as the first time I felt discrimination in the school. Jewish boys were constantly harassed, shoved and mocked, but not so much the girls. Once war broke out, the distinction between Jewish boys and girls vanished.

~

In early October 1940, the Nazis ordered us to leave our homes, forcibly resettling us in the ghetto they had set up in a very poor area of
Pruszków where Polish workers used to live. They ringed the area
with barbed wire and an SS soldier guarded the one gate. The Nazis
established a Jewish Committee, who designated a place for everyone to live. We were assigned one bedroom and a kitchen in a house
where there was a little garden. An elderly couple and their daughter,
who used to own a little dairy store, lived upstairs. Dad immediately
started to dig the soil to plant potatoes and cabbage in case our circumstances didn't change quickly. My father tried everything possible to assure our well-being, but he couldn't improve our lot. The entire Jewish population was suddenly in the same confused situation. I
can't erase my memories of the ghetto and the misery we all felt.

Because the Nazis were rounding up the Jews for forced work and
beating them on the way, Dad could no longer go out to continue his
business. As my sister was older than me, my parents thought that
she would be in danger too, so I was the one designated to sneak out
of the ghetto, get to the outskirts of the city and go to a woman in a
nearby village to ask for food. I brought back potatoes, molasses and
bread. I had money to pay for it, but the woman wouldn't accept any
money because she knew my father.

Although my mother and Aunt Dina still didn't get along, my
mother asked my father to bring Dina and her daughter Toby to stay
with us. Toby had worked in a bank but they wouldn't employ her
any longer because she was Jewish. It didn't matter that Toby was associated with the Polish scouting organization and had served as a
guard at the municipal building. Dina's other daughter, Marysia, had
fled to the Soviet Union when the Germans invaded, but returned
to Poland when she gave birth to a baby girl. Almost everyone from
the Synalewicz family perished in the Holocaust. Only Aunt Dina's
younger son, Benjamin, survived, and that was because she had pleaded with him to leave Poland and avoid being drafted into the military,
as his father had been. In 1931, he was able to get to Argentina with

his new wife, Sofia. My father had tried to persuade Benjamin not to marry her for some reason, so we weren't invited to their wedding, nor did Benjamin come to say goodbye before he left for Argentina.

~

During our time in the ghetto, my mother fell ill. Despite the ghetto curfew, I ran to a friend's place to get some kind of remedy. But she didn't get any better by the morning. Dad managed to sneak out of the ghetto and get to Dr. Stefen's private clinic to ask him for help, and the doctor took his bag and hat and followed him. He knew our family because my grandparents used to deliver food supplies to his clinic. At the entrance to the ghetto, Dr. Stefen explained that one of his patients was sick and the soldier let him in. The doctor diagnosed my mom with a liver disorder, gave my father some medication for her and recommended light vegetable soup. We had vegetables in the cellar that Dad had prepared for winter. I didn't know how to cook, but I figured that vegetables had to be peeled, cut up and cooked in water with salt. Aunt Dina offered to cook for my mom, but I wouldn't let her or anyone else do it. After a few days, she felt better.

Life in the ghetto was intolerable. We coped because there was nothing else we could do. The young people I knew held meetings in different houses to avoid being detected by the Nazis. A teacher, Mr. Koziebrodski, often came to our meetings. It was only a distraction – there was nothing we could do to help ourselves.

No one came to our rescue. The Catholic Church chose to be silent in the face of our torment. Maybe one word from them to stop the hatred in the name of God would have had some effect, but maybe not. Antisemitism was often taught in church. Polish priests such as Father Trzeciak, who worked at a parish in Warsaw, fervently preached hatred toward Jews, without any encouragement from the Germans.

That January in the ghetto, in 1941, was my last birthday with my parents and sister. Friends dropped by and one of them, Zachariah

Artstein, brought a poem he had written as a gift for me. Years later, I learned that he had been one of the heroes who fell in the Warsaw Ghetto Uprising.

Although we lived in precarious conditions, we still hoped that our lives would soon improve. But, little by little, stressed by the on-going danger and daily humiliation, we began to feel hopeless. Then, we heard a rumour that we were going be deported to the Warsaw ghetto.

From One Ghetto to Another

On a dark afternoon at the end of January 1941, we heard a sound like somebody forcing the door. In the blink of an eye, my father reached the door and secured it so it couldn't be opened from the outside. Awaiting the worst, my father passed by the window to put the light out. One of the bandits glanced through the glass and must have recognized my father because they walked away, axes in their hands. Perhaps it was his conscience that had made him pass us by. It was frightening, and everybody felt shaken all night.

The next day, we were told to get ready to move – the rumours of evacuation we'd been hearing proved to be true. We saw that all our former Polish neighbours and the neighbours of other families were now waiting at the wire fence to loot our possessions. They had been told about the move beforehand and that was why those men had tried to rob or maybe kill us the night before. Before we left the ghetto in Pruszków, my father destroyed everything that was left of our belongings and, in a rage, poured naphtha over the provisions in the basement. His anger was justified. An injustice was being done to us. Those people who came to loot didn't deserve better.

The weather was strangely beautiful the day we were deported to the Warsaw ghetto. It was white all over, and sunny. The glistening snow crackled under our boots as we approached the trucks the Germans had prepared to transport us. With bundles in our hands, we waited for orders from the Nazis. Elderly people climbed into the trucks with difficulty while the Nazis yelled at them.

I begged an SS officer to let me go in the same truck as my mother and sister. He refused, yelling at me. I had to obey his order to go to the last truck. This was the first separation from my family and later I wondered if it was possibly the very moment that determined my destiny. The truck was loaded full with women and I stood in the middle, observing their faces. Meanwhile, my father, in yet another truck, volunteered to help the old and sick through the ordeal. Surprisingly, during the journey, what I remember was silence, although sometimes I heard a deep sigh. People looked resigned. Few of us knew each other and no one was in the mood for socializing. Everyone was in a state of shock.

When we got off the truck near the train station, an SS officer told me to go to where the trains stood ready to take their human load to the Warsaw ghetto. The first load of people, including my mother and my sister, was nowhere to be seen. The train cars were empty, as empty as my heart felt while waiting there alone, desperate to see someone from my family. I felt as though my senses of sound and sight were blocked out, as if I were isolated from the outside world.

Hours later, some women arrived and got into the train car where I was waiting. They had been washed and "disinfected," and their heads were bowed from this shameful experience. I asked them if they had seen my mother and sister. "They will be here soon," one of them told me, without adding any further explanation. My mother and sister didn't end up coming into the car. We met up later in Warsaw, in a big holding space that looked like a school gymnasium.

My father found us all sitting on the floor of the large hall in Warsaw with thousands of other people, feeling hopeless. There, I heard what happened to my mom and sister. Mom told Dad that they all had to undress to be disinfected. Mom pushed my sister behind her so the beasts could not see my sister's naked body. She cried as she told the story. At this moment, Mr. Henryk went by and gave us a few lumps of sugar to strengthen our spirits. In the morning, we were allowed to disperse within the ghetto. Our cousin Yadzia gave us her apartment to use and went to stay with her in-laws, where they had spare rooms.

Yadzia was married to Izik Wainfeld and had a little blond son with the same blue eyes as his father. My cousin Itzhak, Benjamin's older brother, lived with his family in a different building in the ghetto. I also remember that my cousin Mindy, who was married to Aaron Rosenberg, was in the Warsaw ghetto. I don't know exactly what happened to Aunt Gela and her son and his family. As far as I know, all perished in the same way – in the camps.

The Warsaw ghetto was already overcrowded with Jews who had been brought in from the outskirts of Warsaw and other surrounding towns. On the streets, Jews were indiscriminately beaten or shot. Little children, instantly orphaned, could be seen everywhere, crying, hungry and sick, abandoned. The older ones begged. Homeless, near-skeletal people were wandering the streets, their stretched-out hands looking like sticks wrapped in dry, yellow skin. Corpses covered with paper lay where their exhausted bodies had exhaled their last breath.

I remember waiting with my mother and sister for my father to come home from synagogue while we were in the ghetto. Every few minutes, I would look out for him. When I finally saw him, walking with his prayer shawl still on his shoulders and his prayer book in hand, I ran to meet him and clung to his neck. I was so happy to see him! Not long after that, I was alone, without a family, without roots, lost.

During this horrendous time, many youths chose to enter the training kibbutzim that had been established within the ghetto area by the Zionist movements Hashomer Hatzair and Dror. Their main hope was to organize resistance. Not all of the members shared the collective ideals of a kibbutz. Some were simply without family, without means and without a home. However, many became loyal members of the movement, even though conditions there were just as tough as anywhere else in the ghetto, often with only one meagre meal a day. For the idealists, of course, the kibbutz represented the hope that some day they would get to Palestine, the dream of their lives.

The kibbutzim in British Mandate Palestine were first created at the turn of the century. They were a refuge for youths who had escaped the pogroms of Russia and the antisemitism of Poland by immigrating to Palestine in the hope that it would become an independent Jewish state. They started new lives as pioneers, developing skills in agriculture, building and self-defence, providing role models for kibbutzim in the Diaspora. The kibbutzim were successful in attracting young people in Poland to *hachshara* (transition training), where they, too, prepared to immigrate to pre-state Israel and rebuild the land of their ancestors.

In British Mandate Palestine, the young pioneers first banded together in small groups or *kvutzot*, then in communities as larger aliyah and other groups of people joined them. This was the beginning of the kibbutz way of life. Women lived in separate housing. Like the men, they had a hard time finding work. Apart from working in the kitchens and doing domestic chores in rich people's houses, nothing was available. Soon they realized they would have to look for nontraditional jobs and show their ability to perform in trades that up until that time had been reserved exclusively for men.

As these women became accepted on the very jobs that had been denied to them before, they initiated an era of emancipation. As the girls achieved recognition, the kibbutzim became mixed. The idea of mixed kibbutzim raised moral questions, since religious and traditional families frowned upon mixed groups. However, overall, the cooperative life on the kibbutzim began to flourish.

In Warsaw, the Dror Zionist youth movement had a training kibbutz, a type of commune. However, with the outbreak of war in 1939 it became impossible for the people there to carry on as they had before. My sister decided to join the kibbutz Dror group not long after our arrival in Warsaw in 1941 because she was drawn to the idealism of the movement and was driven by the hope of resistance. My father helped her move her belongings to the group's house in the ghetto, but his sensibilities were hurt by the idea of his daughter living under the same roof as boys in a place with a questionable reputation. He didn't say a word because of the dangerous and hopeless situation in the ghetto – perhaps he thought this was her best means of survival. But after she had gone, he sat at the table all afternoon with his head in his hands, saying nothing. The next morning when we woke up, my father was gone, without leaving any message behind. We heard nothing for two weeks. Then a letter was delivered to us along with a big loaf of bread. My father had escaped to Siedlce, a city about one hundred kilometres to the east. In the letter he wrote, "I couldn't bear it that my daughter chose to join the kibbutz." He told us to find a smuggler who could help us to leave the ghetto and join him in Siedlce.

My mother and I felt torn: we didn't want to leave my sister in Warsaw, but we also wanted to be with my father. My mind was in turmoil and I felt thrown into a whirlwind. I was young and inexperienced – I had never travelled alone, and everywhere I was used to going was close to home; I had only walked to school and to the library or visited my friends. Although I had been working at the photography studio for more than a year before the war broke out, I was still naive in facing life's problems. In the end, I didn't solve my problems by myself, anyways. It was destiny that guided me, I'm sure.

I thought back to my life in Pruszków only a year earlier, which now seemed so far away. When I had decided to apprentice in photography, it was with my mother's knowledge. When I got accepted and told my father, he was shocked and very much against it because he thought it improper for a young girl to be working. Although the studio was only two blocks from home, he always waited for me after work, afraid to let me walk alone in the late afternoon.

Now, I was forced to make a major decision. If I went with my mother to join my father, I thought my sister would feel abandoned. I couldn't do to her what my father did to us, walking away from the family because he couldn't accept his daughter joining a progressive movement. Despite my anger, I understood my dad's need to find a way to avoid the ordeal. Meanwhile, my thoughts were still with my sister.

I'm sure that it was never easy for the pioneers to leave their homes and parents and join a kibbutz in Palestine. But in peacetime they had their romantic ideals to keep them going, the excitement of learning how to build a new society. For many of us now, it was a sudden and unexpected decision in the face of seeing our previous lives crumble. Suddenly, the family didn't exist any more. It was hard for me to decide what to do. Sleepless nights didn't help either. In spite of the fact that my sister initiated the separation, my initial thought was that I couldn't fail her. I made up my mind and decided to join the kibbutz group as well.

From then on, I wouldn't have to make any decisions: the movement would make them for me. In the kibbutz, I would only have to follow orders. In a way, I imagined it would be easy, since I didn't really know what I wanted anymore, and to stay close to my sister, I felt I could do it. I convinced myself that my father could protect my mother and I should stay near my sister. As it turned out, none of what I imagined was right.

Mom and I found out the name of a man who, for a fee, smuggled people out of the ghetto. We wrote a letter to my father telling him when she would arrive and a few days later I took my belongings to the kibbutz house. That same day, I accompanied my mother to the place where the smuggler waited. We kissed goodbye. It was the last time I saw my mother. This was the end of my tender family years.

～

There was no room at the Dror house for the new people arriving every day, but no one was turned away. The old-timers, as we called the original kibbutzniks, did their best to accommodate the newcomers, although they would reproach us with a certain amount of bitterness, saying we had only joined because the war had forced us to. In many cases, they were right. We learned that the idealists had worked for years, waiting to go to the Promised Land, but their dream was as unattainable as any of ours.

In the early spring of 1941 it was still very cold. The ghetto was severely overcrowded, as was the kibbutz, and it got worse every day. Fearing a typhus epidemic, Lidia Zamenhof – the daughter of Ludwig Zamenhof, who invented the international language Esperanto – came to inoculate us. Another visitor was Dr. Janusz Korczak, an experienced educator who ran the orphanage in the ghetto. He noticed that we had to eat our meals in three shifts because of our large numbers and commented that it was depressing to wait so long for a meal. "Besides," he said, "the people that eat in the first shift are hungry again by the time the third shift goes in." But there weren't enough dishes for everyone to eat together.

A solution came a few weeks later, when the committee presided over by Yitzhak Zuckerman and Zivia Lubetkin announced that they had found a place for a group of boys and girls to work in the countryside, on a privately-owned farm in Czerniaków, a suburb of Warsaw about ten kilometres away. Yitzhak told us, "The farm carts will take you there tomorrow. Chavera [Comrade] Leah will be in charge of the group. Shalom." He walked out of the room. I was one of those chosen to go to the farm, although I had been in the commune for only a short time. I was shattered by this decision. It meant leaving my sister, who was the only reason I had come in the first place.

I realized then that my decision to protect my sister wasn't wise at all. My brilliant idea of staying close to her had quickly ended in separation. I had to leave and I knew there was nothing that Regina could do about it. No one argued with the kibbutz's orders, not even my sister, who was well liked by the kibbutzniks. Regina had to leave for work so early in the morning that she couldn't even wave goodbye to me when I left for the farm.

Czerniaków

The farm carts we rode in to Czerniaków were large and deep, usually used to transport vegetables to the market in Warsaw. When we arrived that afternoon, the farm's administrator, Otto Müller, greeted us and showed us where we would sleep. It was a large empty stable divided by a wall: the east side for the girls, the west side for the boys. Along the length of the longer wall was a shelf made of wooden planks, which were our beds. The stable was dimly lit. Straw was brought in to cover the planks and a few spare blankets were spread on top of the straw. We placed our belongings under the shelf and went outside to look around.

Crossing over a narrow ditch was the way to the kitchen. Near the entrance to the farm was the house of the Polish owner, Mr. Zatwarnicki. Further on lay Mr. Müller's house, past which was a construction site where contract workers who were mostly from the Polish-Ukrainian border area worked. The local farmhands lived within walking distance and went home after work.

Leah Perlstein, the girls' leader, went with Mr. Müller and a few of the other old-timers to look at the kitchen to find out about the provisions. Otto Müller respected Leah, who had been a schoolteacher before the war. She wore a grey suit with a navy blue blouse, her brown hair was cut short, and she had a fresh round face with hazel eyes that narrowed when she smiled. She was sincere and responsible on the job. Müller, who admired her wit and attitude, treated her as an equal and chatted with her often.

As soon as she and the others got back to the stable, Leah told us that we had to get up early in the morning and should go to sleep. It wasn't a question of looking around to find a comfortable spot: wherever one stood, that's where one lay down. I stood in the middle of the stable, looking at the large shelf. There was a momentary silence, then Leah broke the tension, saying, "I will sleep beside Balbinka. She has a duvet!" For a moment, the uncertainty was gone. When we were all lying on the shelf, ready to go to sleep, Leah raised her head and added, "We look like canned sardines." We all laughed.

The real *chalutzot*, pioneers, were Chana, Necha, Masza, Dvora and Malke, the nurse. The boys' *madrich*, leader, was Aaron. All had belonged to the Dror movement for many years. Being experienced in the kitchen, they assumed management responsibilities. They woke us up early for breakfast. As soon as we were ready, Otto Müller came to assign everyone to different jobs.

The farm specialized in breeding hogs and growing vegetables. The horses, cows and chickens on the farm belonged to the estate and the arrangement between Dror and the farm owner, Mr. Zatwarnicki, was that we would work in exchange for food. Boys worked in the stables with the cows and horses, as night guards and as shepherds. The girls were sent to the hotbeds, where wooden frames were filled with soil for the germination of seeds. The gardener, Mr. Lipowicz, had graduated from the Warsaw Agricultural University and instructed all those who were working at the hotbeds with vegetables, his specialty. He was in charge of producing the early seedlings, which would then be taken across a lake that divided the farm, and transplanted in the fields there.

The lake that divided the land was large and we had to cross it in a raft every day. The raft was a wooden platform with two steel cables attached to each side one metre high. The cables were tied to pillars on both sides of the firm ground across the lake. To move the raft forward, we had to hitch the handles on to the cable, and then turn the handle backward. It was fun in the beginning, but after a long day of hard work we were tired and it didn't seem so entertaining. Yet, we always sang going there and back, trying to forget our reality.

Nastka, Otto Müller's favourite local worker, would wait for us at the raft, guide the group to the fields and give us our instructions. She was a large young woman, dressed nicely for the job. The head scarves that covered her blond hair had colourful flowers on them. Nastka was shy, responsible and well behaved in contrast to the other farmhands, who were loud, disobedient and lazy. She never got angry with us, and we appreciated her help.

In almost all the workplaces, there was someone who knew what had to be done. Everything was well organized under Otto Müller's orders. The local workers, though, didn't show any tolerance or sympathy toward us. We were fresh blood, experiencing an endurance test. Our mission was to survive at any cost.

Otto Müller was a *Volksdeutsche*, an ethnic German born outside Germany. In his late-forties, he was tall and heavy and tanned from being outdoors all day long. He was married to a slim and fragile dark-haired woman who was always sick. His two small children, a boy and a girl, were fragile like their mother. No wonder he liked to tease Nastka. When Mr. Müller gave her the day's orders, she listened to him attentively, while her face blushed rosy red. Heinrich, one of our boys, soon became Müller's favourite. Heinrich came from Gdansk and spoke both German and Polish. He was fifteen years old and tall for his age. He had ash-blond hair, greyish-blue eyes, a smart-looking face and he smiled often. One of Heinrich's jobs was to hook up the horses to the cart and ride to the restaurants in the village to collect leftovers for the hogs, mostly on Sundays. It was too heavy a job for his age, but he never complained. Müller also liked me and called me "daughter" from day one. He relied on me when an extra job had to be done. Being appreciated by the boss was fine, but it definitely had its good and bad sides – the extra jobs sometimes meant overtime or work on Sundays.

In the kitchen, the *chalutzot* worked in two shifts. They badly needed help, so Gucia, Hela Szuster, Rushka Borenstein and Cyla Kifkowicz, all from my hometown, occasionally took turns helping out. There were also two boys assigned there to help with the heavier duties. I preferred the back-breaking labour in the fields to working in the kitchen. Besides, the old-timers were better at it. I liked the fields and the fresh air, which made me feel like I was part of nature.

One of the boys who helped out in the kitchen always served my food on a plate decorated with forget-me-nots – the only one of its kind and the prettiest plate in the kitchen. I still remember him and how flattered I felt. Gucia reserved the basin to wash my hair. I couldn't complain of lack of privileges.

One night, a few days after we settled in Czerniaków, we heard someone knocking at the door. Otto Müller called out, "Wake up, children! I need you to do me a special favour. The forecast is for frost tonight. We have to cover the hotbeds with straw mats, otherwise the early sprouts will freeze. Be ready in fifteen minutes; I'll show you the way." We all jumped off the shelf and got ready quickly. When Mr. Müller came back after waking up the boys, Leah asked him why he chose us to help him out. "The others are uneducated and irresponsible," said Mr. Müller, which made us feel worthy. We later realized that it was because the seasonal workers wouldn't go.

The couple who dealt with the seasonal workers were local farmhands. The husband was always in a good mood, but his wife was demanding and used to yell at them. We occasionally heard her colourful, earthy vocabulary, which was utterly new to us. "You are staring like a bull at a painted gate," she would say. Or, "What are you waiting for, the hen to lay an egg?" We had fun listening to her and would repeat her sayings at Oneg Shabbat, which was celebrated on Fridays after work. Chana lit the candles, and we sang. We always sang, as an antidote to our sad thoughts. Leah relished the jokes or unusual events told on Friday nights and she was interested in our well-being. From time to time, we read essays over dinner and I would write a humorous monologue. We put all our adolescent energy into that new experience. We weren't unhappy, although we worked hard. The skin on my hands got so chapped that it bled, but I didn't complain.

In late spring, a month or so after I arrived at the farm, I received a letter from my parents. Most of the letter was taken up with their worries for my sister and me: they were anxious to hear how we were and asked how we were managing. They mentioned that they had rented a room in Mrs. Kartofel's house and that there was no ghetto yet in Siedlce. Although they wrote little about themselves, I perceived the misery that they must have been going through. Still, as I read the letter, I felt hopeful that somehow my parents would find a way out from everything that was happening. My father spoke German, Polish and Russian fluently and was good-looking, with excellent manners. He knew many Polish people. My mother was a loyal and serious woman, and highly educated. If any of these qualities counted, surely they would make it, I thought.

I also got a letter from my sister, who was still with the kibbutz group in Warsaw. The *chalutzim* and *chalutzot* were taking any jobs that remained in the ghetto. We exchanged the news from our parents and agreed that they might need money – although money wouldn't be enough to save them – but we had none to send. We had nothing to offer but our good intentions. I felt useless and powerless to do anything. It was a terrible feeling.

Leah knew what was happening back in the Warsaw ghetto, but not all the news was transmitted to us. It was getting increasingly difficult for anyone from the Dror committee to smuggle themselves out of the ghetto and visit us in Czerniaków, as they had before. Still, sometimes other *chaverim* (comrades) would come in, those who worked outside other ghettos as messengers between various cities. Mostly, they were gathering news or smuggling weapons at the risk of their lives. Sometimes, Leah would get news about the situation in the ghetto from Mr. Müller. Because he was a *Volksdeutsche*, he had permission to listen to the radio, which was a secret that only a few of us knew about.

One of the messengers outside the ghetto was Lonka Kozibrodzki, also from my hometown, and a university graduate. Once, she came to Czerniaków and invited a few girls to the cinema in the village. The movie was *The Great Waltz*, which told the story of Johann Strauss II. I was so excited that I followed the melodies quite loudly and Lonka had to shush me. I'd forgotten my manners after living far from civilization.

One day, the gardener confided to me that the following day, he was going on strike. "I don't know how long I will be away," he said, "but you know what needs to be done. Watch the hotbeds. They must be watered daily. The sprouts must be transplanted in two weeks. The cucumbers need a lot of water. Those ten rows have to be covered at the end of the day: they still need warmth. I'm trusting you to do everything."

The next morning, Otto Müller approached me, asking, "Daughter, what do we have to do today?" With an inquisitive smile, he added, "I know Mr. Lipowicz is devoted to his work. He wouldn't leave if he wasn't sure that the plants would be looked after." To me, looking after the plants was not just a matter of obeying orders, it was important to ensure that they grew properly. Mr. Müller knew how responsible I felt, so he put me in charge. It was not always easy to go along with my duty. I had to give orders to a few of the local workers and some small problems arose. They didn't like us because we were Jewish, and liked taking orders from me even less.

After a week, Mr. Lipowicz came back. He had negotiated with the owner for better wages. He returned to his job with a new project: to grow mushrooms, which we referred to by their French name, *champignons*. He ordered that a large, empty cellar be thoroughly cleaned and its walls painted with lime. He asked the administrator for a few boys and girls to help me carry down the soil to form beds for the mushrooms. Filling the wooden boxes with soil, lifting them and carrying them down the eight steps was quite a heavy job. I came up with the idea of putting a plank over the steps and sliding down the boxes, which made the job a lot easier and faster, too. Leah heard about my idea. For outstanding jobs, she always received some extras from the owner's kitchen for all of us, and this time was no exception.

When the cellar was ready and the beds made, the gardener called me in to show me how to plant the pads into the soil. He instructed me to water the mushrooms every day with a fine spray and gave me the keys to the cellar. "In a few weeks, you will see tiny white points," he instructed. "Once the growing begins, promise me you won't allow anyone in here, not even the owner's wife or her housekeeper."

The *champignons* were a delicacy, worth a great deal on the market. I took great care to water them daily with the fine spray, as the gardener had told me. It seemed amazing to me that, in spite of the war, some people could afford to buy expensive food. However, the order to prevent anyone else from coming into the cellar proved impossible for me to keep. The farm owner surprised me on more than one occasion by suddenly appearing while I was at work. One day, I happened to mention to the others at the table that the rosh gadol (big head) often came to visit me. The *chevra* didn't believe me. Everyone laughed. "He comes to see how the mushrooms grow? What do you mean?"

One Sunday, a group of us were chatting outside the kitchen when the housekeeper came to us, agitated. She recognized me because I had helped her to take out the pits from the cherries for jam. "Balbinka," said the housekeeper, breathing heavily, "People are waiting at the cellar to see the mushrooms." Mr. Lipowicz didn't work on Sundays and I was the only one who had the key. Mr. Müller could have asked me for the key and showed the cellar himself, but he refused. Since I had been the only one at the farm instructed by the gardener, Mr. Müller had sent for me. When I got to the cellar, four SS lieutenants were waiting there for me. They were agronomists. "Guten Morgen," (Good morning) they greeted me in German. "Dzień dobry," I answered in Polish.

Knowing they wanted to see the mushrooms, I didn't have to ask them what they wanted. I knew with whom I was dealing. I wasn't afraid, but I was thinking, if they knew that I'm Jewish ... I opened the door and lit the oil-burning lamp. One of the Germans courteously took the lamp from my hand, a gentlemanly gesture. What an irony! One of them translated their queries into Polish and they asked me how the mushrooms were planted. I answered all their questions, satisfying their curiosity. The whole thing took an hour. They were grateful to me for explaining to them the procedure and care these plants required. Just as they were walking away, the housekeeper asked for a few mushrooms. "I have to prepare supper for them," she said, looking at me pleadingly. I couldn't refuse. Anyway, it wasn't a crime, only a few mushrooms were given away. The next day I told the gardener what had happened and he laughed, praising me for how much I had learned.

The gardener's next project was to plant honeydew melons. The greenhouse was a high, large steel structure with glass walls and roof. I got the key to the greenhouse as well, and the reputation of being a good worker. Because I was careful with the plants, the gardener offered me cookies he bought especially for me. Since it was strictly a kibbutz life and everyone had to share everything, I didn't accept. How could I explain to him that if I ate the cookies I would be cheating on my comrades?

~

As the weather warmed, the seedlings were ready to be transplanted to the fields across the lake. Bent all day with our legs wide open, planting, we all suffered pain in our lower backs and aches in our leg muscles. It took a few days for our bodies to get used to this unaccustomed posture. When we had to step over the ditch to get to the kitchen for supper, everyone groaned from pain. We were so stiff that we could hardly walk. We all laughed, but it really wasn't funny at all.

In the summer, we harvested tomatoes. It was a very busy time, with a lot of people working together in the field. Even Otto Müller showed up to help. On this occasion, the good Mr. Müller, though twice as tall and three times as heavy as me, chose me as his partner to lift the boxes full of tomatoes and carry them to the raft. The boxes had to be loaded onto the raft, ferried across the lake, and then carried from the raft to the waiting carts. We made many trips back and forth before the work was done. Finally, the last cargo of tomatoes was brought from the field and sent to the market.

It was good to be young and healthy, far away from immediate danger, for the time being at least. What would happen later, no one knew. We rarely talked about the circumstances that had brought us to the farm. Everyone had heartbreaking stories. Ignoring sadness made it easier to exist.

One night, a few of us had the idea of sneaking across the lake to visit the night guard on the other side. It was silly, but we were young and trying to have fun. We took a big casserole from the kitchen and I brought mushrooms and a honeydew melon for dessert. One of the shepherds brought meat to cook. We picked up some potatoes and carrots from the field, and then cooked it all together for a soup. I was particular with food at home, so I didn't eat any of the soup they made. I just went along for the adventure. We laughed about it later, when we remembered the quick trip at night to the field. We wouldn't dare to do it again. If the raft had been needed, we could have been in big trouble.

Another time, in a rebellious mood, Heinrich asked me to go with him in the raft to the field and back. I hesitated. "Come on, he won't be angry at us, don't worry. We are privileged." I enjoyed the adventure but was afraid of the possible consequences if we had been discovered. We also went for a ride in Otto Müller's boat. I never knew what Heinrich had in mind. On our boat trip, though, he was serious. He warned me to be careful with boys. "Don't trust anyone; don't get too close to them," he said. Even though he was a few years younger than me, he treated me as a kind of younger sister. "Take care of yourself," he said, "That's exactly what I would tell my sister." I was happy to step out of the boat. I was afraid of drowning.

Otto Müller used to ride his mare at night, dressed in a black cape. He would check up on the night guards in the fields, surprising more than one sleeping. For him, six in the morning was almost midday. He worked hard and expected the same from everyone. Once, he hitched two horses up to a carriage and invited me to go for a ride with him around the huge property. Another time, he invited Leah for a ride in the boat. Generally speaking, Mr. Müller didn't complain about us, but there were a few incidents. Once, he caught a boy sucking milk directly from a cow. Later on, the cow got sick and Mr. Müller sent that boy back to the ghetto. Another misfortune occurred when one of the seasonal workers reported to him that someone had made a joke about him at the Oneg Shabbat. Mr. Müller spoke to Leah and threatened to send all of us back to the ghetto. When a few of us went to ask for forgiveness, assuring him that it wouldn't occur again, he shouted angrily, "I will tear the Zion out of your heads!" He also reproached us for wasting food. He allowed us to eat as many vegetables as we wanted, but some would have a bite and throw the rest away. He was right; this happened often.

Leah couldn't control everyone. A few of us were negligent, and some wouldn't wake up in the morning to go to work. Those few didn't seem to understand that we had nowhere else to go other than back to the ghetto, where death from hunger or disease was a daily event. Mr. Müller knew what the conditions were like in the ghetto, and that if he sent us there, it would be the end of us. He agreed to let us stay.

Mr. Müller told me that he was asking among his friends for a place in a private German home where I could work, and thus, survive. With a touch of cynicism, he said that he wanted me to survive so the Jews would have a chance of reproducing again when the war was over.

While we worked on the farm, the resistance organization in the Warsaw ghetto was preparing fighting groups. We heard this from Hela's brother, Szlamek, who had arrived in Czerniaków from the ghetto. He was just recovering from typhoid fever and was pale and weak. Typhoid fever, along with dysentery and starvation, killed thousands of Jews in the ghetto. Szlamek was only fourteen years old, short, with wide shoulders and unusually light eyes. He offered to stand *shmirah* (guard) outside the kitchen for us, and I stood beside him and asked about my sister. He was grave and gave short answers to questions about the ghetto. He told me that my sister was still at the kibbutz house. Later, he admitted that the situation in the ghetto was desperate. "People are dying from hunger or are shot on the street, their bodies thrown into mass graves. No help is coming from any-where," he said sadly, despair on his face. After the war, I found out that Szlamek fell as a hero in the Warsaw Ghetto Uprising. He had smuggled weapons into the ghetto through the sewers for the Jewish Fighting Organization, the resistance group in the Warsaw ghetto.

~

In spite of all the vegetables we were eating, the lack of protein and the dirt that accumulated deep in our skin caused us to develop ab-scesses. Almost no one escaped this plague. Malke, the nurse who also worked in the fields, was busy dressing sores after supper. She did her best to help but there were so many people to attend to that she asked a few people to help her. Because no one wanted this kind of a job, she asked me. Actually, I was happy to be able to help her clean the wounds and change the dressings.

Everything was fine until one day, a rumour was spread that Malke and some of her friends, Masza and Abram, were plotting something against Leah and the others in charge. I realized that it wasn't a good idea to be associated with Malke. I was naive about intrigues and so forth, and I had nothing to do with any plot. Apparently an incident had happened when a messenger arrived for a visit in Czerniaków with chocolate, a gift from Switzerland. Someone had seen some of the old-timers eating it. I didn't see this because it was during the day when I was in the fields, but that is what I heard.

In any case, a plot of some sort was reported to Leah and Aaron, the boys' leader. Aaron called a meeting with the organizing committee, who voted that the penalty would be to send the conspirators back to the ghetto. Among the inner committee members was a boy from Germany who wanted to be friendly with me. Because I hadn't responded to his wish, he voted against me, even though I was not involved. In the end, no one was sent to the ghetto. Malke and Masza were old-timers and besides, Malke was a nurse and very much needed in Czerniaków. Abram was a good worker, and, as for me, I had a fine sister and they wouldn't dare make her suffer. It didn't affect me, but I had learned a lesson, to avoid all this gossip and gossipers. My duty was to work, at which I excelled. That was enough for me. This wasn't an isolated case of a rumour; in fact, in the kibbutzim, just as in any small place, there was always someone who wasn't happy with something or somebody.

It was not easy to overcome the resentment of being treated unjustly after this incident. It burnt within my body. Soon afterward, it was very rainy and a perfect time to harvest cabbage. I had a wicker hamper strapped to my body. The people cutting cabbage threw them over my shoulders into the hamper. Their impact and weight, together with the inclement weather, was a kind of relief for my feelings of resentment. Carrying hampers full of cabbage and rhubarb, soaked to the bone, helped me overcome my anger and bad feelings. It was anger out of grief and sorrow. I was hostile for a long time, and racked with feelings of loneliness.

One day as I was working in the field, someone came to tell me that a man was waiting for me. I brought the raft to the other side of the lake and ran to the kitchen, where I introduced myself to him. He was about twenty or twenty-two years old, with dark blond hair and blue eyes, dressed in a sports jacket and black trousers. He got up to greet me and told me that he had a message for me from my father. "How are my parents?" I blurted. "How did you happen to meet them? Where are they?" – a cascade of words and questions came out. I asked so many things. He didn't know the answer to some of these questions. Others, I suspected, he wouldn't answer because he knew too much. He told me that he had seen my father where he worked and that my father had asked him to come and see me. He continued, "Your father wanted to know how you were. He asked if you had heard from your sister." The man was a priest, although he was dressed in civilian clothes. He had not seen my mother. He told me that they were now locked in the Siedlce ghetto at night. In the morning, the SS took them to work outside the ghetto.

We talked for a while. Chana asked him to stay for supper, but he excused himself and left. I tried to think of something that would help my parents in some way, but nothing occurred to me. I wrote a letter to my sister, telling her about the priest's visit. I said that if Dad had been able to contact a priest, perhaps he was also able to do other things to ensure their safety. I wrote that I was in a state of nirvana in my passive existence. I enjoyed my work in the fields. In a way, I was even happy there, being useful. As I couldn't help anyone, I had stopped worrying about it, I said. This wasn't strictly true: I was actually angry with myself because I couldn't do anything to alleviate my parents' unhappy existence and also because I hadn't been allowed to stay with my sister. I felt trapped, unable to do a thing about it. I also wrote that Mr. Müller had said he might be able to bring Mom and Dad to the farm. But that had been quite a while ago and nothing had happened. I believe he had good intentions, but after what the priest had told me about Siedlce I knew it was impossible. Who could pull Jews out from between the Nazis' paws once they were caught?

Another thing that rankled was that one of the old-timers from the kibbutz had told me that the reason I had not been allowed to stay in Warsaw with my sister was that the committee felt I wasn't suitable. They felt I would somehow spoil my sister, but I didn't believe that was true.

When I next received a letter from my sister, in answer to mine, she wrote, "You crazy poet, think seriously. This is no time for fantasies – the ghetto is closed, no mail comes now. Do you know anything else about Mom and Dad?" Although my sister called me crazy, being crazy made existence easier. I tried to make things into a game, but reality was revealed to me day after day like a dark cloud hanging over my life. That was the last letter I got from my sister. I never saw her or heard from her again.

~

During the fall of 1941, I heard Mr. Müller calling me across the fields early one afternoon. When he came up to me he said, "Go and sleep for a few hours. At eight o'clock tonight, after supper, I will take you to the barn to grind wheat." When I asked him why, he told me that a local farmhand had refused to do the grinding unless he was paid more. Since there would be no bread without the job being done, he knew that he could count on me. Night after night, for a week, I had to grind wheat by hand in a small grinder for enough flour to make bread for a few hundred people. It took twelve hours every night, from eight in the evening until eight in the morning.

When the night watchman began his shift, he would pass me a coffee and a sandwich that Gucia sent me from the kitchen through the small grated window into the barn. We would talk a little and then he would be off on his rounds and I would speed up my grinding. Rats ran all over the place all night long, jumping, staring at me. I looked away and went on with my job. This was the prize for being responsible.

The last night of my grinding duty, the watchman handed me a letter that had been left in the administration office. When I read it, I saw that it wasn't in my father's handwriting. Someone else had written it. It said that my father was sick with typhus, that my mother was fine and that they missed me. It was clear to me that my mother had asked someone to write because my father was either too sick or he was no longer alive.

At eight o'clock in the morning when my shift ended, Mr. Müller unlocked the door and let me out. For security reasons, I was always locked in like this, but if there had been a fire, I wouldn't have been able to escape. I walked off by myself, as far as I could. Alone, I cried for a few hours. My family was broken up and the world was falling apart. Merciless. This chapter of my life with my parents, who had given me my first feeling of love and affection, was coming to an end.

~

In the late fall of 1941, it grew cold and the ground was almost frozen. We were sent to dig ditches where we would later bury the harvested root vegetables for winter, before the frost got them. Local workers had been doing the job, but they were deliberately going at it very slowly, sabotaging Otto Müller's orders. They hated him. Because the job had to be done quickly, we were sent to help them out. The local workers laughed at us and mocked us, making despicable comments like "Jews don't know how to work," and "the Germans will kill you," and so on.

One of the last jobs before the snow fell was to roll up the wires from the tomato field. These wires were strung over the plants, which were attached by strings. At the end of every season, the wires had to be rolled up and put away for the next summer. This time, Mannfred and I were assigned to finish the job. The lake was already frozen, and we had to walk on the ice to the field. We worked as fast as we could, but there was still a lot to do.

Mannfred was born in Germany. He had come to Poland when Hitler expelled all the Jews of Polish origin. He was small for his age, always apathetic. He couldn't conceive of what had happened to him and why. He was also angry and talked only when he needed to. When it started getting dark, he wanted to go back to the farm but I said I thought we could do a few more rows. Without a word, he walked away. After a while, I got tired and decided to return to the kitchen. By then, it was really dark and, as I began walking over the thick ice, I didn't notice the wide holes that had been made by fishermen. People say that this kind of hole has a power of attraction because of the flow of water underneath. Perhaps it's true. In any case, I fell into one of them. My quick reaction saved me. I didn't panic and managed to support myself on my elbows, lifting myself out. Of course, I was wet all over. One of the fishermen a few metres away saw what had happened but made no move to help me. He was one of the local workers, a man three times my age who hated Jews and hated Mr. Müller. He was one of the ones who had mocked us as we dug the ditches to preserve the winter vegetables, and had worked under me previously, when the gardener put me in charge. Now, he had the opportunity to avenge the humiliation of working under my orders. He smiled as he watched me walk away.

When I walked into the poorly lit kitchen, no one noticed that I was wet and I was too ashamed to tell anyone what had happened to me. Then I realized that everyone had their jackets on, as if ready to go somewhere, and that they had been waiting for me. A strange feeling came over me, as though something very heavy were pressing down on me. The others had had supper already. I don't remember if it was Chana who prepared a sandwich for me. It was late. An order had come from the local authorities. We were to be "disinfected" and we were to go to the village immediately. Why us? We were disciplined workers, we worked hard, we were cultured ... of course, because we were Jews.

The menacing cruelty hung over our heads. We walked to the village almost silently, frightened, not knowing what to expect. After a while, Leah approached me. "Don't worry, Balbinka," she said, "I brought some money. Perhaps it will be enough to save your hair." I had no idea that in other places the SS had been cutting off women's hair. But Leah knew and she was worrying about my beautiful long hair. We arrived at a building and had to undress and hand our clothes to the Polish employees who were working under the orders of the Germans. Luckily, they had not been told to cut our hair. The heat of the disinfection ovens dried out my clothes and I felt lucky for that. On the way back to the farm, I sang at the top of my voice, trying to revive the spirit of the group.

~

Winter had come. It was freezing cold in the stable, where we had slept since we arrived in the early spring. Leah repeated endlessly, "I can't do anything. We depend on the administrator's good will. We have to stay here as long we are allowed. It's gaining us time." But she did ask Müller for a warmer place for us to stay during the winter.

Not far from the entrance to the farm was a three-storey house still under construction, and Mr. Müller asked the owner for permission for us to stay there temporarily. We were allowed to occupy two rooms on the ground floor, the only rooms that had glass panes in the windows. Carpenters had made bunk beds of wood for us. It was as cold inside as outside, and there was no water or washrooms. We washed our faces and hands with snow. On the walls, the icy frost glimmered day and night. Miraculously, no one got ill.

For Sundays, our day off, Leah had organized shifts to pick up breakfast from the kitchen. It was about fifteen minutes' walk from the brick house where we slept. When they arrived, the milk and the coffee were cold. Leah had the idea that whoever could learn a song after hearing it once could have the first mug, the warmest. Every Sunday after that, I got the warmest coffee. It still wasn't very warm, but better than before.

In the winter, there was always something to do on the farm: the stables had to be cleaned and we had to dig up the rest of the potatoes, carrots and other vegetables and send them to the market. It was a hard job to dig with pickaxes in the frozen soil. We also had to sort the dry onions in the attic. Then, when the weather got just warm enough to melt the ice, the soil had to be prepared for the beds in the field. Then once again we would begin to transplant the early vegetables from the hotbeds. Life might have gone on and on like this if Hitler had not had other more sinister plans for us.

In the middle of the summer of 1942, we were coming in from the fields one day when someone said that Leah wanted to see me. She was in the kitchen with another woman, chatting. Leah introduced her to me as Irena Adamowicz. Irena was a leader in the Polish scouting organization. Outraged by the injustice done to the Jews, she helped out however she could. Irena travelled across the country, making contact with *chalutzim* in the major ghettos and telling them about how the underground resistance operated. Although travel was dangerous for Jews, a few *chalutzot*, like Lonka who had come to the farm earlier, successfully fulfilled their mission as messengers too. The messengers were purchasing weapons, which then were smuggled into the ghettos through the sewers. Most people in the ghettos couldn't communicate with others about what to do in case of a massacre but through Irena, they knew how the others were preparing for such a time.

Irena talked to me for a while. She told me that I was being sent to Krakow. She asked how I felt about resistance work and whether or not I knew Christian prayers. I told her I knew many of them by heart after so many years of hearing Catholic students saying the prayers every morning at school. She seemed satisfied with my answers. Irena gave me the address of a convent and told me to send a letter to the Mother Superior on the seventh day of every month as a sign that I was still alive. Whenever the underground needed me, they would let me know. She handed me a prayer book and said only, "Be careful and good luck." That was the only advice I was to receive. The rest of my training would come from real-life situations. I would have to trust my intuition to keep me out of danger, just as animals do. They don't think about it, they simply know when danger is near.

The next day, the resistance had organized for Hela and I to go to the village to have pictures taken for our identification documents. Dvora lent me a pretty blouse and combed my hair, so I would look my best. We walked through the village, afraid that someone would recognize us as Jews. The photographer took me by surprise when he asked me my surname. In shock, I didn't think but just said the first name that came to my mind, a surname connected to the aristocracy. That name, Elżbieta Orlanska, was the one that was used in my forged documents. This was a stroke of luck because later it was useful in getting other documents required by the German authorities.

A few days later, with a forged document that stated that I was from Rzeszów and a letter from Leah for Laban, the leader of the resistance movement in the Krakow ghetto, I was sent to Krakow on the morning train. Hela was sent to another city in the afternoon.

After the war, I discovered that the rest of my group back on the farm in Czerniaków were sent to the Warsaw ghetto about four months after I left for Krakow. In April 1943, when an order came from the Nazis to concentrate all Jews in the ghetto for a massive deportation, some of the group, who were living at 18 Mila Street and belonged to the underground Jewish Fighting Organization, rebelled. Others simply dispersed. Most of them did not survive.

To my friends from Czerniaków who were killed while taking part in the Warsaw Ghetto Uprising, as well as to those on missions who were caught outside the ghetto, dragged to the *Umschlagplatz* – the assembly point inside the Warsaw ghetto – and killed indiscriminately, I offer my eternal homage.

Marking Time

In the Krakow ghetto, Laban, who was in charge of the underground movement, brought me to an attic where many other young people lived. He provided us with food and forbade us to leave the attic. We slept on the floor. With a few exceptions, we didn't know each other. The boy who had given me the prettiest plate back at the farm was there and protected me at night, so I wouldn't have to suffer any unwanted advances from the other boys. We were all waiting our turn to get out of the ghetto. Many were from distant cities, from different organizations, but in spite of that we were all united in the same objective: to survive, no matter what, or at least go down fighting, with weapons if possible. Everyone agreed that we would resist, regardless of the outcome. As it turned out, the confrontation would erupt in less than a year, and it would end with the uprising of the Warsaw ghetto.

Two days after I arrived, Laban sent me back to Czerniaków with a letter for Leah. I had to smuggle myself out of the Krakow ghetto. When I got to Czerniaków and handed the letter to Leah, I begged her to intervene so that I could bring my sister along. Many times, I asked to be together with my sister. As usual, her answer was no. Anyway, she added, my sister wasn't at the kibbutz in Warsaw anymore. Regina had been sent with a group to another commune in Ostrów Wielkopolski, a town in central Poland. Leah sent me back to Krakow.

From time to time, new people arrived in the attic in Krakow. Others disappeared as they had come, almost without notice. They had been sent out with forged papers. The rest of us waited for an order from Laban.

The Jewish police in Krakow had had orders to round up a contingent of Jews for transportation to Płaszów, a forced labour camp. The police were looking everywhere for people who were not bona fide Krakow residents. The first to go was always the outsider. Because we were all outsiders, Laban was concerned for our safety. While all this was going on, he again sent me back to Czerniaków with a letter for Leah.

A week or two later, after carrying out this mission and then returning to the Krakow ghetto for the second time, Laban explained that it was dangerous for me to stay there any longer because the police could come and get us at any moment. "You must go outside and do your best to survive," he said. "I haven't been able to arrange a safe place for you to hide." He put his hand in his pocket, took out some money for me that he said should last two days, and said that he hoped I would manage to get a job somewhere.

It had been about three years since I had handled money and I honestly had no idea of what it might buy. "Is that enough?" I asked. "If I can't find a job or place to sleep in two days, what am I going to do?" He smiled. It was obvious that I wasn't a true *chalutza*. "In the old days," he explained, "a person heading to a distant kibbutz was given only enough money to get to the first stop. From there, he had to get the rest of the way on his own." He was obviously trying to teach me a lesson, one I knew nothing about. Years later, it dawned on me what the message was: if destiny determined I should survive, this amount of money was obviously going to be enough. On the other hand, if I were to perish and lose the money, which was badly needed for buying weapons, it would be a double loss for the organization. The money itself was no guarantee of anything.

I listened, trying to deal with my present reality. I appeared to be equally in danger whether I stayed inside the ghetto or left it. That was all I could see. Laban told me that in the afternoon, Cyla and I would leave the ghetto with the night-shift workers. I assumed Laban had already spoken to Cyla separately because until that moment I had no idea that she would be leaving with me. We hadn't been particularly close, despite the fact that she was from my hometown and we had been together in Czerniaków. Now, I was taken by surprise. No guidance or instruction – just go. I don't blame anybody for this. They had no more idea of the difficulties we would face than we did.

It was almost the end of the summer of 1942. The Jews were lined up waiting for the gate to be opened so they could go to their night-shift in the factories. When they were all in their places, Cyla and I managed to sneak into the line. I remember the eyes of the others at that moment – they looked fearful and anxious, as though they were also part of the conspiracy.

Because of Cyla and me, the SS soldier in charge of counting came out wrong. Finally, he simply gave up counting and when the other soldier asked him if it was all right, he simply grunted "Jawohl." (Yes.) The soldier on guard duty opened the gate and the column marched out. If we had been found out at that point, we would have been shot on the spot. Later on, when I was really on the run, I found myself envying people who had been shot. They had instantly been freed from the degradation of the chase. But I wasn't thinking this way yet. It was just the beginning and things were happening so quickly. It was important not to be slow-witted.

We were in the middle of the line, marching along with the night-shift workers. It was dark. The column was long and it took time for us to get out to the street. We kept shifting where we stood, slowly edging forward from the middle of the column closer to the edge so we could get out to the street. On the left walked the SS soldier. Half the people were still inside the ghetto, the other half outside. The moment we reached the street, we broke away from the line, crossed the road in a hurry and in seconds disappeared through the gate of a house. The others shook their heads with fear.

As quickly as we could, we untied our armbands with the star. "Let's get away from here," I said to Cyla. "Someone might come out of one of the apartments. If we're seen, we'll be in trouble."

"I'm not going with you," Cyla said, turning her head away. She must have thought she would have a better chance without me. Either she didn't rate my chance of survival highly or maybe she felt that two Jewish girls travelling together would stand out. Whatever her reasoning, it was too late to go back and I couldn't persuade her to go with me. This was hardly the time or the place for an argument. She walked away, without looking back. Cyla was taller than I and had beautiful honey-coloured hair. No doubt, she hoped to pass for an Aryan. I found out later that she had walked in the city until she came to a Nazi barracks, where she had asked for a job in the kitchen. She was immediately arrested. She was later shot and her body brought back to the ghetto. Forged documents were no guarantee of survival.

When I no longer heard the sound of marching boots, I walked outside, heading directly to the streetcar stop. I must get away from this place, I thought. Roaming the area was dangerous. I was still thinking positively. I didn't panic. I would take the streetcar to the last stop to gain time until I could decide what to do. I soon realized, however, that I was worse off than before. I was alone, in the dark, and there was no one to turn to, no one to ask for advice or for instructions. Up to this point, there had always been someone else making the decisions for me. Now, I was alone with my worst thoughts.

I boarded a crowded streetcar. No one paid attention to me. The last stop was at Dworzec Główny, the main railway terminal. The ride there was more than half an hour and I had time to think, which was what I needed. I still didn't know what to do. I got off with all the people who were rushing to take a train. A paperboy passed, yelling, "Goniec Krakowski! News ... Latest news!" I bought a paper and crossed the street. Right in front of the station was a square surrounded by trees and shrubs. The shrivelled flowers matched my state of mind. I sat on the bench and opened the newspaper, looking for the page advertising rooms for rent. I soon found an ad for a place that offered beds by the night, which wasn't far from where I was sitting. I also had the time to look up jobs. Suddenly, I noticed an ad that read, "Retoucher Wanted Immediately."

The hotel was two blocks ahead. At the entrance there was a sign, "Bed for a night, knock at the janitor's door." Anywhere would be a good place, as long I could stay off the street. I couldn't afford the luxury of pretensions. I knocked at the door and a short, middle-aged woman opened it. "I'm sorry to bother you; is it here where the beds are for rent?" I asked. She nodded, letting me in. Still holding the newspaper in my hand, I asked how much she charged. She showed me a miserable, gloomy place. There were twenty or more iron beds with dirty mattresses and blankets that looked as though they had never been washed. The beds were on the left side of the basement, each a half-metre apart from the next. On the right were the janitor's bed, a stove, a table and a few chairs.

The woman seemed gentle and because of her kind behaviour, somehow I trusted her. My stomach ached with hunger. I asked her if she would make some tea for me, explaining that so many hours in the train had given me a stomachache. I'm sure my pale face made my story seem convincing. It was a risk, but I had to start trying my luck sometime. She put the kettle on the stove and invited me to sit at the table. While she served me the tea, she asked me where I was from. When I told her I was from Warsaw, she asked if it was true that Warsaw had been badly destroyed. "Yes," I said. "The Germans left the city in ruins." This was old news. The war had broken out in 1939 and it was already the summer of 1942.

The woman asked about my family, so I told her that they had perished in the bombardment and that when an old aunt I was staying with died, I came to Krakow to find work. She looked at me sympathetically, saying, "You are so young. It's not easy to be on your own here anymore." Her husband came in while I was asking her how to get to Karmelicka Street, where the photo studio was located, and he gave me the directions. I thanked her for the tea and I stood up, saying that I would be back later. She said, "Show me your document and pay me now or I will not reserve the bed for you. A lot of people will come in later on, looking for a bed for the night." I paid her the price she asked and showed her my document. Since it was in the basement, the bed cost less than Laban had calculated.

The streetcar stopped one block before the studio. On both sides of the entrance, pictures and portraits hung in frames under glass. Who would imagine that a few months later my portrait, beautifully framed, would be hanging on the wall in one of the showcases outside the studio? By the time I walked into the studio, my mind was clear. No one had given me instructions, other than Laban's "Try to survive." It was like an order, wasn't it? I was trying to do what I had been told. No one said, "Do what you have to do, according to the situation." I had to figure that out for myself as quickly as possible.

The waiting room was large, with chairs placed around the wall. The receptionist stood behind the desk. She had dyed blond hair that was permed and parted in the middle, brown, round eyes, and a large mouth, with thick lips. She wore a flowered blouse and a black skirt. She spoke German and, later, I was told that she was a *Volksdeutsche*.

"Dobry wieczór," (Good evening) I said. "May I speak to someone about the ad in the paper?" A man appeared from a side door, wished me a good evening and extended his hand to shake mine. He was of about average height, in his late forties or early fifties. His hair was silver-grey, cut short, and he wore a grey suit. He was handsome and I also noticed, especially when he turned, a kind of discipline in his movements. I introduced myself, offering my hand, and told him I was a retoucher. He said he was sorry, but Mr. Bielec, the photographer, had gone for the day. Speaking very gently, he asked if I could come back the next day for a test. "I will be here at ten," I said. Then we shook hands again.

I rushed to the hotel. It was crowded with people who had come in just before the nine o'clock curfew. All the beds were taken except for mine, which was the first one nearest to the entrance. The travellers who slept there were smugglers selling homemade products like salami, bacon and cheese on the black market. I went to bed with my clothes and shoes on because they were the only ones I had. I hadn't made any mistakes, but still I was tense and struggled to stay awake. I was tired, hungry and sleepy. I must have slept for a few hours because I awoke feeling a little better. I got up and went to the washroom, where there was a small washstand. Since I didn't have a towel, I wet my hands and passed them over my eyes. I stroked my hair a little and walked out. The minute I was in the street, I regretted not asking the janitor if I could sleep there one more night. I turned round to go back in and what I saw made me shiver with fright. One wall of the building was covered with a canvas on which was painted in big letters: *SS Zug Kommando* (SS Platoon Command). I had slept in a building filled with Nazis! Perhaps the reason I hadn't been caught was that no one would suspect that a Jew would hide in such a place. I never returned there, or even went near it, during the whole time I was in Krakow.

A glance at my watch, which I still had from home, a present from my parents on my fifteenth birthday, showed that it was still too early to go to the studio. I was hungry again. No wonder – it was another day and I had not eaten. I walked a few blocks and saw tables ahead with baskets piled high with fruit. From the villages around the city, the peasants had come to sell whatever they could, in order to buy other goods they needed for their households. I asked one woman how much she would charge for one apple. The woman looked at me, then said that I could take it without paying. The cost of one apple didn't make a big difference in my budget and I was proud; I wouldn't accept alms. I thanked her and left some money on the table. I ate the apple as I walked down the street, which I wouldn't have done before the war. Eating on the street was considered ill-mannered in Poland, but I was hungry. I also stopped in a bakery, where they looked at me strangely when I bought only one Kaiser roll. These were little mistakes, but luckily things were working in my favour.

I got to the studio on time. I had been taught punctuality at home and remembered the lesson. A moment later Mr. Bielec, the photographer, came in. He was a very gentle man, around fifty years old. His black hair was combed away from his face and parted on the right side. He wore a dark blue three-piece suit with a white shirt. After greeting me politely and shaking hands, he asked me to follow him to the room on the left side of the waiting room. In a corner of this room was a table with four retouching stands.

Two retouchers, whom I was introduced to as Niedzwiecki and Gargas, were already working. Mr. Bielec asked me to sit on the second chair beside Niedzwiecki, behind Gargas. Mr. Bielec brought in a few negatives and some pencils. I felt that my hands were heavy from working in the fields. However, I concentrated on my job. It was a test and it had to be done well. About midday, Bielec asked me for the negatives I had finished. He took them to the office, where he checked my work. Meanwhile, the others went out for lunch. After a while, Mr. Bielec returned. He approached me, discreetly taking some money from his pocket. With a smile on his face, he said, "Panna [Miss] Orlanska, go for lunch and then come back." I truly appreciated his discretion. I came back and I got the job.

My first impression of the two retouchers was not promising. Niedzwiecki teased me and made jokes at my expense. Gargas didn't take part but kept smiling at Niedzwiecki's witticisms. This made me uneasy, as I knew nothing about them or what they were really thinking. I didn't pay too much attention to them, though, as I was more worried about where I would sleep that night. We worked until seven o'clock and then as soon as I was out on the street, I bought a newspaper again and started looking for a bed where I could rest.

This second day of tension was a test of my abilities. I had nowhere to go. It was dark. People were rushing home. I hadn't eaten since my one o'clock lunch, but I wasn't hungry. Under a street lamp, I found another bed hotel advertised in the paper. It was cheaper than the other, and wasn't that far from the studio; however, considering the time and the darkness, it was safer to take the streetcar. It was amazing how confident I felt the second day outside the ghetto. I didn't hesitate to do what I had to do.

At the very first stop, a girl got on who had been in the Krakow ghetto attic. She was tall and heavy, with straight blond hair. I recognized her in a glance as a member of Hashomer who had gone outside just two days after I came into the attic. The streetcar was crowded and to keep her anonymity, and mine as well, I avoided approaching her. I had never talked to her before, but she seemed somewhat arrogant. Maybe because she thought she was privileged, with her Aryan look. She recognized me, too, but didn't make a move to come closer. She happened to get off at the stop for the address given in the ad, so I got off behind her. I had no idea that she lived there, and if I had known how she would react, I would have gone one stop farther and walked back. She walked straight to the building advertised in the paper. All the way, she walked as if she didn't want to talk to me, which I understood. However, once inside the gate, she turned angrily and said, "Why are you following me?"

"I'm not following you," I replied, surprised. I showed her the newspaper I had folded open to the "Beds for Rent" section. "I'm going to reserve a bed. It's my second day outside the ghetto. I've got a job but no place to sleep."

She looked at me as though she didn't believe a word I was saying. It made me angry that she should accuse me of following her. She wanted me to tell her more, but I wasn't interested. I remembered Cyla – a strong desire for survival makes people forget the basic rules of human behaviour. I understood that and I listened to her as she calmed down and told me she lived on the second floor, then gave me her apartment number and asked me to visit her. By then, I felt indifferent and turned to go in. "The beds are in the basement," she said with contempt. I didn't respond and knocked at the door. A man opened the door and asked me what I wanted. "I'm looking for a bed for the night," I responded. He told me the price. It was late, so I paid what he asked. I also had to show him my identity document. With the balance left from the lunch, and cheaper accommodation, I had enough money for two more nights. It was almost the end of the week and Saturday was payday. The studio paid me by piecework, so the more work I finished, the more I could earn. I worked as fast as I could. I was truly learning how to take advantage of time.

The man showed me the first bed near the door; as at the first place, the mattresses looked dirty, the blankets never washed. It was good to be young: no pain in the bones, a fresh face, clear thinking. The resource that opened many doors during my ordeal was my parents' legacy – good health and good manners. They were my principal tools. What else did I have? Again, I spent the night fully dressed with my shoes on. This time, though, I was more relaxed in the morning. I was happy to have a job. I asked the janitor before leaving if he would reserve a bed for me that night, and he told me not to worry, that I could sleep there again.

Almost thirty people worked in the studio and the workshop. We all started at nine o'clock and lunchtime was at one. I bought a Kaiser and an apple again to save money, just in case. The two retouchers soon changed their attitude toward me as we engaged in daily conversation. Niedzwiecki, who sat beside me, was of average height, with dark brown hair, brown eyes and a thin moustache. Gargas was blond with blue eyes and his forehead, nose and chin formed a sharp profile. Niedzwiecki was a retoucher by profession whereas Gargas was an artist – a painter and sculptor. He had graduated from the Szkoła Sztuk Pięknych, a world-famous Krakow art school. Hard times during the war had brought him into the studio as a means of survival. Almost no one working in the studio was what she or he had been before the war. Most of us were in the same boat – a rocking one. This included Mr. Lesniewski, the man I talked with the first afternoon. I had noticed his disciplined movements right away and it turned out he had been a captain in the Polish army.

Mr. Bielec supervised everything, correcting the negatives and positives until they were delivered, mostly by mail, to the clients. Mr. Lesniewski was the administrative partner. Evidently, it was a good arrangement: there was no noticeable friction between them and the staff respected each other. Two years before I started working at the studio, Mr. Bielec had married a retoucher half his age and they had had a little baby boy. Mrs. Bielec sometimes came into the studio with the child, strictly to see her husband. Bosses' wives never took part in their business. Mr. Bielec was a serious person, dedicated to his work. My place at the table had been Mrs. Bielec's before me.

On the other side of the room where we worked stood a cabinet with many drawers. Next to this were a table and a chair where a very elegant woman sat. She took care of the negatives, which she arranged in numerical order. She was middle-aged, tall, with wavy grey hair, dressed in clothes whose glory was well behind them. She had been an opera singer and she taught me the "Ave Maria." She frequently sang the religious songs I knew from school. She was often bored and always welcomed a chat. After we finished retouching a negative, it had to be slipped into an envelope and initialled and handed to her to be added to the archive.

Mr. Bielec asked me to initial my work with an O because I came after Gargas. Since his name was Eugeniusz, I couldn't sign an E for Elżbieta. Whenever I had time, I practised my signature so that it would look like the signature of someone accustomed to doing it. Even small details were important then. Most important of all was not to forget the situation I was in. I was careful. It was like being on stage, with a few differences – I had to invent a personality without a model to go by, a name without a background, a modus operandi without instructions. It is true that life is the best teacher: I knew that if I failed, I would never get a chance to correct my mistake. It would be the end of the show.

That night was the third that I slept at the same place. Although it was a miserable place, I felt as though I were going home after work.

However, the following morning, the janitor, who owned the bed hotel, asked me to look for another place to sleep. He was extremely polite about it, but he said that I couldn't stay more than three nights, as it was the law. "I can't risk my business," he said. "We like you and you are a very nice young lady, but you must find a place elsewhere."

I was evasive, telling him that I worked all day and had no time to look for another place that late. Besides, this place was close to where I worked. He considered my arguments but still said there was nothing he could do about it. He refused to let me stay, since I would be putting his business in jeopardy. But in the end, he was kind, and told me I could stay on the Saturday and Sunday because the police didn't check on those days. Monday after work, he would take me to a friend who lived alone. He had already spoken to her and she had agreed to take me in.

On Saturday, we worked a half day. When I walked through the gate, the girl who belonged to Hashomer Hatzair whom I had seen on the streetcar was waiting for me. "Would you like to go for a walk on Sunday at two o'clock?" she asked. It sounded like an attempt to be friendly, so I agreed. Then, she quickly walked away. On Sunday, we met at the gate as arranged. She told me that she worked in a hospital. How well she had adjusted! She lived in a room by herself. I was almost speechless. We walked for a few hours and then parted ways. The next day, I moved out. I never saw her again. On Monday, I finished the daily quota of negatives, signed them, and picked up my bag to go out. While I was doing that, an idea came to me to ask someone in the studio if they knew of a room for rent. But I instantly rejected the idea as too dangerous. At work, no one could know my problems. With a heavy heart, I headed toward the same place.

The janitor was waiting for me. "Let's go, Panienka," he said hurriedly. The janitor was short and skinny and walked very quickly. Night had fallen over the city and the streets were dimly lit, almost deserted. The windows were covered with black paper or dark material, on German orders, to prevent the enemy from tracing the city by its lights. We looked like two shadows moving swiftly through the streets. He sped up every time we finished a conversation. We walked for more than half an hour until finally, he stopped at an old two-storey building. He entered and went straight to the basement, with me following. At a square table, four elderly men were playing cards. A lamp hung on a cable from the dirty ceiling.

The janitor approached a door on the right side. He knocked but received no answer. He knocked again and again. Finally, he turned to the men, asking them if they knew where the laundress had gone and whether she would be back soon. They didn't know. He explained that I was from Warsaw, that I had found a job here in the city and that he couldn't let me sleep in his place because of the law. He added that I was a gentle *panienka* and had nowhere to go. The janitor was eloquent and convincing.

Then, a man stood up and broke the silence, evidently moved by compassion. He had short hair and a moustache, all white. A stiff collar was showing under a dark grey jacket, making him look like a clerk from the 1920s. I thought he had, indeed, been a clerk. He said that he would take me to his place and his wife would give me a place to sleep. I must say I didn't feel any emotion or relief at that moment. It was a continuation of the small miracles, which, at any moment, could fail. Then my story would come to an end, like the stories of millions of others lost in the war and now forgotten.

After the old man's decision to take me with him, everything happened quickly. The janitor thanked him and I thanked the janitor, who disappeared in seconds. The elderly man guided me up the stairs and into the street. We crossed the street, went through a gate to a house, then through a passage. On the right side were iron stairs, at the top of which was a balcony with an iron handrail on the left and two apartments on the right. He showed me to the second door, opened it, let me in and then called his wife.

Their names were Jozef and Victoria Starowicz. She was small and fragile, with a round wrinkled face that showed her to be older than he was. I greeted her and waited for permission to advance, which came immediately. She asked me for my name and where I worked. Right away she called me Elzunia, a diminutive form of Elżbieta. She went to the dining room and got sheets out of the linen chest and spread them on the chesterfield in the dining room. Then, she came back and prepared tea. While I was drinking, she sat at the table in the kitchen and asked me about my family. When I told her that my parents had been killed in a bombardment, her face turned sad, her cheeks rosy. She shook her head and sighed deeply. I continued. "We were all at home at the time, very early in the morning. My parents and sister ..." She interrupted to ask what my father had done and I told her he had been a lawyer. She then wished me a good night and told me to go to sleep.

The old man slept in the kitchen behind a curtain and his wife slept in the bedroom. I said good night and went to the dining room. I took off my shoes and my dress. Such comfort to sleep on sheets after more than a year! I slept so well all night that she had to wake me up in the morning.

Pani Starowicz made tea and gave me a piece of bread, which was a luxury because everything was rationed under the German occupation. In the few days that I had been outside the ghetto, I had eaten only one meal a day, which wasn't even a full meal. At the attic, we hadn't had much more. Before I left, Pani Starowicz told me that she would contact her daughter Vicky to consult her about me, and that I could meet with Vicky after work. "If Vicky agrees, you can stay with us as long as you want. It depends on her," she said.

How could I stay calm all day? How could I think positively? It would be nice to live there, I thought, although it wasn't the best place to hide. Unfortunately, the layout of the building was such that I could be seen entering and leaving the apartment from all the windows of the main building. It could call attention to wicked minds. I had a whole day to think of something else, but nothing came to mind. Of course, it was better than the basement. As in the past, I thought something would happen at the very last moment. Curiously, this time I didn't fear anything. I knew that I would do what I had to do.

That same morning, Mr. Lesniewski explained to me that I had to go to a government office to register in order to obtain permission to work in Krakow. He gave me a paper that certified that he employed me in a permanent position as a retoucher in his studio, and politely told me that it had to be done the following day. It was against the law to employ people who didn't have the right to live in Krakow – they were considered foreigners and needed to apply for a special permit because Krakow was now a German city. I promised to go to the office the next day.

After I left the studio, I got on the streetcar, arriving early for the meeting with the daughter. Vicky stood fully dressed right at the door, waiting for me. I greeted her, introducing myself. Vicky was formal, calling me "Panna Orlanska"; later we settled on "Panna Elsa." Although she was good-looking, she had a grimace on her face as if nothing was right for her. She told me that I had to pay eight hundred złoty a month for room and board plus my food-ration card. I agreed to everything. My wages were high, and I could afford it. Fortunately, I made a good impression on her. Pani Starowicz had told me that morning that her daughter was very smart and worked as a legal secretary. I think she must also have told Vicky that my father was a lawyer, as I had told her. I showed Vicky the certification I had to present at the labour office to get permission to live and work in Krakow, telling her that as soon as the permit was issued I would be able to get a food-ration card. She smiled approvingly and said, "You are truly a lawyer's daughter."

Was it good luck or a miracle? I felt like Moses when the Almighty, in order to save him, moved his hand from the plate with gold to the plate with burning coal. As long as no one asked me if I was Jewish, I didn't mind inventing stories. The lies I told were innocent, almost childish, but they were credible. Until now, they hadn't affected anyone else, and they matched my personality without difficulty. Most important of all, they were a means of enabling me to save my life, every moment of every day and night. It was useless to wonder how long it could last.

At the labour office, where I had to get permission to live and work in Krakow, my noble last name made an impact. Within seconds, I obtained the all-important paper. I rushed back to the studio and showed the permit to Mr. Lesniewski, who thanked me. "Sometimes an inspector shows up to check the staff," he said. This turned out to be quite true. Periodically, a German inspector would come to the studio, asking us if we were well treated or if we wanted the boss to install a kitchen for us. Of course, we didn't complain. How could they come to defend the workers' rights while at the same time murdering innocent people, dragging them from their homes and torturing them? How could they reconcile their concern for workers with the enormity of these crimes against humanity? The hypocrisy was incredible.

The next day, I went to the food-provision office, where a young woman asked me for my documents and asked me if I had a permit to stay in Krakow. I handed her the authorization. She looked at it and at the document. "Are you from Rzeszów?" she asked. "So am I. Where did you live there?" My lies fitted any situation I needed and always seemed close at hand. "I was born there," I replied, "but when we were still very young our parents moved to Warsaw. You know how it is, because of my father's profession. At school, my sister and I were often asked about Rzeszów. I don't really remember the street. I think because it wasn't mentioned at home."

"I know," she said. "People go where they have a better opportunity to work. My sister is working in Warsaw. I miss her." Her face turned sad. We had a few things in common that worked just right for me, and we shared our feelings of nostalgia and sadness. But what I needed was what I had come for – the food-ration card. I told her it had been a pleasure chatting with someone from my hometown and that maybe I would find a moment to drop in to say hello. For me,

every moment I was there was too long because I had to keep thinking of new lies to tell. She filled out the papers with care and I thanked
her, wishing her good luck. She had been very nice to me, but I was
happier once I got the card and left the office.

After work, I gave the card to Pani Starowicz. She thanked me,
saying, "You know Vicky – everything has to be right with her." In
a very short time, I had attained the status of a Polish-born Roman
Catholic citizen, living and working in Krakow with all the rights
permitted under the Germans.

Living the Lie

Every seventh day of the month, I sent a letter to the address Irena Adamowicz had given me as a sign that I was still alive. Irena had said the resistance would find me whenever they needed me, but up to now I hadn't been able to give them an address. Now, I could. I was a survivor, but I paid for it with loneliness and insecurity. I missed the warmth of family.

Although the couple with whom I was living had three children, they had only one granddaughter. She never visited them, at least not while I was there. I noticed that whenever Pani Starowicz told me anything about her husband, she always referred to him as Dziadek, Grandpa. One day I asked both of them if they would like me to call them Dziadek i Babcia, Grandpa and Grandma. They both agreed happily. It felt good to me, as well. Grandma was happy to watch me eat and Grandpa was happy listening to my stories about everything I did at the studio. I listened to their stories about their life and work. They enjoyed having someone younger with them.

Grandpa made himself responsible for my moral guidance. He scolded me once with, "What is all this waking up and singing? When you wake up, you should kneel down and say a prayer." From then on, every morning I prayed right after I woke up. They were both very devout Catholics. Their children were also churchgoers. I was certainly learning to adjust to their life. They liked me because I was respectful and if they needed something I was always ready to help. Grandma often needed help with housework, such as kneading dough. I had never done it before, but she showed me how. Also, Grandpa wasn't as strong as he used to be. He asked me to go to the basement once to bring coal for the stove and it was the first time I had ever been in such a dark basement. Alone in the darkness, I was so afraid I could hardly breathe, but I did it.

Although I was immersed in my current life, I missed my family dreadfully. Over the course of a few afternoons at work, I drew my mother's face on a piece of paper. It came out perfectly. I folded it and carried it in my purse. At work, I had more in common with Gargas than with Niedzwiecki. Gargas was highly educated and we talked about books and paintings, while my conversation with Niedzwiecki was limited to work and the weather. After a few weeks, a new retoucher arrived and was given the chair beside Gargas. She was short, freckled, vivacious. She had a wonderful sense of humour and always had a joke to tell, which soon made her popular with the others. Her name was Alina and she called me Panna Elu. She worked rather slowly, earning only the minimum wage.

A man periodically came to visit Alina. She said that he was her uncle. We followed self-imposed rules at work. No one asked anything about the personal life of another. We didn't know much about each other, although we worked together so many hours in the same room. Polish people are traditionally reserved, and for some, like me, it was dangerous to reveal too much about the past.

There was so much work to do that the negatives were piling up. The clients were mostly the German military personnel who had been assigned to Krakow. The secretary called in a freelance retoucher who took the negatives home to Poznań, a city close to the German border. Niedzwiecki already knew him because he was often called in to help move a backlog of orders. This retoucher had a pinkish face and long blond hair, but one day he appeared without his long hair. When Niedzwiecki asked him what happened, the man laughed as he recounted how the German police had stopped him on the street and taken him to the barber. "The Germans don't like men with long hair," Niedzwiecki confirmed. He waited in the retouchers' room until Mr. Bielec prepared some work for him to take home. The next week when he came to pick up more work, he invited me to go for a walk with him on Sunday. I agreed.

I'm not sure why I agreed to go out with him, but I usually trust people and by nature I'm a good listener. However, this time, I should have listened to what wasn't audible. My lack of caution could have cost me my life. I was nineteen, so young and inexperienced. It was my mission to do everything I could to preserve my life, yet I was risking it. Later, I felt devastated and ashamed that I had agreed to meet him.

We met on Sunday at the Sukiennice Plaza, or Draper's Hall, a marketplace for handcrafted goods, particularly merchandise from the mountains. He led me to the outskirts of the city and stopped near a huge pit that had been excavated for future construction. Standing there at the edge of the pit, he said, "If I pushed you down, what would you do?" He watched my reaction.

"Oh, it would be easy to climb up the side," I answered, which was true as long as I didn't fall on a stone. Meanwhile, I was thinking, he knew where he was taking me; he has a sinister plan. Although I could feel my head pounding with an unusual rhythm, I laughed, saying, "You know, I'm a gymnast, so it wouldn't take me long to get out." But I was afraid. I observed a malicious smile on his face. I turned and started walking. He followed me back to the city with little conversation on either of our parts. I thanked him for the invitation and he just walked away. I really do think he had a sinister plan, but once again I was lucky. The whole incident left me very upset with myself. I never saw him again.

At work, Alina and I talked about our homes. I didn't yet know it, but she was inventing hers just as I invented mine, building a past that had to be more or less credible. I thought that I was good at telling lies, but Alina was even better. Besides her incredible imagination, she had even arranged for a fictitious uncle to visit her and reinforce the image of a real Pole with family in a distant city. It was nice that this Polish family gave her support in such uncertain times. Her wages were low and she couldn't afford to buy anything. Sometimes, I exchanged sandwiches with her at lunchtime since hers were just two pieces of bread with nothing in between. She wanted to give me something in return. Once, she brought me a brown velvet dress. "It's my mother's," she said. "Take it, it's your size." I wore it the next day, which made her happy. I also had a black velvet dress that my mother had made for me from her nightgown. During the war, it was impossible to buy material. Now, I had two dresses, one summer skirt and blouse, and the dress that Dvora had given me for the train trip from Czerniaków to Krakow. It was only tacked together, but somehow the white thread didn't show through from the seam.

One day, Alina seemed very sad, not herself. Our conversation up to then had been only casual, our socializing only during work hours. We never asked anything personal and we never visited each other or went out together. At the end of the afternoon, after I had finished my work and was going out, I found her waiting for me in the dark outside the studio. "I have to talk to you, Panna Elu," she said. She then told me that she rented a room from a family in a house and that they were heavy drinkers. Last night, they had been drunk and demanded more money. They threatened her that if she didn't give them this money, they would report her to the police for being Jewish. She was frightened. If I'd had a room to myself, I could have taken her in, I thought. But I too was part of another family with no privacy at all. It was impossible. I suggested she move out and find somewhere else to live. "Not today," she said. "My things are still there." My heart was heavy for her, but I couldn't help. Then I said, "Go on as long as you can." She turned to me. "Are you Jewish, too?" I nodded. Immediately, I felt this had been a mistake, but it was too late now. She said she felt better. I felt perplexed. It was foolish to disclose my secret. We separated at the streetcar stop. In fact, the very next day she found another place with a woman who had been living on her own. I never knew where she lived. The impulse to go on stayed with us. I had suspected that she was Jewish when she first came into the retouchers' room, but her jokes sometimes made me blush and that changed my mind. I was too naive to understand many of the jokes.

Alina was the only one who knew my secret. Later, when we had an opportunity to be alone, we made a pact that if anything happened to one of us, the other would report it to our survivors after the war. Did we really think we had a future? Danger was everywhere. I took care for my safety at every moment, but how long can an artist perform on stage without stumbling? It's good to be alert, but fear does not make a good companion. Besides, there was more than one enemy. There was the risk of being reported by both the Poles and the Germans.

One morning, Mr. Labuzek, the professional photographer who worked at the studio, watched me as I came into work. I was wearing a gold-coloured turban made of a shiny scarf and my face was still tanned from working in the fields in Czerniaków. He was so impressed with how I looked that he asked me to pose for a portrait. Mr. Labuzek was a rather nervous person with a hoarse voice, piercing black eyes and black hair. The portrait was a success. Mr. Labuzek was so pleased with his work that he framed it for display in the showcase outside. First, he brought it into the retouchers' room to show it off. He was proud of his art. Everyone congratulated us for such an outstanding job except for Niedzwiecki. He sarcastically remarked that the picture was well done but, he said, with a cynical smile, "You look like a little Jewess." He said it in the presence of so many people – everyone who worked in the retouchers' room, the four men who worked in the darkroom and their four helpers, and three other employees. It wasn't true at all. I looked like I was from the Orient. Nothing further was said, and I couldn't tell what anyone else was thinking. His remark was intentionally malicious. I felt I had been stabbed in the back, but I restrained my impulse to get into an argument with him and instead praised the photographer, saying, "I love it. It's so beautiful!" It was time to leave this place, but I didn't know that then. Mr. Labuzek went outside to hang the portrait in the showcase and everyone got back to work.

That was the end of the incident – or was it? Later, Alina told me that she had talked to Niedzwiecki afterward and told him that his comment could have endangered my life. Did her comment confirm his suspicions that I might have been Jewish? I assumed the motive for his hatred was that he had asked me to go for a walk with him and I had refused. One experience was enough to learn to be careful. I didn't care for him. Right away I had realized he was no gentleman and I was right. Now he seemed even more despicable.

Niedzwiecki had a friend named Szwarcenberg-Czerny who often visited him. At one point his friend seemed to have disappeared, staying away from the studio for a long time, until one day he came in with a clean-shaven head. Also, I met him once on the stairs when he was drunk and Niedzwiecki was helping him to stand up. After the war, Alina told me that Szwarcenberg-Czerny had been thrown in jail for something, then released on the condition that he denounce Jews hiding in the city. Niedzwiecki had apparently been one of his informers. When the war ended, Alina told me, Szwarcenberg-Czerny was caught by a couple whose daughter had been killed after he denounced her. They handed him over to be tried in Krakow. Alina had been in the courtroom when he was found guilty and went to jail.

New apprentices often came in to learn photography. One boy was sent to the darkroom to learn how to develop negatives and copy positives. Another, a girl, was told to help out wherever she could, either in the retouching room or at the front desk. She was young, pretty and helpful. We called her Panna Jasia. In Poland, no one was addressed simply by his or her first name. She would often bring me some sweets or pastries. I asked her once how she got them and she answered in a discreet, low voice, "My sister works in a German office." "Why do you bring them specially for me?" I asked. "Because I like you," she replied. She was a darling.

The third newcomer, a boy whose last name was Schwartz, was assigned to me to be instructed in how to retouch negatives. Mr. Lesniewski had asked me to do it as a special favour. He was tall and thin, around eighteen, a violinist who had been unable to get on with his studies because of the war. I tried my best to get him interested in the art of retouching, but it was clear his heart was in music. He had music in his head all the time. One day, he wrote out the notes of a melody on the glass where the negatives were usually put to be retouched. I didn't know much about music, only what I had learned at school, but with his help, I was able to recognize the melody, an aria from the opera *Cavalleria Rusticana*.

He paid more attention to me if the topic of conversation was music, although he was making a little progress in retouching. One day he had the courage to ask me to a matinee symphony concert the following Sunday. His violin professor was playing in the orchestra and he very much wanted to hear the concert. It was exciting for me, too. It had been a long time since I had had any entertainment. When we met on Sunday, I asked him how he had been able to get tickets for the matinee. He laughed. "My father and my whole family are Volksdeutsche. We are privileged and we take advantage of it. It's easy for us to get what we want." It made me shiver. Once again, right next to danger. As we approached the concert hall, I saw a girl waiting for someone near the door. She wore a white blouse and a black pleated skirt. She kept turning her head, looking in both directions. Something about her behaviour struck me and I was sure she was Jewish. I very much enjoyed the concert and even recognized melodies from various operas. Schwartz walked me home and thanked me for coming to the concert with him. The next day at work, he told me that he realized his future was in music and a few days later he quit his job.

After the incident with my portrait, Niedzwiecki tried to be friendly with me. He invited me to go out with him many times, but I always refused. Later, I realized he had been trying to lure me. I didn't want him near me, he was false and I didn't like his personality or his manners.

Once, indiscreetly, I happened to say that a picture Mr. Bielec had painted, enlarged from a small photograph of a man riding a horse, seemed to have its proportions wrong. Niedzwiecki obviously passed this on because a few days later Mr. Bielec came to me with the painting. He told me that the proportions had to be right because he had copied it faithfully from the photograph, enlarging it exactly ten times from the original photograph. "Maybe it is an optical illusion," he suggested. I realized I couldn't trust Niedzwiecki with anything. Maybe I should have taken this as a warning that I should leave, but at the time, I sensed no immediate danger.

Working for the Underground

Twice in the same week, two people from the underground tried to contact me. One day after I got home, Grandma described a woman who had been asking for me. It might have been one of the messengers working outside the ghetto, on the "Aryan side"; she hadn't left a message. The other, from Grandma's description, must have been the boy from Czerniaków who had served me on the only plate with the tiny blue flowers.

I was astonished: why were they putting my life at risk like this? Since they knew where I was, it would have been wiser to send me a letter or wait for me in the street as I went to work or returned home. Despite my anger, I was also concerned, thinking it could be a sign that they needed me. Although none of us had had to take any kind of an oath of loyalty to the movement, morally I felt as though I belonged to them.

That evening after work, I took the streetcar to the ghetto. I walked close enough to the fence to be able to communicate to someone on the other side that I wanted to see Laban, who was well known there. Laban came immediately, with another man behind him. He told me that I had to go to Warsaw and that someone would be contacting me about it soon. I asked him who the people were who had found out where I lived. He didn't answer. As Irena had instructed me, I had addressed my monthly letters to the Mother Superior, and as far as I knew, absolutely no one else was aware of where I lived. It couldn't have been the girl from the Krakow ghetto attic, as I had moved since I last saw her. Since then, I hadn't met a single person I knew. Yet, these people knew where I lived. I thought it was strange and I couldn't understand it. I wasn't really thinking clearly – I agreed to fulfill a dangerous mission to Warsaw, which wasn't so bright.

Mietek, the man who had been standing behind Laban, met me outside the studio one day soon after that. He then hailed a horse-drawn carriage and directed it to a street I wasn't familiar with. There, we stopped at a small shoemaker's store. Behind the shop was the shoemaker's apartment, a single dark room. Mietek and the shoemaker huddled together, then Mietek turned to me and told me not to worry, that he was "ours," meaning a member of some resistance movement. We left the room and climbed upstairs. It seemed that the man who opened the door already knew Mietek and again, Mietek said, "Don't worry, he is ours." I held out my hand to him and my watch fell off my wrist. A flood of superstitious thoughts came to my mind, but I soon forgot the whole incident. So many things happened during the time I was living under an alias that I couldn't take every incident seriously. I didn't know how to avoid trouble and I knew I would have to put up with whatever came my way. After a few minutes, we went out into the street. Mietek told the driver who had been waiting for us to take me home, and he paid for the ride in advance. We agreed to leave for Warsaw in a couple of days, on Thursday.

At work, I said that I had to go to Warsaw for a funeral. Mr. Lesniewski didn't object. Mrs. Pola, the positive retoucher, sold me her high-quality veil. Everything was working out. Thursday morning, I met Mietek at the main railway terminal, Dworzec Główny, where he bought tickets to Warsaw. The train was crowded. We sat together on the left side of the car, talking only when necessary. When the train started moving, a Polish guard came and asked the passengers for the tickets. When he approached me, he asked for my ticket and personal documents. It was packed and the air was thick, practically unbearable.

I couldn't bear to wear my veil and shoved it back from my face. The guard looked at my photograph and then at my face, twice. I don't know if he was wondering about my age, which was incorrect on my document, or if he recognized me as a Jew – probably both. He asked if I was travelling alone. Mietek answered that he was going with me to a funeral. The guard stood there for a while, shaking his head doubtfully. Then he slowly turned and walked on. The ticket was paid for – why did he have to scrutinize me so carefully and single me out like that in front of the other passengers? Was this another small miracle?

The probability of a Pole denouncing a Jew was much greater than that of a German recognizing one. The Polish people could have saved many Jewish lives by not reporting us. For many of them, it seems, their anti-Jewish feelings were so strong that it completely overcame their innate humanity.

Once we arrived in Warsaw, Mietek gave me two addresses. One of them I already knew – it took me to the Mother Superior to whom I had been mailing my monthly contact letters. I entered the door to the left of the main entrance and found a nun folding sheets. I gave her my name and told her that I wanted to see the Mother Superior. She left and returned a few minutes later, continuing to fold sheets without a word, as though nothing had happened. I went up to her and asked her how long I would have to wait. She did not answer.

Perhaps the nun had orders not to talk, no matter what, although she had gone into the convent with my message. In any case, the Mother Superior didn't come out. Eventually, I left. In retrospect, I think I probably should have waited, but I was feeling frustrated. They had been receiving my letters and they had to know who I was. I couldn't figure out why they wouldn't make contact. Mietek was outside the church waiting for me. When I told him what happened, he muttered, "They are afraid." But we needed help. The second address was that of a man named Anielewicz, whom I didn't know personally, but later I found out that he was head of the Jewish Fighting Organization. A young man let me into the apartment. When I asked to see Anielewicz, he made me wait, going into another room every now and then, not saying a word. I didn't talk either. Finally, I asked once more. He didn't answer. Again, after I got tired of waiting, I left. I had been careful but both times came back empty-handed. Mietek repeated, "They are afraid." I had no idea why they would be afraid of us.

I wondered if the issue was that Mietek belonged to a different organization. And what was my role in all of this? If something had gone wrong or they hadn't been advised to expect me, a contact, even with the right person, wouldn't be trusted. I would never know what the problem was. I couldn't blame Mietek. I didn't even know him, really. He was sent to me as a contact and that's all there was to it. I had never been trained for underground activity.

On another occasion after this, when I was working at the photography studio's branch on Zielona Street, I looked out of the window and caught sight of two men running into the entrance of a house across the street. I recognized Mietek and Yitzhak – who also went by the name Antek – Zuckerman. I suspected that they were hiding there for some reason and the next time I saw Mietek, I asked him what had happened. He was evasive. After the war, I was told that they had killed some Germans. So I can't accuse Mietek of lack of loyalty or wrongdoing.

Now, it was late. It wasn't safe to walk on the streets, so we had to go to a hotel for the night because of our tight train schedule. We shared a room, where I slept in the bed and Mietek on a sofa. In the morning, a plainclothes policeman knocked at the door. His job was to check on the guests in the hotel. The policeman first asked Mietek for his documents, then passed them back, satisfied. He turned to me and, after looking at my document, said, "Say the Lord's Prayer."

"Here?" I replied. "Come with me to the church. I will not pray here." He looked at me, surprised, and then said, "Everything is in order," and left. When he had gone, Mietek laughed, but I was trembling. We immediately went to the railway station and left for Krakow.

~

Maria was the secretary at the studio's branch on Zielona Street, where I was sent to work for a few weeks. One Sunday, she invited me for a walk. Afterward, she asked me to come and meet her mother at their home. The apartment had one bedroom, a dining room and a kitchen. In the dining room stood a table and chairs and in the corners of the room were empty crates covered with white sheets. All the other furniture was gone. Maria shook it off with a good sense of humour and, laughing, told me, "We sold it because we didn't have any money. Now, things are better. I'm working, and Mother and I are managing to stay alive." Her mother served tea. She was as depressed as Maria was cheerful, not taking much part in the conversation.

After tea, Maria walked me to the streetcar stop. As we walked, she told me that her father and brother were in jail. They had been caught listening to the news on a radio concealed in their attic. Neighbours – former friends – had tipped off the Polish police, who had arrested them. I couldn't understand how people could do such things to their own neighbours, friends and their own people, yet, it happened often.

Months had passed by while I lived and worked in the city of Krakow and it was nearing the winter of 1942 and getting cold. I hadn't brought my beautiful coat with me from Czerniaków because it had been summer when I left and I had been afraid that carrying it might attract attention. My father had had coats specially made for my sister and me by the best tailor in Pruszków. The coats were similar, only the fur collars were different. The memory of it brought nostalgia, but memories didn't help right then; I was cold. At the apartment, on the chair in the dining room, there was a black knitted vest that belonged to Grandma. I asked her if I could wear it to keep warm and she let me. But when Vicky arrived, she said that she had knitted it herself especially for her mother and that I was not allowed to use it. I could see why she might feel that way, but I didn't know how else to keep from being so cold. Then, at work, I asked Mrs. Pola if by chance she might have a coat for sale. She brought me an over-dress. It had sleeves and was open in front, with ties. It was thin, with no lining and shorter than my dress. Its colour, dark blue, matched my dress perfectly, but it wasn't warm. Still, I convinced myself, it was better than nothing.

In December, I sent a season's greetings card to Mr. Müller with my photograph on it, but, as a precaution, I left off the return address. After the war, I was told that Otto Müller had appeared in the Warsaw ghetto with two huge carts loaded with vegetables for the group who worked in Czerniaków. He also showed them my picture on the card I had sent him. Much later, as the Allies advanced, Otto Müller was ambushed by the local workers at Czerniaków and killed.

Eugeniusz Gargas invited me to his home for Christmas dinner, asking me to come early to help decorate the tree. It was far from where I lived and since the streetcars didn't run after curfew, he had prepared a place where I could sleep. He had told me in the past that he lived with a woman, Jadwiga, and that he had an older brother, Tadeusz.

When I got there, Gargas was out and Jadwiga was cooking. She greeted me in a very friendly manner. Then she told me to call her Hedwig, the German equivalent of Jadwiga. She explained that her father was a German and her mother a Gypsy. She told me all this right at the beginning of the conversation. As the Gypsies were being persecuted like the Jews, she was more or less in hiding there. Despite her mixed parents, her skin was white. She had an oval face, with grey-green eyes and a beautifully formed nose and lips. Her long hair was strikingly gathered into one braid. She was really beautiful.

Hedwig cooked many different dishes for Christmas dinner, typi-cal of Polish custom. I decorated a Christmas tree for the first time in my life and really enjoyed doing it. After that, I swept the floor. Everything was ready when Eugeniusz and his brother came in. Tadeusz was a very handsome man. He was tall with sandy hair and blue eyes. The brothers were alike, but Eugeniusz wasn't as handsome. Tadeusz was a professor of mathematics at Jagiellonian University in Krakow. Like his brother, he was also skilled in drawing and sculpture, although it was Eugeniusz who had become the professional artist. They had been rich before the war, with land and other property, until the Germans had confiscated everything. Their stepmother had left them two apartments in the same building, where they had lived before now. Their father died of tuberculosis and both brothers suffered from it. I found out later that Tadeusz was actually sick when I met him.

We ate and sang. I knew all the Christmas carols from school. Then, we talked late into the night. I slept over, as arranged, and after breakfast I went home. After the holidays, back at work, Eugeniusz and I never discussed the visit. He invited me to his home again a few weeks later. I told Grandma this and, cautioning me, she said, "Elzunia, where people like you, go once, to the others, never." However, I had already promised to go and I couldn't disappoint them. I only stayed one hour and left. It was clear that, little by little, Tadeusz was dying. He spent more time lying in bed than up. It was the last time I saw him and also the last time I visited that home. After that, I heeded Grandma's advice.

～

Mr. Lesniewski's wife appeared one day at the studio with a lot of packages and asked the darkroom assistants to carry a table into the retouchers' room. When everything was in place on the table, Mr. Lesniewski was called into the room. It was his birthday. Despite war rationing, there was a cake, vodka, canapés, salami and cheeses. We toasted him with vodka and sang the traditional song "Sto Lat" (One Hundred Years). We called him Panie Szefie (Chief), which he liked.

We all ate and joked around, although I wasn't completely sure of myself there. I wasn't used to this kind of celebration, and it was the first time I had ever tasted vodka. All the other employees were having a great time. Alina climbed up on the table wearing a paper bow and recited a childish poem, which made everyone laugh because of its double entendres. It went on and on. The chief was happy and everyone wanted to toast everyone else. I didn't realize I was getting drunk, and I didn't know the consequences of alcohol; I just drank.

I think that Mr. Lesniewski was aware of what was happening. When the party was over, he asked a few men to accompany the girls home. I was feeling good until I tried to straighten myself up. It wasn't easy. I felt as if I were walking on the air. The man who had been assigned to take me home was the buyer of studio supplies such as chemicals, papers and negatives. Loyal to the boss, he would do anything for him. He was a colourful character, with a fox-like face and a fox's manners. He smelled with his long nose and listened with his big ears. He moved fast when on assignment, his small grey eyes sparkling all time.

I was having trouble walking. I was lifting my legs too high and I didn't seem to be able to find the ground. I didn't even know if I had revealed my secret identity or anything else that might have doomed my efforts to survive. When we boarded the streetcar, he carefully helped me up. I remember that there were no empty seats and that I hung on to a pole near the door. The buyer watched, ready to help me if needed. When we got to the stop where I lived, he wanted to walk me home. I remember refusing, saying, "I can manage to get home myself, thank you."

"Be careful! Goodbye!" he answered. I made it home. Grandpa was playing cards in the basement across the street. Grandma made supper. I went to bed early. When I was able to think clearly again, I realized I had put myself in danger. The experience taught me a good lesson: to be careful with alcohol.

The studio was flooded with work, so Mr. Lesniewski suggested that I take negatives home to retouch. Grandpa agreed to let me work in the kitchen after supper and Mr. Lesniewski lent me a spare retouching stand from the studio. It was old and heavy, so instead, Grandpa told me where to find a carpenter who could make one to my specifications. It was beautifully made, light, polished, a work of art. I thanked Grandpa. I was able to work a few hours every night, adding a lot of money to my wages. Mr. Lesniewski used to say that I was earning more money than Mr. Hartman, a man twice my age who had worked for twenty-five years developing negatives and copying positives in the darkroom. On the one hand, it was satisfying. On the other hand, I was working more than twelve hours a day. If I was tired, I couldn't complain. I later found out that Mr. Hartman was Jewish too.

Once, Mr. Lesniewski surprised me on my way home from work by appearing just as I was crossing the street to enter the gate to where I lived. "What a coincidence! I didn't know you lived here," he said, observing my surprise. It wasn't true that he didn't know where I lived. He was coming from the direction of the bridge, which meant that he had taken an earlier streetcar and gone one stop beyond mine. When he had seen me getting off, he had started walking toward me.

"What brings you to this neighbourhood?" I asked.

He smiled and said, "I have to meet someone." This wasn't a very obvious place to meet someone. It wasn't a commercial area, but a residential district, very close to the Wawel, the ancient royal castle. When he asked who I lived with, I wondered whether it was mere curiosity, or if there was a reason for his questioning. I thought the best thing was to tell the truth. After I replied, he simply shook hands with me and walked away.

Suddenly, one day, Grandpa got sick. When I asked him where the pain was, he told me that it was his stomach. "Maybe I can get something in the pharmacy for the pain," I said. He smiled, seeing me so worried. I explained to the pharmacist that Grandpa was in pain and asked if he could help with something. He gave me a bottle with some liquid in it, which I took back home and left, since I had to go to work. Meanwhile Grandma had sent for Vicky, who came with a doctor. When I came back from work, Grandpa was calm.

That night, I had a dream. I saw a woman enter the house. She was tall, with long hair and wore a long white dress. She moved around the room a few times. Then, she sat on my bed and told me not to worry. She looked at me for a while. She stood up and went to look at Grandpa, who slept in the kitchen behind a curtain. She came back, watching me again. She circled around the room and disappeared.

I went to the studio the next morning, trying to understand the dream. By the time I got back home, Grandpa had died. Grandma had tied a dishtowel around his head to keep his mouth closed. An hour later, Vicky came with the undertaker and he took Grandpa away. The next day, Jozef, their son, a chemical engineer, arrived, followed by their other daughter, Wanda, a school principal. They lived in different cities. The funeral was on Sunday. Grandma wasn't allowed to go because of her health, so the siblings had decided that Grandma would stay home with me. I had never been in such a situation before. Everything was new and strange for me. I still couldn't understand the message of the vision in my dream. Had death come to advise me not to worry?

I was sad and I didn't know how to behave in this time of mourning, just sitting there with Grandma. Grandpa had been good to me. After the funeral, all three of the children came to stay a while with their mother. She asked them how everything had been at the cemetery. She shrank as she listened to the details. She moved her fragile body over to a chair and sat looking into space, pensive.

Vicky, Wanda and Jozef talked in low voices. Their mother watched her children placidly, all grown up and all highly educated. She was proud of the fruit of her labours. Grandma had been a governess in a duke's palace in Austria, teaching his children for many years before she married. Breaking the silence, Vicky said to me, "Panna Elżbieta, my father's last wish was that we take care of you. You will stay with us until you get married. It was very important to him – it was his only wish before he died. He repeated it many times. He died with your name in his last breath."

Tears came to my eyes. They all smiled, watching my reaction. It must have seemed strange for the siblings, whose father, I gathered, had never really shown his inner feelings to them. Jozef left later that day, as he couldn't stay away from the responsibilities of his job. Wanda spent the night with her mother. In the morning, she suggested that I go to church with her before work. She accompanied me to the nearest church, a few blocks from home. We knelt down, made the sign of the cross and sat on the bench, praying with devotion. "Go to work now, Elzunia – you will be late," she murmured after we had been there a while. As we left the church, she added, "Promise me that you will do this every day before going to work." Perhaps she was suspicious of me. It was possible she had invited me to the church to see for herself if I knew how to pray, but I didn't let it bother me. By then, I had been living under a false identity for nearly a year. I was playing a role, supposing that at some point the curtain would fall and I would be able leave the stage.

I did what Wanda had asked. I prayed in the church every morning on the way to work. It was a good place for meditation and a place to grieve over the loss of my parents. Sometimes, it felt as though I was standing in the middle of nowhere, in a storm, unprotected. I prayed for the soul of my adopted grandfather, Pan Jozef Starowicz, who had saved me that day when I stood before him in that basement, completely helpless. I knew that my parents and grandparents would have blessed him, too, for saving me.

Life with Grandma

In the apartment immediately next to ours was a family of four – a father, a mother, their daughter, Helga, and their younger son, Genek, who was perhaps two or three years older than me. Genek worked as a technician for the railways. In his spare time, he played mandolin with a band that sometimes broadcast on the radio. He was of average height and blond, handsome, with blue eyes, a round face and an easy smile. Helga was a seamstress, with the same dark hair as her mother. We greeted each other whenever we passed outside the apartments. I imagine that because the Starowicz children were older than Genek and Helga, there hadn't been much connection between the two families. Maybe the social class was different, too. I always greeted them and they were very friendly in return.

Genek came to pay his respects to Grandma the evening after the funeral. She thanked him, adding, "Please stay here for a while. Talk to Elzunia. She needs company." Since Grandma went to bed early, Genek often came after supper to keep me company, with Grandma's approval. She was happy because she had been worried that I was thinking too much and working too much. She felt I needed someone to talk to, as a way to take my mind off my problems. Little did she suspect how major these problems were.

While I was working on my retouching at home, we would talk. He told me about the mandolin band in which he played. He was gentle and kind to me. We were never able to go walking on the weekend because the members of the band often practised together on Sundays. The band had programs on the radio, but radios were forbidden to the Polish population. As I mentioned earlier, people had been arrested for listening to radios.

Genek also belonged to a youth organization and a few weeks later, he invited me to go along on one of their weekend excursions. I was excited at the prospect of a change in my routine. But two days later, after supper, he said, "Even if I take good care of you, Elzuś, you wouldn't like the company of these people."

"If that's true, why are you going?" I asked.

"Because I know how to go with the flow. I avoid taking part in what I don't like. We would have to sleep over there for two nights. It's not for you." He was a caring friend. I was sincere in my feelings for him, but I couldn't reveal my identity to him. I knew everything about him and his life. Who knows what might have happened if he had known the truth about me. Sometimes, I regretted having to tell lies, but what else could I do? It wasn't easy for me to carry my load of suffering, but my survival depended on my ability to remain constantly alert and above all, not provide other people with information that could prove fatal to me.

Genek's family was also good to me. His sister, Helga, adjusted the navy blue dress that Dvora had given me, changing the style and sewing it on the machine. She was quite amused that I had been wearing a dress that was unfinished. I told her that I had been in such a hurry to come to Krakow, I had removed it from the dressmaker's. As I tried on the dress, I noticed a photograph on the top of a corner cabinet, leaning against a picture of a saint. Helga's mother followed my glance. "She is the landlord's daughter. We don't know where they are or what happened to them. They were very nice people. She was Helga's best friend. Now, a Volksdeutsche couple live there, in their home, both of them fat, riding in a carriage on Sundays to the church. Bad times, Elzunia."

"What a disgrace! Poor people," I said. Helga adjusted the dress to the over-dress at the upper part. It matched perfectly. I bought a beautiful housecoat and matching slippers at the Rynek Główny, a huge medieval market building still in use. The slippers, called *kierpce*, were handmade by indigenous people from the Tatra mountain area.

Soon, Helga's birthday arrived. I was invited, but suddenly I felt shy and not in the mood to attend. I was anxious because I didn't know their friends. On my way home from work, I entered a florist's store and bought a potted chrysanthemum as a gift. I wished her well and gave her the plant. I had forgotten that in Poland chrysanthemums are used to decorate graves on All Saints' Day and are not for birthday presents. How could I have forgotten such a traditional religious custom? They were in bloom, beautiful. She put them outside the door. Up to then, I had made a series of mistakes, but this one, I was ashamed of. I could find no excuse not to go. Then, I got the idea to wash my hair and give them the excuse that I couldn't go to a party with wet hair. It was too childish and it didn't work. I was in my beautiful deshabille, wearing the *kierpce* and a towel made into a turban, when Genek appeared. He picked me up and carried me straight into their apartment. His father looked so happy to see his son carrying a girl in his arms. Everyone approved of his gesture. His mother said, "It's only an informal house party. You look fine as you are." Then a friend said, "Genek chose the most beautiful girl." His parents were really happy to see me. Despite my mistakes, things were still going in my favour.

One day soon after that, Vicky told me that Grandma and I were to move to her apartment and Wanda's married daughter would move into Grandma's apartment. We could take our personal belongings, nothing else. I could pack my personal belongings into one suitcase and I could carry my retouching stand in one hand. Grandma had more clothing than I had.

Vicky lived right in front of the Krakow ghetto, in the house where

Cyla and I had run to for cover when we escaped from the ghetto. It was a nice apartment, richly furnished, containing one bedroom, a dining room, a kitchen and a bathroom with a tub and shower. In many ways, it was far better than what I had been used to – not all houses in Poland had such comforts. Vicky accommodated us as best she could. Grandma slept in the dining room and I had a settee in the bedroom Vicky and her husband shared. Vicky was keeping the promise she had given to her father to take care of me. She also permitted me to do retouching in the kitchen after supper. I had seen Vicky's husband, Vincenty, only once, the day of Grandpa's funeral. He was a high-ranking officer in the Polish military. He was a nice-looking man, always in a good mood. His friend Zygmunt, a military man who visited often, had the same easygoing style as Vincenty. I didn't know at the time if he was single or not.

Vicky worked out a church schedule with her husband and me. On Sundays, I would go to church with her husband for nine o'clock mass and she would stay home and cook. Then she would go to eleven o'clock mass. That way, Grandma wouldn't be left alone too long. Later, she reversed the schedule. Vincenty and I attended the Franciscan church. We liked it there and they had an excellent choir. Sometimes, Zygmunt came along with us, but not often. Vicky criticized us because we weren't that religious. She attended an old-fashioned, much stricter, church. There was no shortage of churches in Krakow.

When Vicky went to mass at eleven, we had an hour to roam before having to get back to Grandma in the apartment. Usually, after church, Vincenty and I sat on a bench in the Planty gardens. On both sides of the length of the Planty were trees and benches. We would sit there looking at the crowd going by, usually laughing and commenting on the passing parade. Afterward, we would tell Grandma all about our adventure, talking about the people we had seen. Grandma would shake her head, saying it wasn't polite to gossip, hiding a smile.

Vicky didn't approve of Vincenty's sense of humour and, even when she was relatively content, her face still bore a grimace of disapproval. It wasn't bad staying there, but I felt exposed. One mistake could ruin everything. I noticed that Vicky opened a window on to the street every morning when the Jews were marching from the ghetto to work, and that she had tears in her eyes. One morning, Grandma asked, "Did you see him?" She nodded and cried. One day, I asked Grandma why Vicky cried every morning. She told me that when Vicky watched the column of Jews pass by, she saw the lawyer for whom she had worked for twenty years walking to work in a factory supervised by the Germans. She couldn't stand it. "Elzunia," Grandma said, "this lawyer is a smart, very intelligent man. Always nicely dressed. Now, Vicky sees him in rags, hungry and humiliated. That's why she is crying. She had been his secretary for twenty years. Every morning, she opens the window to see him and it breaks her heart."

It was good to know that these people felt sympathy for us but I wondered how she would react if she knew that I was Jewish. Would she protect me or report me? That question, like many others, remains unanswered, but I know they had good feelings for me at the time. Perhaps my fantasy that I would find someone to protect me was childish.

Vicky asked what I thought of Zygmunt, Vincenty's pal from the military. I had never given him a thought. What could I say? "He is a nice person," I responded, without enthusiasm.

"Would you like to marry him?" Vicky pressed.

"Yes, I like him, he is always in a good mood."

"But it's a serious decision, to marry someone."

"I don't know. He never asked me, anyway." He did show up at my work once, in a luxurious carriage. He took me for a ride, then home. Vicky changed her mind a week later.

"He is too old for you," she said. She was still worrying about me.

Sundays, Vincenty served us breakfast in bed. That had been their own custom since they got married and, as I slept in the same room,

I got the same service. They took Grandpa's last wish that I be taken care of as an order. I wondered how long this could last.

Watching Vicky open the window every day and cry, I started to yearn. I knew that something was missing in my life. I missed my family. One Sunday afternoon, I went for a walk and sat on a bench in the Planty, waiting for the Jews to pass on their way back from work. I was thrilled to hear them speaking in Yiddish, the language I hadn't heard spoken since Czerniaków. A week later I went back to sit on the bench and read, waiting to hear the language again. That was the last time I did it, though. I realized that it wasn't safe; it looked too suspicious. I had forgotten that I was still in danger. But the temptation to try my luck was always with me. Perhaps I was being careless because I had had enough of this hide-and-seek life.

I decided to walk further on, wearing the veil I bought to go to Warsaw for the fictitious funeral, and I walked into a little place that stood alone near the railway station. The sign on its roof said "Wine and Honey" and the façade was ornamented with concrete lions and flowers. The doors and windows were supported on iron hinges, gothic-style, and inside, heavy gold trimmed drapes hung from the windows. Dim light from brass and crystal chandeliers cast shadows over the whole room. Every detail suggested past glories. It must have been a place where music lovers went to enjoy themselves. In a corner, a musician played piano. A violinist chatted with the newcomers, asking what piece they would prefer. The audience, well-dressed men and women, listened attentively, enjoying the music.

The bartender served wine and hot liquid honey, moving among the tables silently. He was bald, with a thick moustache and sparkling eyes. When the bartender approached to take my order, I asked for hot honey, which I had never drunk in my life. I told him I wanted to talk to the violinist, who had been playing the same piece since I came in. I had never played an instrument, but I knew the names of many composers and compositions. When the violinist approached my table, I asked him to play Schumann's "Träumerei." When other guests arrived, the musicians changed the tune. I paid and left. Once outside the bar, I disappeared, walking as fast I could.

I worked hard and money wasn't a problem, but I felt lonely. All communication with Genek stopped the day that Grandma and I moved to Vicky's. He hadn't tried to contact me. Vicky had told me that I was allowed to invite Genek to her place, but I was afraid to go back and invite him because of something that had happened shortly before we moved.

The Germans had surrounded the streets around the block one morning, demanding to see everyone's documents. As I walked out the gate, I found myself fifty metres from the checkpoint. I remembered Irena handing me the prayer book and asking if I knew how to pray. I soon realized what was going on. I couldn't go back, as it would look suspicious and call attention to myself. And what kind of explanation would I give to Grandma, or my bosses, if I arrived late? Besides, there were so many SS soldiers everywhere that it was impossible to do anything but comply. I knew that I was in big trouble.

With no idea of what to do, I stood in line, thinking. What did Irena mean when she asked if I knew how to pray? Was I supposed to entrust myself to the Almighty in the last moment of my life? Had she thought that if I prayed, it would help me to survive? My father had prayed, but it had not helped. While these thoughts went through my head, the moment of crisis approached. I knew I could get caught, here and now, and shot. As I got closer to the SS soldier at the checkpoint, it was too late to pray. "Zeigen Sie Ihre Dokumente!" (Show your documents!) shouted the SS soldier. The people advanced slowly, talking in low voices. They seemed surprised by the checkpoint.

"What do they want?" a woman asked.

"Are they looking for a thief?" asked another.

"They are trying to catch Jews," someone answered.

"There aren't any Jews here."

"You never know."

"I knew such a good Jew. They killed him. Damn it!" a man said, angrily.

"They were cheaters," one said to him.

"There were decent people among them," the man answered.

Krakow was not a cosmopolitan city. The population was mostly Polish and Jewish. I had never seen tourists from other countries or people of other nationalities, except at the embassy. One of the times that my father had taken me to Warsaw when I was a child, we had seen a live promotion for coffee in which a black man stood behind a big shop window roasting beans. I remember how unusual it was because we never saw black people in Poland. The Polish people rarely saw people of other races or customs. They learned about them in school, but this was not enough to make them accept people who were different. In general, the Poles hated the Jews or barely tolerated them, although there were exceptions.

Why did the Germans fear the Jews? By this time, it seemed that half of all the Jews in Poland had been killed. The great majority of the others had been locked up in ghettos, harmless and hopeless. They weren't a menace to anyone. But Nazis were determined to hunt down every last Jew. If someone reported that Jews were hiding somewhere, I was the target. It would be the end of my life. Every second counted now and I still hadn't decided to whom I should pray. I couldn't pray to any God: it offended my own sense of religion to pray only when it was convenient. Only a miracle could save me now.

I was getting closer to the checkpoint and still hadn't prayed. What God would accept my prayers? I was a fraud. I carried forged documents. I lied all the time. I robbed decent people of their trust. I wasn't who I said I was. In peacetime, for all these criminal offences, I would have gone to jail. But I wanted to live. On the other hand, if those people had known that I was Jewish, all those decent people, what would they have done?

"Dokumente!" shouted the SS soldier repeatedly. I got the document ready in my hand. Looking at it, I asked myself: Who am I? I had adjusted to the situation so well that no muscle moved in my face. Pray, pray now! I handed him my identification.

"Where are you going?"

"To work," I answered.

"Where do you work?"

"At the Bielec Photo Studio."

The studio was well known. The Germans always came in to have their picture taken there.

"Do you have a permit to work in Krakow?"

"Yes." I showed him another piece of paper.

"Weitergehen! Schnell!" (Go on! Quick!)

Luckily, he hadn't noticed the age on my identity document, which said that I was ten years older than my real age – a mistake on the part of the forger. I felt that I had somehow betrayed the Creator, but I was too honest to pray to Him only when I needed him. I had denied my true faith to save my own life. Yet, whoever He was, He had protected me.

It was because of this incident that I was afraid to return to the old neighbourhood to see Genek once we had moved. The people there all knew each other, having lived for decades in the same neighbourhood. It would be easy for someone to report me; it wasn't at all unusual. Besides, Genek was from a working-class family and I think would have felt uncomfortable in Vicky's home, although he was very well mannered. The families of Grandma's children were all highly educated, middle class. I put my survival before our friendship.

~

Grandma was always at home and I wanted to do something for her. She didn't talk very much and she walked very slowly. One day, I asked her if she would like me to take her out. She was so happy and responded that she would go wherever I wanted. I told her that on Sunday I would take her to St. Mary's Basilica and that we could pray at the main altar. When Sunday came, she put on her best clothes. We walked down the stairs carefully. I stopped a carriage and helped her into her seat. It was a beautiful day. The church was in the middle of the city and when we got there I took her by the arm and slowly guided her to the main altar. We knelt down and prayed for a while.

She couldn't have been happier. "Elzunia, dear," she said, "it has been a long time since I was in this church. Usually, I go to mass at the chapel in Wawel. When I couldn't walk that far, I prayed at home. Thank you, dear Elzunia, I will remember this day."

Weeks later, when I took her to the cemetery to see Grandpa's grave, Grandma's eyes sparkled with emotion. Vicky explained where it was and asked me to water the flowers while we were there. Again, I took a horse and carriage to get there, since Grandma was too weak to walk. She was silent the whole time, lost in thought as we prayed together at the grave. Then, while she continued praying, I watered the flowers. "Elzunia," she asked, "pray a little more for Grandpa. He loved you very much." I prayed. He deserved an Our Father. He truly deserved it. I stood beside her until she got tired and asked to go back. Vicky looked happy when we arrived. Grandma was excited and told Vicky, "Elzunia is a golden child; she was so nice to me." The truth was that it made me happy, too.

At Easter, we fasted and went to confession at the church. I found it much easier to confess my sins than fast. Walking to the church, I was thinking of what the priest would say if I told him I was Jewish. Silly thoughts! I was becoming obsessed with the idea of telling someone my secret. Each day, the pressure seemed harder to bear. When it was my turn to approach the priest, I said, "Father, I cut a piece of cheese and didn't tell the truth when I was asked." The priest was busy and my sin wasn't important. He said, "My child, don't do it again. I absolve you; go with God."

My work at the photographic studio continued without incident until, at the end of one day, I stood up and as usual handed the envelopes with the negatives to the woman in charge of the archive. As I left the studio, a German officer was waiting for me in the street. He greeted me and asked if he could walk with me to the streetcar stop. I agreed. As we walked down the street together, I felt shame in my heart for being with a German. He explained to me that he had been waiting for me for almost an hour. When I asked him how he knew me, he said that, for the second time, he had looked at me through the open door. The door to the retouchers' room was always wide open and anyone coming up to the reception desk could glance in. He had asked the receptionist when I would be leaving. I started to feel uneasy and resentful. I wanted to run away from him, but he knew where I worked. From past experience, I had found that it was better to wait and deal with whatever was going to happen.

The German officer was tall, good-looking, and about twenty-five years old and seemed like an intellectual. He had only one eye; the other he had lost in the battle of Stalingrad. "I'm going home tonight," he told me. Inwardly, I breathed a sigh of relief, so what he said next completely knocked the wind out of my sails. He told me that he loved me and wanted to marry me and take me to his home in Germany. He was crazy with excitement. "I'll get permission from my superiors to take you with me. My mother would be delighted to meet you. You would have everything you needed. My parents love me very much. My happiness would be theirs."

When we got to the railway station, he begged me to wait for him while he went to talk to his superiors. That gave me some time to think. It wasn't a bad idea to leave Poland, where the danger of discovery pursued me every day. But, heavens! How could I stoop that low, even to preserve my life? After a few minutes, he came back. He had been refused permission to take me with him to Germany, he said, but he would return for me. Meanwhile, he would write. Two weeks later, I got a letter from him at the studio. He wrote that he missed me badly and was planning to see me soon. On a separate sheet, he had written out the most beautiful love poems. I never answered his letter.

I didn't deliberately set out to look for adventures. Neither did I look for trouble. But things happened whether I wanted them to or not. One Sunday, I had a very bad headache and Vicky suggested that a walk would be the best thing for it. I liked to walk and I would often walk for hours. The last time I had done so was the time I ended up at the wine and honey tavern. This time, I was looking for a pharmacy, but when I found one that was open, I decided to continue on to the next even though the walk didn't seem to be doing my headache any good. Finally, I decided to head back home. I remembered that on the street that marked the border of the ghetto, there was a home occupied by a pharmacist. The rear of the house was actually inside the ghetto limits.

The pharmacy was open and I walked in to get some aspirin. I paid for them and had just walked back out into the street when two policemen approached me, asking for documents.

"What are you doing here?" one asked. I still had the aspirin in my hand. I explained that I had a bad headache, had gone for a walk and then decided to buy some aspirin.

"Where do you live?"

"Just across the street. If you wish to accompany me..."

"Give me your address."

I told them my address. I couldn't allow myself to panic. As before, it seemed the best approach was to go along with them, to wait to see what lay in store. Besides, they hadn't actually asked me if I was Jewish. The policemen finished writing down my address. When I asked if they were coming with me, they just said that they would call on me another time to confirm that I lived there. I said goodbye and walked away, trying to put the whole incident out of my mind.

That same night, in my sleep, I heard, "Panna Elsa, wake up. Don't be scared. Some people have come to see you. They are policemen. Be calm, don't worry." It was Vincenty, Vicky's husband. I had been sleeping like a log and hadn't heard any knocking at the door. I put on my nice housecoat with the slippers. My hair was long, curling down over my shoulders. "Good evening," I said. They didn't answer. I put out my hand to shake theirs. They did shake hands with me.

"Documents, please," one asked.

"My purse is in the kitchen. May I get it?" They allowed me to enter the kitchen. I returned with a smile on my face, the documents in my hand. There were four men and only one entrance, so there was no way to escape. Two of them were the uniformed policemen who had spotted me coming out of the pharmacy. The other two were secret agents in plainclothes, black raincoats with hats. They were standing outside the open door. What would they get, if they discovered I was Jewish? Sugar, salt, butter? Was their conscience that cheap? It wasn't any risk to them if they looked away. How many Jewish people had died the same way? No one knows. No one remembers them.

I showed all my documents to the police. They were satisfied. One even mumbled a few words of apology, excusing himself and the others for interrupting my sleep. I shook hands with them again and then they left. I explained to Vincenty that the police had asked for my documents. Then I told him how I had met two of them at the pharmacy. "Dranie" (Bastards) he said, visibly angry.

The next morning, I left the apartment as usual, jumping down the steps. Outside the entrance, I saw one of the two policemen who had interrogated me at the pharmacy and again the previous night. As a photographer, my eyes were trained to observe rather than merely look. I recognized him at a glance, even though today he was in civilian clothing. He greeted me elegantly, apologizing for waking me the night before and waited for my reaction.

"Good day," I said, smiling.

"Good day," he answered, perplexed. I saw a carriage waiting. I didn't know what else to say, but I knew I had to be careful. "I couldn't think of any other excuse to see you again," he said. "Will you please allow me to escort you to work in this carriage?" He helped me into the carriage and gave the horseman the order to go. The carriage was one of the best; it looked brand new. Even the horses gleamed.

"Do you like Krakow?" my escort asked.

"Very much. Krakow is more than a beautiful ancient city. The old buildings with their artistic ornaments fascinate me – and all the churches, with their domes turned green with the verdigris of time, the statues of saints, the arabesque and flowers made of concrete. I love it all, it's a great city," I said enthusiastically.

"It was a capital city before Poland became a republic," he explained.

"I know, I learned that in school," I answered, as if to say, Don't teach me what I already know.

"I'm sorry about what happened last night."

"It doesn't matter anymore. Your surprise has flattered me." In such a situation, how long could I continue to act offended?

The horses drew the elegant carriage along the stone-paved street. Because I didn't know what to do, how to behave, I looked shy. The policeman didn't press me to talk all the time; for much of the ride, he just gazed at me rather happily.

"Are you still angry with me?"

"I was angry – two policemen and two detectives checking someone's address in the middle of the night. Isn't that rather extreme?"

He was handsome, with a witty smile. In seconds, he could become a murderer. "It's common police procedure. Jews are hiding in the city."

"That was the purpose of your visit, to catch a Jew?"

"We have orders to do so."

"I'll try to forget."

This appeared to make him happy. I quickly changed the subject. "In the afternoons especially, the sunbeams reflecting from the old metal roofs lend a mysterious appearance to the city," I offered. He looked at me as if he were charmed by my descriptive powers.

"Besides being a pretty young lady, you are romantic too," he observed, not taking his eyes off me. "Thank you," I returned, smiling at him. In reality, my brain was whirling with thoughts with each clop of the horse's hoofs. Clop, clop, clop, my home, my parents, my sister. Clop, clop, my father giving me a beautiful doll that walked and talked. Clop, clop, my mother making me a velvet dress for my fifteenth birthday. Clop, clop, where is my sister? If I am shot, I want to be thinking of them at the very moment. But how will they know? How will they know how much I loved them?

"You are lost in thoughts," the policeman said, observing my silence.

"Oh! It's nothing. Sometimes I get so excited that I become tongue-tied. I'm really surprised that you did this. I'm also a little tired, after last night's events."

"Don't worry, it won't happen again."

"I hope not," I said, looking him squarely in the eyes.

We went past the Planty, two rows of trees and benches lining a walkway. In the middle of the Rynek Krakowie, the town square that was also called the Rynek Główny, stood Sukiennice Plaza, the large Romanesque-style building with long, symmetrical archways. At the end of the building was a clock tower. Every hour, a watchman sounded a trumpet. The clanging of the streetcar bells mixed with the sound of the horse's hoofs. The city was alive.

"I love early mornings in the city," I said. "Especially when you come in by train and see the lights going on one by one." "Yes, mornings in the city have their charm," he agreed.

My eyes captured everything they could, almost as if I were bidding farewell to the scene. I saw Germans everywhere, uniformed, with shiny boots. They were so neat and clean, I thought; why were their minds so dirty, so perverse? Meanwhile, the civilian population calmly went about their daily routine. We continued talking until we arrived at the studio and he spoke of hoping to see me again. The policeman ordered the carriage to stop at the studio. He got off first, then helped me down the steps. Then he smiled, shook my hand and planted a kiss on it. He watched as I entered the studio, then he climbed into the carriage and left. I was uneasy all day, with new fears added to my troubled thoughts, wondering if this carriage ride was the last luxury of my life. I was satisfied with my performance of my assumed persona. I had to live, no matter what. That was my only goal.

～

Vicky had lent me a collection by the famous Polish poet, Adam Mickiewicz. I knew many of the poems by heart. At the studio one day, I was enthusiastically reading his poem "Żeglarz" to the other retouchers. Written in Odessa in 1825, it tells the story of a navigator in a boat, suddenly separated from his ship by a hurricane. I liked it; it reflected my life a little. Unfortunately, whenever I forgot to concentrate on my problem, even for a moment, it seemed that bad things happened to me. Just as I was halfway through the poem, Mr. Lesniewski passed by. He didn't say anything, but on Saturday, as he distributed the week's wages, he observed that I had spent work time reading when I knew there was so much work to be done. He said that I had to go in on Sunday for a few hours to retouch the most urgently needed negatives.

He was the boss, so I had to obey. Weekend work replaced going to mass for the next few weeks. I took advantage of the sunny day and walked to the studio that Sunday morning, which took nearly an hour. I arrived at the same time as the secretary and started to work straight away. A few minutes later, Mr. Lesniewski arrived, greeted me and entered his office. At one o'clock, he emerged to say that was enough, but that I had to come again for a few hours the following Sunday. Mr. Lesniewski was a military man; he knew how to punish his subordinates. But I felt the discipline was out of proportion to the actual infringement, since I was already working every night at home. I was really working hard. The drawback was that, while working, I had too much time to think about everything that had happened to me. The good thing was that I had money to live in a good home, with a family that really cared about me.

After that, when I saw an ad in a newspaper for a position working in the forest, I showed it to Eugeniusz and told him I was interested. He laughed, telling me, "You know that is not for you. You don't know what you are going to expose yourself to." I told him I was tired of working so hard and that I needed a change, but he didn't think it was a good idea for me to be among a group of foresters. I didn't understand what he meant, but I didn't mention it again. The truth was that I still feared Niedzwiecki. Worse, I had a premonition of evil, which I couldn't discuss with anybody.

The next Sunday I took a shortcut to the studio and as I was approaching the bridge, I was surprised to see my admirer, the policeman, in uniform. He noticed my astonishment but didn't acknowledge it. "I'm happy to see you," he said, shaking my hand. We talked as if he was an old friend, but I feared the worst. He started walking me to the other side of the bridge. Maybe I was under surveillance. No, I mustn't panic. Surely if they suspected, they wouldn't play with me. It would be a fast end. I explained to him that I liked to walk and that I chose to walk to the studio because at work, I sat for many hours at a time. We chatted until we had reached the other side. Then at the end we said goodbye, shaking hands again.

Occasionally, in times of desperation like this, I used to reproach my parents and my sister for abandoning me. I knew that it was silly, that what had happened was not their fault. Many families had been broken up, their members isolated from each other, at a time when they most needed each other. I knew in my heart that my parents were not alive. The emptiness of not having anyone to turn to was overwhelming. To know that I was alone was devastating.

Betrayed

It was a Saturday in the early summer of 1943, a working day, just like any other Saturday, and it was payday, as usual. The only difference was that it marked the start of a two-week vacation period for me. And that very Saturday at noon, two Polish secret agents walked into the studio and came up to me, ordering me to take my belongings and follow them. Instantly, I knew that this was the end of my adventure. The agents didn't tell me why they were taking me away. I didn't ask. It was clear they had a reason and I had a pretty good idea of what that reason was. Besides, I was too proud to argue with them. I was not going to give them the opportunity to be rude.

As I crossed the room on my way out, the other employees stood there, petrified and silent, holding their breath. I had no idea what they were thinking at that moment. Certainly, except for Niedzwiecki, they had all been friendly and polite the whole time I had worked there. I couldn't apologize for what I had done because I didn't feel sorry. For me, it had been a necessity. I couldn't even say goodbye to anyone because it might suggest complicity on the part of that person. To tell the truth, although they were, on the whole, very nice people, I had no idea how sympathetic any of them were toward Jews. Therefore, I said not a single word as I walked out.

Outside, I thought of confessing everything to the agents, admitting that I was a Jew and begging them to let me go. Obviously, this wouldn't have worked – there was a reward for catching Jews, and

I still had my pride. I walked silently between them to the streetcar stop, where they stood on either side of me. They ordered me to pay my own fare and at this, I smiled. We got off at Gestapo headquarters. I was shown into a large room where two high-ranking Nazi officers sat at a pair of desks pushed together. They asked me to sit down and began to interrogate me.

As I answered their questions, looking straight at them, my eyes fell on a whip that was lying on top of a stack of files on one of the desks. It was a long leather whip like the kind used to control circus animals. My brain raced with thoughts – I won't let them torture me; it will be easier to be shot at once. I wasn't afraid of them, but I was afraid of being beaten. What worried me most was that I might not be able to endure it and might divulge something important. One way or another, it would be fatal.

If the whip hadn't been there, I wouldn't have been so unsure of my capacity to keep silent. At first, they were treating me with respect, perhaps because they were still not sure who I was. It might, after all, be a mistake. I stared at the instrument of torture, anticipating the humiliation and pain I would suffer. I became obsessed with one thought: If I told them right away that I was Jewish, they wouldn't have to beat me up. If they killed me immediately, I wouldn't be humiliated. I still had time to lie, up to the moment when they asked me if I was a Jew. They didn't seem to be in a hurry, either. While one officer examined my documents in detail, I had time to think again. I saw myself lying on the floor, crying out in pain. No, I made up my mind: I would confess.

In fact, the only fake document was my personal identity paper, which had been forged. All the other papers were genuine, obtained from various German administration offices, giving the initial impression that everything was in order. That was why it took them so long to decide. As I sat there, waiting to be questioned more, from time to time they would sneak a look at me. I realized there was some disagreement between them. There was the issue of the age stated on my document and perhaps the other point of interest was my aristocratic surname. However, these two points weren't what they were looking for. I had been reported as Jewish.

I heard one of them saying, "Vorsichtig, sie könnte eine Gräfin sein." (Careful, she could be a countess.) They both seemed impressed and nodded to each other. They had agreed to ask me directly. There was a pause, then the first officer asked suddenly, "Sind Sie Jüdin?" (Are you a Jew?)

"Yes."

"Who gave you the identification document?"

"Someone at a Volksküche [soup kitchen]," I answered.

"Do you know the person?"

"No, I had never seen him before. One day, he took a picture of me. The next day, he gave me the document and helped me out of the ghetto."

It wasn't my best lie, but it sounded credible. Why had I been in such a hurry to give up? I suppose it was destiny, which knew better than I how to keep me alive. They called the Polish agents to take me away. In spite of my emotional turmoil, I noticed that they didn't seem at ease. Something was unusual about their behaviour. After the war, I found the answer when I ran into Mr. Lesniewski on a street in Lodz. He was amazed to see me still alive. He told me that when he heard that I had been taken away by the police, he had gone to the Gestapo headquarters, arguing that he needed me in the studio. Every German military man stationed in Krakow knew Mr. Lesniewski from the photo studio. He pointed out that all my documents were in order, that I had a permit to live and work in Krakow – he had seen the documents himself – and that he wanted me back in the studio immediately. He told me that the officers had promised him that after the interrogation, if they were satisfied I wasn't Jewish, he could take me back to the studio. Although he was happy to see me, there was a reproachful tone in his voice as he went on to ask, "Why did you confess? I was waiting there to take you back."

"I didn't want to be beaten," I replied. I told him about seeing the whip and making my decision to confess.

"I was waiting there to take you back, to the studio," he repeated. "It was really too bad."

"I confessed right away and that was the end of it. I'm sorry," I said. "I knew I would be kept under surveillance after the interrogation, even if they had let me go back to the studio. It would have been dangerous for all of us if I had gone on working there. Those who reported me would have looked for revenge. I'm sure of that."

Mr. Lesniewski listened attentively. He knew that I was right. He wanted to give me more details of what had happened that day and we stepped into the entrance of a building to avoid being seen together on the street, which would have put both our lives at risk, since we were both moving around under false papers and it was safest not to raise suspicions. He told me he was on a secret mission, that he was living under a false identity because he had the names and addresses of people who had collaborated with the Nazis and he was trying to find them. I learned later that this mission cost him his life. While he was waiting outside a courtroom to testify, someone pushed him out of an upper-storey window. He hated the collaborators, I was told. I think of him as being a thoroughly honourable Polish citizen. Maybe if I had told him my whole story at the beginning, things might have been different. Who can ever know?

But that was all much later. On the day that I was picked up, the two agents escorted me to the Polish police headquarters. The officer at the desk grabbed the silver monogram pinned on my overcoat, which I had bought myself. He asked for my watch. From my purse, he removed my money and a silver cigarette holder, a name-day present from my co-workers. In Poland, people celebrate the day that honours the saint for whom they were named. A policeman took me downstairs to a basement cell, a small triangular enclosure where temporary detainees were kept. The door had an iron grating and there were dirty old rugs lying in disarray on the floor. A stale crust of bread and a cup of putrid water had been left by the previous occupant. On the walls were names, messages and days of detention marked off. I was there alone from Saturday afternoon to midday Monday. During that time, I got a piece of bread and some fresh water.

On Monday afternoon, a policeman took me upstairs to the office. There stood Alina, in front of a stenographer typing out notes. The typist looked at us and started to cry. I suppose she knew better than we did what awaited us. We didn't cry. We just stood there waiting to be told what to do next. What else could we do? We were surrounded. No one was likely to hide us or let us escape. People wanted rewards, many hated Jews and others feared the consequences for helping Jews.

Once the paperwork had been finished, we were taken to the detention cell in the basement. Alina told me that when she returned to the studio from her two-week vacation, the employees told her what happened to me, suggesting that she escape. But she had had enough, and she stayed. The Polish agents came in soon after and took her away. After we had spent a few hours in the cell, two policemen put us in a car. They drove fast, taking the curves sharply. We kept tumbling into each other and laughing. To the right, to the left, we laughed hysterically. It was weird, but so was everything else that was going on. Besides, we had never been told what to do if this happened, nor did we know that people could stoop so low – lower than we could have believed possible.

The two policemen turned toward us, puzzled by our reaction. To bring us back to our senses, they asked, "Who wants to die and who wants to work?" We got the message. The policemen were in their forties, well-nourished and cynical, smiling at the hunt that had bagged them two prey at once. During the war, sometimes destiny depended on the executioner. Not this time. The policemen would neither kill us nor let us go. They had only one thought – the reward they would get for catching two Jews, criminals whose only crime was to still be alive. My little miracles seemed to have come to an end. Or had they?

I didn't know at that point that just surviving for so long was lucky. I still had a long way to go before I had seen the worst.

We were taken to the maximum-security prison for criminals, Montelupich. All I remember is a very large building with iron bars in the windows. I couldn't take in any more details, since everything was happening so quickly. The agents took us upstairs to a large room where a number of gentile women were being detained. Among them were teachers, professors and important government employees. In spite of sharing the same fate, they were still segregated into the usual social classes.

The floor was relatively clean, considering that it served for walking, sitting and sleeping. Light entered through a wide window. There wasn't anything more to do than walk, talk, sit or sleep. Because I was relatively uninhibited, I talked to people, asking why they had been detained and how long they had been there. I also answered their questions, without telling them my true story, of course. We weren't safe in jail. A hostile reaction against Jews was always possible.

Later that afternoon, I was shocked when a girl was brought in from the interrogation room. She had been beaten and tortured there. It was terrible to look at her, lying on the floor, writhing in pain, turning over and over, moaning bitterly. She was young and looked strong. I asked the other women about her, but they were used to seeing her in that hopeless state and had stopped paying attention to her. No one would go near her for fear of becoming involved and having to suffer the same fate. It turned out the girl was Polish and had been reported by her Polish neighbours for belonging to an underground organization. She had been beaten to force a confession, but she wouldn't tell them anything about her fellow workers in the movement.

I wondered if I could have been as brave. I learned later that she survived. Long after the war, by sheer chance, a neighbour of mine received a book from Poland about the partisans during the war, which he said was about his sister. Every night at the neighbour's house, I read a chapter or two. Subsequently, I realized that she was the girl who had been so brutally interrogated at Montelupich. With my neighbour's permission, I wrote to her. She wrote about the events of that time and mentioned people I knew, including Mietek, my failed contact with the underground. She had married after the war and worked as a teacher. She was surprised that I could still write Polish without mistakes after so long. We corresponded for some time, until 1982, when I read in the newspaper of an antisemitic rally in Poland.

The days in Montelupich were empty, the nights filled with nightmares. Alina and I were the only Jewish girls there. After a week or so, I became acquainted with a girl who said she knew how to foretell the future. She had special cards and talked in a low voice. She shuffled them and made me divide them into three piles. "You will walk out of this jail, but only to go to another closed place," she predicted. The same afternoon, two agents came and took us to the ghetto.

The streets of the Krakow ghetto were virtually deserted. By this time, the ghetto had been liquidated and I later found out the Jews had been transported either to the Płaszów *Zwangsarbeitslager*, a forced labour camp, or the Auschwitz-Birkenau death camp. The only ones remaining were those caught hiding somewhere on the Aryan side, many of them turned in by Poles. They were now housed in the ghetto jail. A few Jewish policemen remained to keep order, but that was no guarantee of any understanding or sympathy, I'm sorry to say.

A Jewish policeman seated behind a table asked our names. As he raised his eyes to me, he said, "I know you but can't remember from where." A well-trained policeman doesn't simply see; like a photographer, he observes and remembers. Of course, I remembered him. The few times I had sat on the bench outside the ghetto to listen to Yiddish being spoken, he had been escorting the Jews to and from work.

"How did you get caught?" he asked.

"We were betrayed by a co-worker," I responded. He lowered his head.

Afterward, he took us to a room where a woman and her two children were locked up. I can't remember her first name, but she was known as Pani Rafalowicz. What is fresh in my memory is her face, her hair and her figure. I thought she was around thirty-five, but almost four years of war had made her look much older. She was taller than average. Her hair was pulled back and gathered with hairpins, showing grey streaks near the forehead. Her face was oval, her eyes round and big. She looked healthy but very, very sad. Her two children were clutching her dark pleated and wrinkled skirt. Their big frightened black eyes reflected the horror of their experience. The girl might have been ten years old and the boy two years younger. Both had very dark, curly hair. They took shelter behind their mother's body, with only their little clenched hands and their faces showing.

"Were you caught on the Aryan side?" she asked.

"Yes," we responded.

"Are you hungry?" she asked. Answering her own question with, "Of course you are!," she reached for a loaf of bread hidden under a pile of clothes, cut two slices and handed one to Alina and one to me. We were hungry, but, looking at the children's faces, we thanked her and told her to keep it for them. She replied at once, "If we are lucky to stay alive, we will have bread." With an empty look she added, "If not, what's the point of keeping it?"

Pani Rafalowicz told me her story. She had been hiding with her husband and their children in a village near the forest. Her husband got sick and since no doctor or hospital would help a Jew at that time, he died. She carried his body to the forest and dug a grave. By bad luck, or destiny, an SS patrol drove by just then. Because it wasn't a cemetery or an official funeral, they wondered what she was doing. She explained that she didn't have money for a burial.

Tears didn't help, nor did they have mercy on the two frightened children glued to their mother's skirt. They forced her and the children to walk to the car and took them to the ghetto jail. The short time we were together in that room, she was kind and supportive.

A man who knew her before the war told me that she had been a rich woman, known for her generosity, but she never spoke of her former wealth. We knew the jail in the ghetto was a transitional place. What we didn't know was when and where it would end. There was no safety and no hope. Soon, we heard the jail would be liquidated. Where would we be sent next?

From Płaszów to
Skarżysko-Kamienna

After three or four days in the ghetto jail, in the summer of 1943, the order came for all prisoners to line up. The squad on duty arrived, Lithuanian *SS-Totenkopfverbände*, soldiers in black uniforms with skulls on their caps. They were the most bloodthirsty unit, walking on both sides of the line with their rifles ready to shoot. We heard that we were going to Płaszów. It was quite a long march and we were a large group.

Just as we arrived at the camp's entrance checkpoint, the SS man guarding the gate heard the telephone ring. He went into his booth. We waited. He was obviously entertained by his conversation. We waited. Finally, in a state of rapt amusement, he glanced up and saw us still standing there. Wanting only to continue his conversation, he waved the group through the barrier. We will never know who was on the other end of the line entertaining that Nazi, but he or she saved almost a hundred people. On the other side of the barrier was a Jewish policewoman. As we got through, she shouted, "Run! Quick!" Within seconds, we scampered far away from the entrance, out of sight of the SS man in the checkpoint booth.

"I ordered you to run so he wouldn't have a chance to change his mind," she explained. "You are the lucky ones. Yesterday, a group of people were taken from the checkpoint directly to that hill and every one of them was shot." It's difficult for me to describe what I felt at that moment. I may have felt apathy or resignation or nothing at all. For sure, I was frightened. I was awaiting the worst.

Very soon, I experienced another humiliation. The policewoman guided us to a building with a central partition and large bathrooms on either side, with showers lining the walls. The drain was in a big circle of concrete one step down in the middle. The men were brought to the other side of the central partition. "Take off your clothes and shower!" shouted the policewoman, threatening us with her stick. One had to show one's naked body to so many people. The fact that we were all women was no consolation. Discomfort and shame was on everyone's faces. When we hesitated for a second, she shouted a few obscenities at us. I felt miserable, incredulous. She was Jewish, the same as we were! There were no Germans around – why would she behave in this hideous manner? Then I remembered my mother telling my father in Warsaw about how she and my sister had been disinfected in Pruszków, how she had put my sister's young body behind her to shield her from the eyes of the beasts, the Nazis, but, here, no Nazis were in sight. "Quick! Get your clothes off and start showering," she yelled. She was determined. We knew she would use her stick on us if we hesitated any longer. We were right. Later, we discovered that she used a whip to discipline women who didn't follow her orders. Twenty-five lashes on the naked body was her usual punishment. The water from the showers running into the drain was mixed with blood running from more than one woman, who had been caught menstruating.

A lady in her forties, with grey hair and a very pleasant smile, looked at me with resignation. I don't know what kind of expression she saw on my face. She said to me, "Wróbelku, my przezyjemy." (Little sparrow, we will survive.) I couldn't answer. I had nothing to say. I didn't know what my chances of survival were. The whole matter appeared to have been taken out of my hands. Nothing depended on personal ability any more. I stood under the shower, helpless, my arms hanging beside my body. The lady's name was Celina and her remark gave me momentary relief, but it wasn't enough to kindle the hope of survival. I met her a few years later in Germany after the war. She was working at the branch of the American Jewish Joint Distribution Committee, an organization working internationally to make it possible for survivors to emigrate from Germany to different countries. She recognized me. "Little sparrow, we did survive!" she exclaimed. "I'm happy to see you." She stood up from behind her desk and came around to embrace me.

When the policewoman thought that we had showered enough, she ordered us to get dressed. Two men with cans of white paint were waiting for us outside the door to paint our clothes. Each of us had stripes in the form of a ladder painted on the front and back. Alina and I also had an additional brand, a large yellow sphere, to signify that we were particularly dangerous because we had knowingly used forged documents. To cap our humiliation, Alina and I were sent to live in the men's barracks, in order to embarrass us for what we had done. There, we heard the details of the mass killings at the foot of the hill, Chujowa Górka. We heard that people would often be shot coming from work. The tractors would come and mix the corpses with soil. The men seemed amazed that we were still alive.

Actually, Alina and I had no troubles living with the men. The *Blockälteste*, the man in charge of distributing bread and maintaining order, was from Krakow. He was serious, honest and fair. He immediately saw to it that we were given bread and soup. We soon got acquainted with his younger brother, Henek, by having a long conversation with him. Henek was friendly, sometimes sharing a bit of marmalade or a candy he managed to get. A few months after the war, Henek's older brother came to see me while Henek was in hospital. He told me that Henek had been shot through the head during a forced march from a camp. Wounded, he had managed to endure for seven days until he found help in a hospital. Henek survived and later he married Alina. Someone else had experienced a miracle. I'm glad it was him.

My first job in Płaszów was to clean up an area of wood planks. We worked in pairs to carry the planks to another place. The girl assigned to be my partner was a thin blond who was a few years older than I. As we lifted a plank and straightened up, I felt momentarily distracted from the job. "You have one blue eye and one brown," I said, amazed. I had never seen such a thing before. She smiled. She was used to people mentioning it, always reacting the same way. After work, she introduced me to her sister. I recognized her at once – she was the girl I had seen waiting outside the Symphony Hall in downtown Krakow. She had been betrayed, too. She would never talk about it or tell who had made her suffer.

After a few months, by late fall, my dress wasn't enough to keep me warm. I hesitated for days before overcoming my shame to go to the clothing warehouse to ask for a sweater. I knew there were tables there covered with clothing and shoes of all kinds. When I finally decided to go, the reaction of the Jewish policeman in charge was brief and to the point. "What for? Who knows if you will be alive tomorrow?" He smiled maliciously. It was hard to believe anyone could be so cynical.

"But I'm cold today. I don't know what will happen tomorrow," I answered, turning to leave. I wondered if he had any idea how difficult it had been for me to have to come begging like this. He called me back and gave me a sweater. It wasn't the best, but it was better than nothing. It wasn't as if these clothes belonged to him – they had been left behind by those who perished. But this was Płaszów.

I soon learned to not even ask why the police were so low-minded, so utterly hostile. They had learned the skills from their Nazi bosses quickly. We never knew whom to hide from first. Besides, in Płaszów, at any moment one could be shot on the street by the Nazis, who came to entertain themselves, shooting for pleasure. Also, the police, themselves Jews, acted like wild animals. My anger grew even stronger against them, but what chance did I have among thousands of other people also enduring this brutality?

One late fall afternoon, we were told that everybody had to gather in a large hall, a former factory. It was empty and dimly lit. The Nazis waited until everyone was inside the hall. Then, on the orders of their superiors, the Nazis and the police grabbed the children from their mothers' arms and loaded them on trucks. The children's screams pierced my ears; they stretched their little hands out into emptiness. The police shoved the mothers away, widening the gap between them and their children. Powerless, they cried, moaned, flung their bodies against the police. Everyone was deeply touched by the awful pain and sorrow. When the mothers tried to cross the line, they were beaten.

There are no words strong enough to describe the helplessness I felt. This was a night to ask the world, Where are you? Is nobody listening? The violence, injustice and atrocity that took place in that damned hall was heartbreaking. The trucks, loaded with children, drove away immediately. All the adults had to go back to their barracks. Out of compassion, Alina and I marched in the same line as Pani Rafalowicz. Her children had been snatched away from her skirt, where they were holding on for dear life with their tiny hands and sad, scared faces. She was crying bitterly. The agony of these mothers grieving for their lost children was unbearable. The darkness of the night could cover their anguished faces, but it could not diminish the sound of their laments.

Pani Rafalowicz was crying loudly. I began to fear that she would attract attention to all of us, particularly Alina, who was quite a bit shorter than I and might have been taken for a child herself. I begged Pani Rafalowicz not to cry so loudly, explaining that she might be endangering Alina. In spite of her painfully broken heart, she asked in a faltering voice, "If we could save one life, would my children live?" It was a question no one could answer. There was a knot in her throat. In mine, too. Pani Rafalowicz's tragedy is still etched in my memory. Recalling that night brings back all the anguish, rage and fear as vividly as if it were happening right now.

~

We were given many tasks at Płaszów, such as loading stones onto wheelbarrows and unloading them in another place. One day, I was sent to the kitchen to peel potatoes. Mostly elderly women were working there. That is, not what we would call elderly today, but women in their fifties – the older ones had been shot long ago. They were afraid to go outside to fill their pails with potatoes because the Nazis had shot many there for not moving fast enough. They asked me to fetch the potatoes. "You are young," they begged me. "You can move quickly." They were right.

One day Amon Göth, the commandant of Płaszów, stopped with his company to watch me for a while, filling the pails. Then, miraculously, they walked away. I never knew what would happen next. Once, I had worked the night shift and was allowed to sleep during the day. Suddenly, I was woken from sleep by someone yelling, "Down from the bunk! Down, fast!" It was the policeman everyone feared – he was tall, fat, brutal and aggressive. He yelled insults – unrepeatable, unmentionable words. I didn't get the chance to explain that I had worked all night. He hit me with a lash three times on my back. Great red welts suddenly appeared and my skin was scarred for weeks. It hurt, naturally, but no more than the pain of my humiliation. Again, there wasn't a single German in sight; there was nothing to justify his action but his own base nature.

Once, that same policeman came into the barracks and saw a woman sitting on the edge of a table, talking to another woman. He lifted the lash and hit her so hard on the face that she lost one eye as a result. She was a poet. This policeman's mother was also a prisoner in Płaszów. She was old and sick, and was always in her bunk. She couldn't deal with all the complaints of the people who had been beaten by her son. She would answer angrily, "Leave me alone. I can't do anything." It was true, she couldn't. He wouldn't listen to her. Not even his mother could change this inhuman beast. I sometimes reflected on the fact that I had been able to avoid being beaten up by the Nazis a year ago, but not here in Płaszów. Besides the police, we had Nazis such as Göth, who entertained himself by shooting people. And this still wasn't the end of it. In mid-November, orders arrived that some of us were to be moved to another place. I was loaded, along with many others, into cattle cars. We didn't receive any food and there was no toilet inside. It was literally packed so tightly that all you could do was stand.

~

We arrived at our destination at night. Our legs were stiff from standing for such a long time. The Germans opened the cattle-car doors, shouting, "Schnell raus!" (Hurry, get out!) We had to jump down. Some couldn't and fell. We were then ordered to form columns and to march. We had arrived at the Skarżysko-Kamienna forced labour camp, where the Germans had taken over what had been a Polish munitions factory. Now, Jews had replaced most of the Polish workers under vastly different conditions.

Over the entrance was an iron signboard reading "Arbeit macht das Leben süss." (Work Makes Life Sweet.) Of course, we were slaves. The police counted us, then ordered us to enter the barracks, yelling and swearing to make us hurry up. The interior was dimly lit, with mice running all over the place. There were a lot of double-decker bunks, one table and a large round stove, a metre high, with pipes going up through the roof. Everything was in chaos, with people confusedly choosing their bunks, trying to sort out how to stay near a friend.

Suddenly, a Jewish policeman turned to me and ordered me to make a list of the people in the barracks. He was short and bad-tempered. One of the other women found me a piece of paper, another a pencil. I made the list and took it back to the police officer. I was then given a broom with instructions to sweep the barracks' floor and provide wood for the stove. Some of the women in my barracks were originally from Leipzig and had been expelled from Germany because of their Jewish-Polish roots. They said they would help with sweeping the floor and others promised to gather wood for the stove, so I never ended up doing that job.

The next morning, as the bad-tempered policeman entered the barracks, he shouted as if to remind us of who was in charge. Wanting us to fear him, he treated us to a display of what could happen if we didn't obey. A woman, tall, maybe fifty, approached him to ask for a blanket because she was cold. He kicked her viciously in the belly. As she doubled over from the pain and burst into tears, I thrust myself between them to protect her from a further blow, pleading, "Do you have a mother? Why are you doing this?" His brutality was entirely unnecessary, as far as I could see. Again, there wasn't a single German around.

The policeman looked at me and calmly said, "I'm putting you in charge of the barracks. Make sure the floor is clean. In the afternoon, you'll get soup and bread. You have to divide the bread. Sometimes, you may get marmalade – a spoonful for each of your people." He spoke quietly and reasonably, as though nothing had happened. Luckily, I had no problems distributing the bread and the marmalade. I was careful to divide the portions evenly, so nobody would complain. In spite of this, a woman who had been brought to the camp only a week before reported me. She must have said something because one day two policemen hid between the bunks to watch how I cut the bread. When I finished, they emerged from their hiding place, ordered me to follow them and gave me an extra ration of bread and a cup of marmalade to reward me for my fairness. I felt good about that.

The barracks in Skarżysko-Kamienna were large and we slept on bare wooden planks, wearing the clothes we had on. Those who were from Krakow had some blankets. I had nothing besides my life and every second I was in danger of losing even that. Some of the barracks were used as latrines: along the wall was a line of toilets and in the middle was a line of cold-water taps.

Later on, another policeman arrived to assign people to different jobs in the munitions factory. I was sent to unscrew the heads of the large-calibre bullets that had failed to fire. This was tricky because they could go off if they weren't handled carefully. However, this job was preferable to working with the explosive powders such as picric acid and trotyl. It was sad to look at those who did work there. Their skin had become discoloured and they were slowly dying. They were called *kanarki*, canaries – they looked yellow and skeletal and walked like zombies, with their eyes unfocused. I heard that the Jews who worked with these compounds often died within three months.

Two young men delivered the boxes filled with the dud bullets to the place where I operated the machine. One was a medical student who had been just about to graduate when the war started, and the other was a young lawyer. They had run out of hope and told me they didn't think they could bear it anymore. Many times, I talked to them, trying to stimulate their will to survive. "Forget your professions, who you are, what you were hoping for. But don't give up! Don't think about it. Just take it as it comes." But, little by little, they were falling apart. I was hardly the best example. I was not really following my own advice. I was angry and suffered a lot. I could put up with hunger and cold, but not injustice. I remember another young man who could stand no more. I gave him my portion of bread once. Before long, he just faded away.

Shortly after we had arrived at Skarżysko-Kamienna, Alina made friends with an older woman and our friendship cooled. It was a blow to me. She was wise and cheerful and I had enjoyed her friendship. Besides, she was the only person I knew when we arrived because I had been caught so far from my hometown. Most of the others had been together in other concentration camps or had known each other from the same city before the war. One day, a girl approached me and said that she knew me from Czerniaków, that we used to work there in the fields together. It was difficult to recognize her. It was Rosa, but her long, dark, braided hair had been shaved off and she had a blanket over her head.

She was ashamed of how she looked. By contrast, I had all my hair and was less changed because I had only been imprisoned for a few months. Rosa told me that once Czerniaków was dissolved, the group had been sent to the Warsaw ghetto. When the Germans burned the ghetto after the uprising in April and May 1943, she had been sent to Majdanek, where she worked for a few months. Later, the Nazis selected a group to be sent to Skarżysko-Kamienna. She had arrived a few months before me.

Each morning in Skarżysko-Kamienna, we were awakened by a policeman singing this song:

Wake up! Your mothers are whores!

I've been calling for half an hour!

You are still sleeping!

You are sons of bitches!

Remembering this still brings tears to my eyes. We had been oppressed and humiliated by the Nazis. Was it necessary for these Jewish policemen to add pain to our degraded existence? We formed columns and walked to work.

One day, the bread was delivered at the same time as the soup was being distributed outside the barracks. The man pouring the soup into the dishes also worked in the infirmary. I asked him to serve me first so I could get back and divide the bread before it was stolen. "Stay in line!" he yelled at me.

"If the bread is stolen, the others will kill me!" I pleaded.

He got furious with me. "You whore!" he shouted, slapping my face so hard that I couldn't speak for days. I threw my dish down, went into the barracks and divided the bread, then flung myself down on my bunk. I lay there unable even to cry. My face twisted, I felt hatred for him, for the police, for all the oppressors who imagined themselves the lords of our lives. Who could imagine that such low instincts could emerge in other human beings. Especially, I felt rage against the orderly who had hit me. I hadn't been looking for special treatment, I was only worrying about the bread. He could have poured the soup in my dish without a problem, as he had plenty of time. Everyone standing in the line agreed. A girl who had seen what happened to me picked up my dish, stood in line and asked him for my ration of soup. My mouth was so twisted from the blow that I couldn't put the spoon into it.

Some of the policemen were even worse than this man. Remembering the bad ones still brings back the anger. The same night, the orderly who had hit me came to my bunk to comfort me with a blanket. Either he had a conscience or else he figured that it would be easy for him to take advantage of my wretched state. If that blanket could have spoken, it could have told of the many different corpses it had covered, as well as their life histories. Besides, it was infested with millions of bugs. He said, "I don't want you to be angry at me. I brought a blanket to keep you warm." With that, he made a move to climb into my bunk. I jumped out, ran to the table and huddled on it. So he didn't get what he had come for. But he warned me that he would catch me the next time.

This was just another experience of the reality of life in Skarżysko-Kamienna. But this sort of thing was routine there. Even the chief of the camp police was a philanderer. He had a wife and a lover and what's more, his wife had her own lover, who was having other casual affairs, and so on. The chief used to invent ways to amuse himself by humiliating us. He would order the girls to stand naked outside the barracks at night. Some of the staff would then take them away, supposedly to protect them from further shame and would then rape them. There was no such thing as consent. These women were trapped. What made it worse was that so many of these atrocities were committed by our own people.

Once, a policeman ordered me to follow him. He guided me to a large empty room and yelled at me to lie down. I weighed probably around sixty-five to seventy pounds, just skin and bones. Even though the wooden bench was narrow, I fit on it without any trouble. He repeated angrily, "Lie down!" I lay on the bench with my dress on. I was totally stiff, my eyes closed. He looked at me for a while, then, without touching me, yelled, "Go back to your barracks!" He was angrier than ever. I had saved myself, I suppose, by playing dead, without realizing what I had been doing. It had been luck, sheer luck. He was twice my age and, of course, far stronger, as the policemen were much better fed. I had similar experiences at other times, but in all of them I was able to escape. The miracles still came, but they weren't able to save me from some degradation.

One day, I was sent with a small group to gather used bullets at a place where the Nazis practised target shooting, very near the forest. Near the range was a small mechanic's shop where two Poles worked. The younger one, about forty-five years old, would smile sarcastically at us. The older one, about fifty-five, seemed more compassionate. The older man talked to me when the policemen or the SS weren't around.

After a few days, the older man started bringing me sandwiches from home, cigarettes or a few złoty. He told me he had a daughter my age and was sad about what was happening to us. The partisans hid in the forest not far from his house, he said, and his wife often helped them when they were desperately hungry. Every day, the older man tried to convince me to keep looking for a chance to break away from the group. He told me how to find his house. "If any of the neighbours spot you, I'll get you to the partisans in the woods," he said. Another time, he told me, "I know when the war ends you'll fly away like a bird that has been uncaged. But I want to save your life. My wife and my daughter know about this plan. I have my daughter's clothes here to give you when the time is right." He also made me a beautiful aluminum soup dish with a handle. The soup given out there was better than the soup from camp. Sometimes, I got many chunks of meat. But one day the policeman who took us to and from work saw me talking to the older man. On the way back, he grabbed my cigarettes and money and walked very close to me. I couldn't even think of escaping.

The SS man in charge of Werk C, where we worked, surprised us one day by searching everyone's pockets as we walked back into the camp after work. We called him V-2, like the rockets. He had one arm and one good leg. He needed help to get onto his bicycle, but, once he was on it, he could ride very well. He was standing at the gate, sticking his hand into everyone's pockets. I happened to be carrying a piece of butter that the Polish man had given me. He put his hand into one pocket only and then waved me through. I was lucky again. If he had checked the other pocket, I might have been hanged, like the man found carrying a small piece of leather he had taken to fix his shoes.

Everyone had had to gather in a big circle and watch that hanging. The SS officer did it only because he wanted to. It wasn't an order. In spite of this cruel spectacle, I heard people saying of the hanged man, "He's better off than we are." It was true: no more humiliation, no more distress. My own miserable life, saved repeatedly by a series of miracles, didn't seem worth living.

The next day, I told the Polish man that I was afraid to accept anything further from him. But he still brought me hairpins and wooden clogs with leather straps for shoes. He did what he could to help me and I remember him with affection. Soon after, I was sent back to the munitions factory.

When winter arrived, my shoes were worn out – only the upper part still held together, the soles had worn long ago. The soles of my feet touched the ice and snow on the ground with every step. I had asked for shoes at the warehouse but had been refused. I waited for a day when I felt courageous enough to show my defiance. The other girls begged me not to do it, but I had decided that one day I would. So one morning, when we were marshalled for work, the head count was one short. One of the policemen came into the barracks, where I was sitting on my bunk. "Come out or they will kill you," he yelled.

"I've had enough," I said, staying put. "I'm not going anywhere until I get shoes."

They went off to the factory without me. An hour later, a German foreman came in, asking me why I refused to get to work. Without a word, I showed him my broken shoes. He smiled, "Come with me. You will get shoes." I walked with him to the factory. I was half his size and one-third his weight. As we passed by the office window, he stopped to ask for a piece of paper. Then he wrote out an order that I be given shoes. As I entered the machine hall, the girls couldn't believe their eyes. After work, I went to the warehouse and got a pair of clogs.

At the end of winter, I caught typhoid fever. My arms and legs were heavy and my head was spinning. Supporting myself by leaning on the walls, slowly, dizzily, I went to the infirmary barracks, even though it was well known that no one left the infirmary alive. I asked the orderly, the same man who had slapped my face, to put me on the sick list because I couldn't walk. He had his revenge; he refused, saying that they would drag me out of the barracks and send me to work. My eyes were blurred as I returned to the barracks. With great difficulty, step by painful step, I managed to get back. Everyone else had gone to work and I lay down on my bunk. I couldn't even lift my head. I became delirious.

When Rosa came to see me, I asked her to curtain off my bunk with a blanket. I didn't want to see anyone but just lay there, repeating, "Everyone is false. They betrayed me." I suppose that the fever had just released all the pain of past betrayal and hatred and my deepest feelings came out for everyone to hear. She did what I asked. Later, someone suggested that I might suffocate, so she took it off.

I don't remember if it was Rosa or someone else who brought another orderly. He applied glass cups to my back and gave me a single aspirin – hardly effective treatment for typhoid fever! After a few days, though, I passed the crisis. I began to talk properly. I still couldn't walk, but I could sit. Because of the fever, I hadn't eaten for a few days and I was hungry. I was weak the first day back to work, but they wouldn't allow me to stay away any longer.

On my first day back, the section foreman, a grey-haired Pole of about fifty, called me to his office. He closed the door and proceeded to press his body against mine, leaning against the wall. As a reward for putting up with his shameful behaviour, he offered me a big onion. When I angrily refused, he said I needed to eat because I had just recovered from typhoid fever, as if he was being decent! Afterward, I went out, carrying the onion. I had nowhere to hide it and I presumed that many of the other girls had experienced the same humiliation. But no one talked about it. I never talked to anybody about it, not even to my closest friends. I can still feel the awful shame now, as I remember the experience.

Another time, a Polish foreman gathered everyone together in a large room. He pointed to a man whom he knew to be a cantor in the synagogue and told him to sing. He sang the *Shema* prayer. It didn't matter that not everyone could understand the words. Tears ran down our faces. Fright and terror brought, finally, only apathy and resentment, which didn't help our efforts to keep up hope.

One day around noon, toward the end of summer 1944, we were suddenly called together in a big circle. The SS had arrived to put an end to the Skarżysko-Kamienna camp. The first thing they did was to separate the old and sick from the rest of us. They were later shot. A female doctor who had been hiding her elderly mother with her all this time, from the moment they had been dragged out of their Krakow home, refused to let go of her mother. She held her mother so tightly that not even the police or the SS could separate them. They were shot there together, still holding on to each other as they fell to the ground. I was standing near a girl named Matilde who had been close to them and I caught her in my arms as she fainted. We got to be friends after this incident. She survived and I met her after the war. By then, she was married and had two children. Each time I saw her, I still remembered that scene and so many other horror stories from Plaszów and Skarżysko-Kamienna, which often haunt me. And this wasn't the end of it.

That night, the Nazis finished their sinister job. We heard shooting and screaming. In the morning, we heard that some of the Jewish policemen had tried to escape to the woods. They had been shot there. The Nazis had no further use for them. The next morning, the first of August, the Germans ordered us to line up. The men were being sent to various camps, the women to the HASAG-Leipzig forced labour camp. As before, we were packed into cattle cars, with no room to move for days.

So Close Yet So Far

We arrived in Leipzig's Schönefeld station three days later, exhausted, hungry, more dead than alive. Despite the Germans' well-organized methods of carrying out orders on time, they weren't ready for us. We had to stand still for many hours outside a building. This sort of exhausting forced assembly was called an *Appell* and was the first of many to come.

Leipzig was a forced labour camp, its mostly female population made up of Poles, Jews, Dutch, French and Gypsies, among others. There were also some Soviet women soldiers who had been captured after parachute landings. They didn't socialize with the rest of us. They were honourable prisoners of war, citizens of a country that was fighting the Nazis. We, on the other hand, were prisoners of evil, with no country to defend our rights, our dignity. On our first day in Leipzig, the SS women guards showed their power over us by refusing to allow us to use the lavatory facilities inside the building or to let us sit on the ground. They knew only too well how to hurt us, how to degrade us.

After a few hours, we were ordered to walk into a large room, undress and put our clothes aside. There went my dress and over-dress, first tacked, later sewn, then painted with white ladders and a yellow circle that looked like a sun, a paradox. Naked, we had to show ourselves at a large window, where the *Obersturmführer* scrutinized our bodies through the glass. Then, we had to shower and get our striped dresses. Later, we were checked for pregnancy and disease. After this process, some of the women were sent to another camp in Ravensbrück, for women only.

In Leipzig, the rooms were ample, with bare wooden floorboards and double-decker bunk beds. Everything was clean. Even the blankets were new and clean. We were in German territory. Apart from the dirty minds of the SS women, everything was spotless. The showers were open twenty-four hours a day with hot water – quite a change from Plaszów or Skarżysko-Kamienna. The next day, we were registered and given numbers. We had to sign declarations that we had been arrested as prostitutes to justify our detention.

The next morning, Wehrmacht soldiers took us to an ammunition factory where foremen were waiting for us. They assigned us to different machines, explaining how they worked. The machine I was put on was the only one of its kind: it corrected the heads of bullets that had come out faulty from the production machine and my job was to make them to measure. I also had to adjust the machine when something got loose. I asked for tools in the workshop. I worked independently and best of all, I wasn't given a production quota because of the high-precision nature of the work. Officially, I didn't even report to a foreman.

The machine was in a relatively quiet part of the large hall. The German production foreman, an engineer, often crossed the hall to chat with me. He would pretend to inspect the pieces or help me fix the machine, but most of the time he talked about what had happened to him and his family during the war. He was bitter. His wife and two sons were in the military and he had no idea if they were still alive. Another time, he told me that he had been shot in the leg and been unconscious for days. The doctors in the hospital had done their best for him, but he still limped, which made him angry and tired of the war. From the hospital, they had sent him to work as a foreman. Once, I told him that he still had hope but I had none. He limped away without an answer. I could talk to this man without fear, which was unusual. Sometimes he told jokes and other times he would play practical jokes like putting steel shavings into my shoes and then watching my reaction as I put them on. On another occasion, when I complained that my throat was sore, he took me to the doctor's office at the factory. The doctor said that it was mere irritation caused by the dust from the machines and therefore not serious.

Many times, I asked him to go easy on the women who couldn't make the daily quota because we stood at *Appell* for long hours outside the building. He pretended not to notice, accepting the smaller production. After one particularly long *Appell*, we found out that the Soviet parachutists had disappeared without a trace. We never found out what happened to them. The rumours were that someone helped them to escape. There was another foreman who was also angry about the war. He told a girl who worked on the other side of the hall that his father was in jail for being a Communist. He would sometimes bring us news about the war.

A Polish girl who worked in the factory had gone to Germany to volunteer to work in a German home but the German family had let her go because they planned to escape, fearing the consequences of their actions during the war. She had actually come to the factory looking for a job. Her husband worked elsewhere in a metals factory. She sold aluminum combs that her husband made in the factory for two rations of bread. I ordered one from her, but someone stole the bread from my bunk. No bread, no comb. Things like this happened every day. We showered a lot in the nice, hot water to make up for everything else we had to do without.

The factory work wasn't too bad. We had no problems with the *Obersturmführer* in charge. However, in the camp, the SS women treated us dreadfully. They beat us and yelled at us, spreading terror. They were beautiful women, mostly German, some Dutch, but so mean and insensitive. Many times, they threw us out of the building for no reason and kept us out there for hours.

At one time, there was a problem with a lesbian SS woman who molested some of the girls. At night, she would come and choose one, taking her away somewhere. When the *Obersturmführer* found out, he sent her away and we never saw her again. There was an air-raid alarm one night when Allied bombers were near our area. We had to go to an underground bunker, where we saw coffins, one with a body inside it.

To pass the time when we weren't working, we altered our striped dresses, shortening them or adding belts made out of spare pieces of material or string. Some women made collars out of a piece of white cleaning rag. This outraged the SS women. They yelled at us and sent us outside for yet another *Appell*. We stood there until the *Obersturmführer* came to find out why we were being punished. He let us go back in. He even seemed to be smiling as we returned to the building. I remember two SS women most clearly. One was Dutch, tall and blond, with a vicious temper, always whacking someone on top of the head. The other, a German, was shorter, dark-haired. We called her "the Doll" because of her delicate looks. She was basically shy, but, as soon as she was on duty, she would start yelling and slapping. Too short to hit people on the head, as her colleague did, she slapped faces. On Christmas Day 1944, one of the Jewish women approached the Dutch SS woman, greeting her with, "Frohe Weihnachten!" (Merry Christmas!) The Dutch SS woman got red in the face and shot back, "You don't have to say that to me." I just stood there, listening to the exchange.

After work, we had our own cultural life, which was tolerated by the *Obersturmführer*. Once, a group of women put together a show, complete with costumes and even a stage with decorations. It looked like a real theatre. They danced and sang – some had been real artists before the war. Others represented their countries with folk songs. This took place at night, so the SS women weren't there and the *Obersturmführer* permitted it. He came in after the show started and stood beside me for a few minutes, watching, smiling. Then he left.

I got to know a girl in my barracks who was a sculptor. She was convinced that if I dyed my hair I would look much better. Fantasies, stupid talk, but harmless. Once in a while, we had to show that we were still capable of thinking. She asked me to pose for a plaster bust she was making for a German woman who worked in the office. There was also an opera singer who would quietly sing beautiful arias to us at night when we were in our bunks. Her younger sister was miraculously spared from the selection in the camp that had sent all the children to their deaths.

The French political prisoners had a day on which they wore sophisticated hats, creating a kind of fashion parade to demonstrate the arts and customs of France by walking through the rooms and displaying their finery. They put so much work and imagination into it, and it was interesting to watch them. We didn't understand the meaning of their traditions, but they explained it to us enthusiastically. I became acquainted with one of the French women. We would chat for a while in one language, then a few words in another.

A girl who was an English teacher before the war kept nagging me to learn English, but I wasn't interested. She didn't give up. She kept repeating, "You are intelligent. Let me teach you. Repeat after me."

"What for?" I answered, "I'm not going to survive." It seemed absurd to learn anything, knowing that our future was not in our own hands. I preferred listening to the Bible stories one of the religious girls told. Once, she told me that we would pass by trees with fruit on them, but we wouldn't be allowed to pick any fruit. It happened just as she said. We passed by apple trees growing in the streets, but we were told that picking up even one apple would mean death.

One day at the factory, I saw that someone had written "Quo vadis?" (Whither goest thou?) on one of the ammunition boxes we had packed ready for dispatch to the front. Ironically, none of the boxes we packed at that factory ever went anywhere. It was too late, luckily. The war ended first. Among the soldiers who escorted us to the munitions factory were Germans who served in the Wehrmacht, together with Polish *Volksdeutsche* in Wehrmacht uniforms. It was cold and dark on our way back from work. Right next to me was a young German soldier, part of our escort. To avoid looking at him, I lowered my head. He started talking to me. "Head up," he said. "The war is nearly over. Endure, don't be sad. Soon, you will be free." This was in mid-February 1945, two months before we were ordered to evacuate the camp in Leipzig.

⌒

It took a long time to find out what awaited me at the end of the road. All sorts of incidents piled up along the way. The journey was arduous. Before the war, I suppose my story might have been about youth and romance. During the war, there was no room for romance. I was still young, but years of suffering, including the loss of my family, had killed my love of life. Love? My heart had stopped feeling long before. Convenience? My brain had stopped thinking. It was utterly blank. On the other hand, the demands of endurance led to bonds of comradeship, sometimes out of sheer necessity, without any of the usual ingredients of fantasy or reciprocity. Endurance was all that counted. Love, if it ever came at all, was a surprise.

One morning in mid-April, the evacuation order was announced. We were allowed to take a blanket and were given a loaf of bread and two cups of uncooked rice each. Rumour had it that Soviet troops were approaching Halle, a city not far from Leipzig. The SS officers were visibly upset. It was obviously a surprise to them. Although they were at home, in German territory, they were frightened. During the war, they had come to believe they were invincible. Now, they faced having to atone for all the atrocities they had committed. As for us, we really couldn't believe it. We had had too many years of suffering to expect that we might ever be liberated. No one imagined that the war would ever end. We had no idea what was going on. Where were my miracles? Would they come at the right time? Who believed in them anymore?

We were ordered to line up outside the building, ready to march. As we did, we saw a group of men from another camp coming up to walk behind our column. The SS men and women were nervous wrecks. They knew that the Soviets would take revenge for all the atrocities they had committed on the civilian population in the Soviet Union. They would now have to pay for all the burned villages, the terrorizing of women and children, the indiscriminate slaughter of all that had stood in their way. That was why they were in such haste to escape, taking us along so no trace would be left behind. As fast as they could, they were heading toward the American military positions because they couldn't expect mercy from the Soviets.

The first day of our march, we covered forty kilometres, not knowing where they were taking us. The Germans screamed at us to march faster. The bread didn't last long. By the second day, people were hungry. Some stepped out of line to grab a handful of grass to eat, and were shot instantly. The marchers grew weaker and weaker, falling, exhausted, to the ground. They were left behind to die. Every day, corpses were left by the side of the road, lying right under the eyes of the German civilians who lived there. Whenever the SS men walked into private homes to eat and rest, we had to stop where we stood, always under the surveillance of the soldiers.

After a few days, we were near a village when a torrential rain began. The soldiers took us to a square surrounded by a thick privet hedge, so that no one in the village would see what was going on. While we stood there in the rain, the highest-ranking SS officers sought shelter in the houses around the square. The young soldiers were left to guard us, but they too crossed the street and went under the roof of a house there. We were soaked, tired, hungry and barely able to stand on our feet.

When we had lined up in the courtyard in Leipzig, each of us tried to stay close to someone we knew. I formed a group with Rosa from Czerniaków, Lodka and her friend Dora from Skarżysko-Kamienna, and Rachel from Leipzig. Rachel had come out of the building late and joined us because we were four and the order was for five in a line. We stuck together during the march, caring for each other emotionally and physically.

In the square, exhausted, we spread one blanket on the grass and covered our bodies with the rest of the blankets. The rain kept falling all night. The overall group seemed much smaller than the line of marchers that had left Leipzig. Apparently, the SS officers had had differing opinions on where and when to rest, and the group had been split up. We didn't know where the others had been taken. Suddenly, in the middle of the night, we heard shouting and someone crying, "It's my blanket, you thief. Give it back to me!" Someone was stealing blankets. We clutched ours firmly to make sure no one got them. What else did we have? We had been robbed of everything, including the right to live with dignity.

The next afternoon the rain stopped and the sun came out strongly from behind the clouds. We were wet and our sodden blankets were heavy. As we stretched our legs, we saw movement among the other groups. People approached one another to find out who had made it, who had died. While the women gathered, talking to each other, the daughter of one woman, out of curiosity, leaned on the hedge, showing her head out to the street. A young Nazi soldier shot her in the head on the spot, from a distance of only half a metre. I saw this and I will never forget it. It was only a few weeks before the end of the war. The mother's lamentations were heartbreaking. Her daughter had been so young, like the murderer who shot her. They had survived all the camps together and now, almost at the end of the war, this tragic end. He didn't get an order. He had acted impulsively. He could have shouted at her. But he had the power to shoot and he did.

My friends dispersed, advising me to keep an eye on the blankets. Soon, Lodka found an old rusty can and a piece of wire. The other girls gathered small twigs to make a fire to cook the rice. Suddenly, a Gypsy girl came running and grabbed the can. Lodka was a tall, strong girl and she fought her until she fell, holding the can behind her. When the girl tried to yank the can away, the rusty wire cut Lodka's skin behind her knee. She didn't feel anything at the time, but a few days later the cut was infected.

The march resumed. We walked more slowly and there were fewer casualties. The Germans' shiny boots got muddy and their uniforms dusty. Their mood had changed. Each day, some of them disappeared. It was evident that they had had enough. One morning, we awoke to find that we were on our own. All the SS men and SS women were gone. They had deserted the army and us. We continued walking in the same direction along the road until we approached a village and spotted a group of Germans with rifles, men who had served in the civil militia. They immediately began to shout at us and try to drive us off, afraid that we might break into their houses. One put his rifle at my back as we were running. We ran away as fast as we could. The Germans ran after us until we left their district. Then, they stopped following us. We gathered together and continued walking, always in the same direction. Finally, near the end of April, we got to the Elbe River.

Destiny Works Its Way

It was dark when we arrived at the river. A battle was in progress between the Germans and the Soviets and projectiles from a Katyusha, a new Soviet invention, flew over our heads. We heard them explode somewhere ahead of us. We bent down, keeping low. Someone pointed to a house in ruins from a previous bombardment, saying that it could shelter us. We stood in the remains of the basement all night, glued to the walls, terrified, listening to the exchange of fire.

In the morning, we heard someone talking. It was a Soviet patrol and they must have heard our voices. They looked through the small basement windows, which were miraculously in one piece. "Out!" they called loudly in Russian. When we were out of the basement, a woman explained to the soldiers who we were and how we had gotten there. They told us to follow them and guided us to barracks not far away that were occupied by Italian troops. The Italians had been held there since the entire group had thrown down their weapons and refused to fight alongside the Germans against the Allied forces. The Germans had abandoned the Italians for the same reason they had abandoned us. The Soviet soldiers put us in a few empty rooms. Every room had two bunks, a sink and a washroom with running water. It had been a long time since we had had a roof over our heads. Unfortunately, we still had no food and it had been weeks since we had swallowed the last grain of our rice. We were hungry, but it looked as though we were, at least, safe for a while.

Outside the barracks, we saw a high-ranking German officer dressed in women's clothes, riding a carriage. The Soviets had caught him. I don't know the end of this peculiar story, but later, we saw another SS officer running through the fields in women's clothes. He was caught as well.

German civilians were also in a hurry to leave the territories occupied by the Soviets. They embarked on boats to cross the Elbe River to the other side where Americans occupied the territory. This had been the plan of our SS escorts on the march, but it was too late for them to make it and they decided to flee before they could be caught. As many people as possible squeezed onto the boats, leaving their luggage on the riverbank. Much later, we understood why the Germans trusted the Americans. They knew that the Americans would not shoot them on sight.

The Soviets saw this but let them go. "Nichivo," (It doesn't matter), they said. "We will get them later." The girls rifled through the abandoned luggage for clothes. They didn't let me go with them because I wasn't a good scrounger, but they thought of me. I was given pajama pants, a blouse, a short synthetic fur coat, a scarf and a large white handkerchief. When the booty was divided, we began thinking about our next move. We were still in Germany and everyone agreed that we couldn't stay there forever. We had to go back home to Poland, where we hoped to find family alive. Ironically, after all we had seen and gone through, sometimes we were still hopeful. A strong desire can fuel the imagination. Miracles did exist. Otherwise, how could we still be alive? Maybe, maybe our families were among the lucky ones who survived. The separations from our families were different for all of us.

I wasn't sure about my sister. Maybe she was still alive somewhere. But my parents? I knew it. Besides, I had a feeling, a deep, sad sense that I was utterly alone. My companions and I hadn't known each other before the war. We didn't really know each other that well and this troubled me; I felt I had lost my identity.

The girls decided that we had to get rid of our old clothes from the camp. Rosa said, "If the Germans see us in these striped dresses, they will kill us. We must throw them away." I wasn't too happy with the idea of taking off my dress and throwing it away. I had had it since we arrived in Leipzig, when the *Obersturmführer* had selected who would stay and who would be sent to some other much worse place. The dress had a history. It had been too long and a girl who knew how to sew had shortened it for me. From the spare piece of material, she had even made a pocket, sewn on the left of the bodice. I had braided the belt from strings. Among the rags the foremen had given us to polish the machinery, I had found a red piece of material, which I used as a handkerchief, sticking it jauntily out of the pocket. I had gone without bread to pay for all this and to pay the girls to launder my dress for me. They dried them on the heating pipes. My dress was always clean. Not everybody could stand hunger, but because I had been a picky eater at home, I didn't mind as much.

The truth was that after so many weeks without showering, we were dirty. Millions of bugs had collected in the seams of my dress. There were so many bugs that the dress could have walked away on its own, that was how strong the army of bugs was. Yet, I still wouldn't give in, arguing, "I earned it. It's mine. Besides, the Soviets are here now." The girls wouldn't listen. They tried to convince me that it didn't matter that the Soviets were here. "We are in danger with the striped dresses," Rosa kept saying. I had to go along with them in the end.

Getting rid of the dresses was the first group decision. The second was that if anyone asked us who we were, we would say we were Polish; we would not admit that we were Jewish to anyone, anytime, anywhere. I opposed this decision – it seemed crazy to have to hide that I was a Jew when I had decided to confess my identity in a much worse situation. I don't know why, but suddenly, I felt proud to be a Jew. Finally, though, we all agreed. The improvised meeting came to an end. I put on the pajama pants and went to wash my face. I was the only one with such a silly idea. I can't forget how the girls laughed at me. My face was dirtier than before.

I had just put one leg into the bed when we heard loud voices outside the room. We got up to look outside. Like a stampede, everyone was running out of all the barracks. In seconds, we had joined them. Rosa had the bright idea that we should all wear white kerchiefs on our heads, so we wouldn't lose each other in the dark. In the commotion, we heard that Germans were hiding in the forest nearby. They were shooting at the Soviets, the Soviets retaliated, and a battle began. Once more, bullets were flying over our heads. We ran so fast, we didn't realize we were passing an entire battalion of prisoners of war being marched away by the Soviets. "Nazad!" (Back!) shouted a Soviet soldier. "Those are prisoners of war! You can't walk ahead of them!" We stopped and waited until they had passed. As we turned around to see where we were, we saw that we stood between two groups. On one side were people from the concentration camps, on the other side, the Italians. We were impressed with the Italian general. He held a map in his hand, explaining to his people the route they would take. While we were listening to the general, still undecided where to go, a few tanks slowed down. One of the drivers opened the hatch, calling loudly, "Amchu? Amchu?" (One of us?) None of us knew what he was saying. He repeated it a few times. We didn't answer. He persisted, "Skąd jesteś?" (Where are you from?)

"Z Polska. Polski." (From Poland. Polish.)

"Are any of you from Drohobych or Lwów?"

"We are from Warsaw."

He wore a strange hat with earphones. We had never seen such a thing before. Whatever he was offering didn't seem as immediately useful as the Italian general's knowledge. We didn't understand a word of what he was saying, but he was a general and he had a map. That seemed important. Rosa said that he would know how to get to Poland. Rosa turned to me, "Ask them if they're going to Poland." I spoke no Italian and limited German, but I somehow managed to convey the question to an officer who was standing near me, who in turn asked his general. With the help of Polish, German and some

hand gestures that the Italians understood perfectly, we were welcomed to join them. We would walk together for some time until we
reached a point where the road forked. There, they would turn off
and we would continue on the road to Poland. It took only a few moments for my little group of comrades to decide to follow the Italians.
We didn't always agree so quickly. Sometimes, we got along and were
reasonably close. There were times, though, when there seemed to be
no cooperation, not even friendliness.

As we left, I realized that out of the whole group only four of us
had decided to follow the Italians. Lodka's friend Dora deserted her,
joining the other group. I discovered years later that shortly after we
had left with the Italians, Soviet trucks arrived and picked up all those
who wanted to go to Poland. Some actually arrived back in Poland a
week before the war ended. Such are the strange workings of destiny.
Luck was not on our side that time. Or, maybe it was. Some went to
their homes in Poland, only to be killed there by antisemitic Poles.

Soon, we realized that we were the only four girls amid a few
hundred Italian male troops. There were officers and soldiers of all
ranks, as well as high-ranking naval officers. Lodka was limping
badly and she could hardly walk. She was also in pain, with a high
fever. I asked if there was a doctor among the Italians and one of the
officers pointed him out to me. I asked the doctor if he could give me
a few aspirins for my friend and he gave me two tablets. Lodka slept
a little better that night. In the morning, we looked around in the
abandoned houses, hoping to find some kind of cart for her to ride
in. I finally found one that was too small for Lodka but it was in good
condition and better than nothing. She couldn't walk. I approached
the doctor several times, asking for aspirins. Finally, he came to look
at the infection. He knew that Lodka was in danger, but there was
nothing he could do.

We weren't as skilful as the Italians when it came to looking for
food. Some of them had found bicycles and used them to ride around
the surrounding countryside, going into villages. They were good

people, sharing whatever food they found, especially the officer I had first spoken to. We took turns pulling Lodka in the little cart. It wasn't too bad, but we were always a little behind the others, always the last to arrive at a break spot.

On both sides of the road, there were German casualties. We saw the corpses of German soldiers who had probably once thought themselves invincible. The Soviet attack had apparently taken the Germans completely by surprise. Some still held playing cards in their hands; some were lying in groups; some had been asleep and looked peacefully at rest. We had seen many corpses since the beginning of the war. It was a common sight. Passing them, we remembered our own tragedies – civilians, the elderly, women and children killed without provocation, without mercy. We walked on in silence. The strong feeling for our families persisted. The trees were cut in half by the tanks. Destruction and death were everywhere.

The Soviets didn't stop the Italians, although they wore uniforms, perhaps because they had eventually refused to fight alongside the Germans. Still, the Italians didn't dare ask the Soviets for anything. As we moved away from the forest area, we approached houses. In the distance, we saw a Soviet soldier telling his comrade something. As we came near them, they asked if we were hungry. The Italians had been as generous as they could have been, but we were still hungry. One of the soldiers invited us into a house in a friendly way. As I entered, I glanced into the far end of the room behind the table. There was a pile of dead Germans lying near the wall. I felt sick to my stomach. The soldiers offered me food, cutting a piece of bread and salami. I backed off. "I can't," I said, refusing to accept their hospitality.

"Don't be frightened," a soldier said. "They're dead. They won't torture you any more. You have to live. Don't forget what they did to you and your families." He was right, but I still couldn't eat there. I walked out without saying a word. One called me back, offering me a whole loaf of bread and a chunk of salami.

After a few days, the houses along the road were completely empty. The Italians rode their bicycles further into the villages to look for food. Sometimes, they couldn't find any. Their doctor, who spoke a bit of German, invited me for a coffee, which was prepared and served by a soldier. I had coffee and smoked cigarettes while we talked for a few hours and he asked about the concentration camps, about my family. He told me about himself and their decision to throw down their weapons. I smoked two packages of cigarettes and drank a lot of coffee, but he wouldn't give away one more aspirin for Lodka. He had reason to refuse – he was responsible for all the soldiers and still had a long way to go. However, he suggested I watch for a Red Cross post where I could ask for help. I had seen improvised Red Cross posts along the road before, but it hadn't occurred to me to seek help there.

At the next Red Cross post, I got some pills from a Soviet doctor. At the second post, the doctor had more compassion, or more time, although he too was very busy. He cleaned Lodka's wound and gave her a pill, then he took me aside and explained that Lodka had gangrene, that it was dangerous and that she needed immediate surgery to stop the infection from spreading. The hospital was still far away. Lodka wasn't a friend of mine, really. She had lived in the same barracks in Skarżysko-Kamienna where I was in charge of distributing bread and maintaining order. She slept on a bunk not far from mine. When I was recuperating from typhoid fever and was hungry, Lodka had sold her boots to buy me bread. Our relationship was something more than the word friendship can describe.

Meanwhile, discord broke out among us. Rosa and Rachel refused to walk with Lodka and me but walked ahead, not even together. Rachel was nicknamed "Moody," and bad moods were not unusual for her. But now, both were cross with me because of an argument over a jar of cream Rosa had found in an abandoned house. I told her not to drink it because the cream was fat and our stomachs were still delicate because we hadn't eaten for a long time. She didn't listen and drank half the jar. Just as Rachel was about to drink the rest of it, I grabbed the jar from her and threw it away. I realized that it wasn't polite, but what if she got sick? Now, they weren't speaking to me. I was too proud to apologize. To make matters worse, I had to pull Lodka in the cart by myself. Indeed, Rosa got sick with diarrhea. The problem was hers; no one could help her.

The Italian officer who most often shared his food with us came to talk to me. Using the complicated hand gestures we needed to communicate, along with a few words, he told me he had talked to the general about me and the general had agreed to protect me all the way to Italy. Once there, he would intervene with the civilian authorities to grant me a permit to stay in Italy. He urged me to think about it. It was a good idea to consider. It would be an opportunity to cut my ties with Poland, all the suffering I had experienced there because of being Jewish. My parents weren't alive anymore and I had no idea what had happened to my sister. I planned to look for her once I got established somewhere, but I knew that, with the experience I had had in living among Christians, I could again pass as one, if need be. I also wanted badly to belong to somebody. I needed someone to take care of me. I guess I was tired of loneliness, of struggling to defend myself, of my occasional failures when my strength gave way. But then, on reconsideration, the whole idea seemed foolish, my dreams illogical and my thoughts silly. Finally, I convinced myself that there was still time to think about it.

We walked more slowly. I had difficulty pulling the cart fast enough and couldn't keep up. Nevertheless, we always found a room waiting for us to sleep in. If it was on the second floor, someone helped me with Lodka and the cart. It didn't matter if we had covered twenty kilometres or only fifteen, the Italians always stopped for the night. Rosa and Rachel were still angry with me, but they slept in the same room as Lodka and me and they shared whatever food the officer gave us.

A few days later, the officer appeared with another officer, who was an artist. The artist held a pad in his hand, ready to draw my portrait. I refused, despite his pleas. I don't know why I refused and I still don't know now. Even the girls were astonished.

The general approached me to explain that, after the next stop, we would have to go our separate ways. That afternoon, we arrived in a small city. The houses were completely empty. There was no food, nothing to eat. In the morning, the Italian officer told me that he had seen a bakery a few blocks away, where the Soviets were baking bread for their troops. He couldn't ask the Soviets for bread because Italy had belonged to the Axis together with Germany and Japan. He wouldn't know how to explain that all of them had eventually refused to continue to fight the Soviet and the Allied forces. At this time, everyone was suspicious. I put on my synthetic fur coat and scarf and went to the bakery. Rosa and Rachel reluctantly promised to look after Lodka.

The man who was responsible for the bakery told me that he had to account to his superior officer for every loaf of bread. War or no war, the Soviets had their rules. But he was concerned that we were hungry. He suggested that I make a list of at least fifty people, constituting an official request for humanitarian assistance to help stranded people. It sounded fair. I returned to the place where the girls were awaiting me anxiously. Searching around, we found a piece of brown paper and a stub of a pencil. We racked our brains to invent fifty names. In no time, I was back in the bakery with the list and was given fifteen loaves of bread. I took two for us and gave the rest to the Italians. I felt good. They deserved it. They had helped us and fed us through the whole march.

Finally, we had to say goodbye to the Italians. I thanked the general and the doctor. The officer who had offered me the opportunity to go to Italy with him came back a few times on his bicycle to hug and kiss me. I was tempted by his offer, but how could I leave Lodka? I hadn't forgotten how concerned the Red Cross doctor had been about her condition. Somehow, somewhere, things would work out, I thought.

It was a warm, sunny day. We slowly advanced a few kilometres through a small city. On the walls were slogans printed to commemorate May 1, Labour Day. It was our first notion of dates in a long time.

We had lived for so long without a calendar, without clocks, forgotten by the world. Suddenly, memories came to me of how my mother hadn't let us go to school on Labour Day because of the frequent clashes between the workers and the police. Here, by contrast, I saw slogans displayed openly and wreaths bedecking the pictures of the founders of the Communist Party. This had been entirely prohibited in Poland.

It seemed that the celebration must have taken place only a few days before we got there. The flowers were still fresh. But now, the streets and the road were empty. Few vehicles were passing. We walked alone, frightened. We looked into some of the houses. The Germans must have abandoned the place in a hurry. The kitchens were still warm and the food was still on the table. I thought they could be hiding somewhere in the house and I was afraid to touch the food. It could have been poisoned, I thought. Sleeping in the abandoned houses might also be a trap. It wasn't safe to walk alone either. At any moment, the Germans could surprise us and take their revenge. The war on their territory had been disastrous for them and in the end they had suffered too. In the present confusion, we could easily be mistaken for other people and pay for it with our lives. The only people who would certainly never get revenge were the Jews whose families had been slaughtered and who had lost everything. The surviving Jews were weakened from everything they had gone through, afraid and widely dispersed.

Lodka was suffering from a high fever. Her blue eyes were half-closed and glazed. Night was coming and we had to find shelter. We hesitated to enter a house but finally decided that it would be even more dangerous to walk at night. We chose to enter a house where a lot of people had taken shelter. A few men wore uniforms and others were in civilian clothes. We didn't sleep, we just sat on the floor, resting in the entrance hall.

Later that night, we heard shooting, like a fireworks' explosion. In the streets, Red Army soldiers were shouting, "Mir! Mir!" (Peace!

Peace!) A man in a uniform murmured, "It's the end of the war." He didn't seem happy with the Soviet victory. Later, we understood that he was part of the Ukrainian force that had fought with the Germans against the Soviets. I didn't translate to the girls the word we had awaited for so long. Besides, one smile on our faces could have meant the end of us.

In the morning, we resumed our journey. The official ending of the war meant little to us. We still didn't know what to expect. We weren't free, because we didn't even know what would happen during the next hour. We missed the excitement and celebration of the end of the war, just as we had missed ceremonies of mourning the deaths of our families.

By the afternoon, we saw a large group of Ukrainians marching in front of us. We had almost passed them, when Soviet soldiers suddenly surrounded us, herding us, along with the others, into a manor-house property, shouting constantly. There were so many people pushing their way into a barn – a few hundred men and we four girls. We found ourselves standing near the only door, barred from the outside to prevent us from escaping. After a while, we got tired and lay down. It was so crowded that I was afraid to close my eyes. I talked late into the night to the man lying next to me, communicating in a mixture of Polish and Russian. Meanwhile, I also had to watch Lodka. I was angry at myself for lacking the courage to try to explain to the Soviets that we didn't belong with the others here.

Early in the morning, the barn door was opened wide. Then we heard shouting again. We were ordered to form a circle in the large farmyard. Two Soviet commanders stood in the middle of the circle, shouting at the men. One by one, they had to approach a table where an officer was sitting. On the table was paper and a pen, ready to record their names, birthplaces and the unit they had served. We stood, waiting our turn. I was trying to think of a way to get closer to the Soviet commanders, to tell them my story, but couldn't think of a way to do it. Yesterday, I had missed my chance and, today, I still didn't have enough courage. The Soviets shouted constantly, with such rage that it was truly frightening. I couldn't step out of the circle. I racked my brain, but nothing ingenious came to mind. By contrast, the people around me were joking scornfully, talking and paying little attention to what was going on.

A man standing beside me asked, "Girl, do you smoke?" I told him I did. He gave me a piece of newspaper, then put his hand into his pocket and brought out a little tobacco. He didn't ask if I knew how to roll a cigarette but watched me as I did, then smiled and gave me a light. When things were uncertain, I always found it advantageous to have something in common with someone. My acceptance of a smoke from this man formed a link between us. He was tall, blond, maybe twenty-eight or thirty years old. He immediately became quite comfortable with me, talking in a very low voice. The girls shook their heads in disbelief, seeing me smoke in the company of this stranger. I didn't know if I was getting anywhere, but I knew I had an ally.

All at once, as we were talking, I realized that the good spirits of the crowd had evaporated. I didn't know why the men had become nervous, until the man next to me inclined his head close to my ear and said, "The two commanders are Jews." In an instant, I had thrown down the cigarette and stepped on it and was walking straight toward the two commanders, a good twenty metres. As I approached, they looked at me in wonderment. I can still see their amazed eyes and expressions and the way their upper bodies leaned forward. How I found the courage to do that, I don't know. I burst out, "I'm a Jew from a concentration camp and these are my friends." I pointed at the girls.

The reaction was incredible. One of the commanders embraced me and kissed me. "Yiddishe Kinder!" (Jewish children!) he said to the other, who also hugged and kissed me, while keeping an eye on the men in the circle. I beckoned to my friends. The first commander took us to the kitchen, but there wasn't much he could give us. They themselves had no food. There was only an old piece of dry bread and some cold coffee. He asked how we had survived and where, and listened to our stories with tears in his eyes. I asked if there was a doctor. This was only a patrol unit, he said. He asked why I hadn't approached him yesterday, since, if I had, we wouldn't have had to spend all night in the barn with the Ukrainians. By then, I was relaxed and told him, "Each time I wanted to approach you, you shouted so loudly that I was afraid to move. Someone had to be afraid of you." He smiled, satisfied that at least one person had been terrified of him. Then he became enraged, talking about the Ukrainians.

"You know what they did? They changed out of their uniforms into civilian clothes, pretending to pass as refugees. They fought with the Germans against the Soviets! They are traitors!" He had good reason to be angry. We had no idea of what had gone on elsewhere during the war, only what had happened to us. I thought it was better to change the topic of this conversation and politely told him that my friend urgently needed surgery, that she was in grave danger.

He replied that, although he couldn't help me, as he was busy and didn't have a vehicle, the hospital wasn't far away. All his men were out on the road, scouting for traitors. He advised me to go straight along the same road until I found a place called Rauscha, later called Ruszów, where the hospital was. He kissed me again and then we put Lodka in the cart. He walked a few metres with us, showing us the way. As we walked away, we could still hear his voice shouting at the Ukrainian collaborators.

There were no more soldiers along the road. On the left side, there were green fields, on the right, a forest. It was spring. A little further along, out of nowhere, a Polish officer in uniform appeared. When he passed by, I stopped him, asking how far it was to the hospital. He was amazed to see us. First he asked, "Amchu, Amchu?" This time we knew what it meant. "Polski," I answered. He knew exactly where the hospital was, as it turned out that he worked as a dentist there. Finally, we managed to get there, right to the door of the hospital in Rauscha.

Our New Protectors

As soon as we reached the hospital, I ran inside, calling for a doctor. One came immediately, a surgeon from Lwów, Poland. He was of average height, grey-haired, about fifty years old. He followed me outside to help me bring Lodka in and put her on a bed. After he examined the wound he confirmed that she needed immediate surgery. I pleaded with him to do it and told him, "We don't have any money, but I can work here for as long as she has to stay in hospital."

"What, you, here?" he laughed. "With all these soldiers around? It's too dangerous for you to work here. But don't worry. I know a few soldiers whom I can trust to take care of you. Wait here."

He walked away, returning shortly afterwards with four men from the artillery of the Red Army. They had been wounded in the battle at the Elbe River that we had witnessed not so long ago. One was wounded in the heel, one in the thigh and the third's head was swathed in bandages. The fourth, a tank-driver, was dragging one leg, had one arm in a sling and his mouth was deformed from a piece of a shrapnel that had split his front teeth in half. If the situation hadn't been so serious, they would have made a comical team. These walking wounded were the only ones the doctor trusted to look after us. They were young, in their early twenties, yet all of them had experienced many years of the cruel war. First, they looked at us, curiously. Then suddenly, the one with the bandaged head enthusiastically lifted me up in the air and whirled me round. When he put me down, he was met with a disapproving glare from the doctor. That was the end of that.

The doctor took Lodka and went to prepare for the operation. The soldiers went off for a while, then came back and led me to a pharmacy. Upstairs, the pharmacist's apartment was empty. In no time, the soldiers brought in mattresses, bread, vodka, cigarettes and candies, all taken from the hospital's kitchen and elsewhere. A few hours later, the soldiers brought Lodka from the hospital and placed her carefully on one of the mattresses. When Lodka's dressing needed changing, they carried her to the hospital and then back to our rooms. They really cared about us.

The news about us, the survivors, went round the military units. A large group of Polish-Jewish soldiers organized a meeting with us to see if we could answer any questions about their families. Lodka was still recovering, so she wasn't there. Rachel was having one of her moody fits and didn't want to attend so Rosa and I walked to meet them, together with our protectors. We sat at a large table and the soldiers stood around us asking questions like, "Did you see my sister? She is about your age." One tall soldier gave the name of the place where they were from. They mentioned cities and villages, names of sisters, mothers, cousins, brothers and fathers. The atmosphere was one of sadness. Disappointment floated in the air. We didn't know any of their relatives. There were so many camps, large and small: transit camps, labour camps, death camps. They were people from different places, with different languages and customs, displaced from somewhere else. The soldiers listened to our stories in silence, smoking cigarette after cigarette. Sometimes, one interrupted with a question. Sometimes, one would mention that he had been in one of the places we described, fighting the Germans. It was sad for us, knowing there wasn't much hope of them finding anyone alive, especially from the smaller cities. We went back to our rooms feeling terrible that we had had to disappoint them.

Another wounded soldier joined our group of protectors. I had the impression that he didn't like taking responsibility for us, but he enjoyed our company. He would appear from time to time, chat for a while and sing tangos in Russian. His name was David. I don't know why they called him by his name, since all the others were called by their rank. I also had the impression that he wasn't comfortable when the tank-driver was around – none of them were, in fact, except the big blond artillery corporal with the bandages on his head. We could feel the tension in the room when the tank-driver was around, but I couldn't tell if it was the result of respect or fear. The blond corporal seemed to be close to him and took orders from him with no difficulty.

The officer that had been wounded in the heel was tall, dark and handsome. I was convinced that he had gotten his rank because of his looks. He was lazy but had a winning smile. He enjoyed Rosa's company and had the knack of suddenly turning up whenever we had cooked anything. Cooking was not my specialty. I didn't know how to cook, although I knew how to make dessert from dry fruit – just add water and sugar and boil for half an hour. The officers came and went, sometimes bringing another soldier from the hospital to visit us. Actually, no one was very keen on the idea of looking after us, with the exception of the very first ones whom the doctor had entrusted with the responsibility. Still, we always had plenty of food. Many times, our protectors travelled to other towns, looking for groceries. We had everything we needed and were just waiting for Lodka, who was getting better every day, to heal. The plan to return to Poland was still in our minds, but we had no idea of how we could get there. Lodka was determined to go. She told the soldiers that she had a premonition that she would find someone from her family alive in Poland. Besides, we couldn't stay in Rauscha. The tank-driver, for one, was getting tired of protecting us.

One day, the handsome officer came to tell me that the doctor's wife, also a doctor, wanted to see me. Her office was in the hospital.

She greeted me with a sunny smile, showing me to the seat in front of her desk. She asked me about my family and how I had survived the camps. We chatted for a while and then she came to the point. "The reason I invited you was because I have seen how loyal you have been to your friend. I would like very much for you and my brother to get together. He is good-looking, a young doctor, very intelligent. He will be back from the front soon and I'm sure he would be happy to meet you. I think you are the right girl for him. Wait for him. You can stay here as long as you want."

At the time, my brain worked slowly. Maybe if I had been on my own, I could have made a fast decision, relying on my intuition. But I wasn't alone. I thanked her and told her that I would think about it. As soon as I was on the street, I began to think about Lodka, who was still weak and needed me. I didn't want to leave her alone, nor the other girls either. On the other hand, would we reach Poland? I wasn't convinced that returning there was a good idea for me. I was sure that no one from my family was alive.

I didn't know what to do. I needed advice from someone and I chose the tank-driver. He was serious and seldom spoke. I still wasn't sure if his comrades feared him or respected him, but I wasn't afraid of him.

The tank-driver was broad-shouldered, of average height, with jet-black shiny hair. He was the one who had opened the hatch of his tank and yelled "Amchu?" near the Elbe River. This was before he had been wounded. He carried his medals for bravery in his pocket, never pinned to his uniform. I told him about my conversation with the doctor. He listened to me thoughtfully, then quickly replied, "How do you know that he'll return in one piece from the front?" He was bitter and continued, "At the very end of the war, I got wounded. It took only seconds. I'm still suffering from a concussion. Who knows if he is alive or dead at this moment!" He paused, then added harshly, "I'm thinking of taking you all to Poland on a military train." With that, he left. It really amazed me how fast he could make decisions when he had to.

The next afternoon he became more outspoken. "I just put a group of people from a concentration camp onto the train," he told me. "I stood with them inside the wagon and when the train started to move, I jumped out." Many years later, Alina told me that she and an older friend of hers had been among this group. When she saw the tank-driver with me, she recognized him.

"What would happen if someone saw them?" I asked.

"Nothing," he said. "But we would travel legally." It was a coincidence that those people had been stranded there and it was another piece of luck that the train had stopped at that station. Yet another stroke of fortune was that the tank-driver had been there to take charge. I assumed he had gone to inquire about trains after our chat of the previous day. Trains were running, but not on any schedule. It was evident that he didn't like the idea of my waiting for the young doctor to come back from the front. The sooner he could take us to Poland the better for him – he wouldn't have to care about us any more. "I wonder what we would do in Poland?" I asked him. "I have no family, nowhere to stay, no money. Besides, they won't let us onto a military train." I was making excuses.

"Leave it to me," he responded. "When we get there, I will put you in a house and send you soldier's wages until you get established. With time, you will find someone to take care of you. Meanwhile, I will find my unit and rejoin the army."

"We'll see," I said, not convinced. As long he was making decisions on my behalf, I felt powerless to act for myself. Yet I knew that, in the end, I would have to look after myself. I would wait and see what happened. Perhaps this wasn't smart, but I didn't have any other ideas. I didn't know what I wanted. On the other hand, Lodka still had a strong feeling that someone in her family was alive. She wanted to go to Poland at any cost. Rachel the moody was quiet; it was difficult to guess what she was thinking.

The other soldiers kept their distance from the tank-driver. When they talked to him or about him they called him *Starshyna*, Senior Sergeant. They noticed that the two of us were talking and began to pry, asking me why I talked to him and what he had offered me. His friend, the corporal, told the tank-driver what was going on. For the first time, the tank-driver warned me to be careful. "They are jealous," he said. "All of them like you, but they don't have the courage to approach you. They say that you are too classy for them, that it would take a lot of money to satisfy your tastes." In fact, I myself didn't know what I liked, even who I was. But I got the picture that the tank-driver was serious about me.

New people appeared in the small city of Rauscha. Some were opportunists. David, the tango singer, once met two of these newcomers in the street and befriended them. They told him they were partisan fighters. One mentioned his surname, which happened to be the same as that of the handsome officer, so David brought them to meet us, knowing that everyone was desperate to find family after the war. The man told us that he was actually a cousin of the officer. There was no way anyone could prove him wrong because the officer had already left to rejoin his unit.

They sat at the table waiting for the tank-driver to show up. When he arrived, he greeted them in a friendly way, especially as David had already told him that one of them was a cousin of the officer. Then David and the tank-driver went off to get some vodka, to celebrate. Everything at that time was celebrated with vodka. We were left alone with the strangers. Suddenly, the one who had said he was a cousin of the handsome officer took out a gun. Playing with it, he put the gun to my head. I was too terrified to move. I didn't even open my mouth. Then we heard a creak on the stairs and the others returned. I was relieved. I didn't tell the tank-driver what had happened and the other girls put it out of their minds too. During the conversation, the tank-driver mentioned to the strangers that he was planning to travel to Poland and take us girls along. The stranger then invited all of us to his apartment in Lodz, where he lived with his wife.

Later, I realized that I had been right not to tell the tank-driver about the incident with the stranger and the gun. He was one of the few wounded soldiers who had been able to keep his pistol and he knew how to use it. He wouldn't have let him leave the room alive for what he had done, even if it was a joke. It was better that I had avoided an unpleasant experience. The tank-driver had joined the army when he was seventeen. He, like all the others, was taught the tactics of war: kill without mercy or be killed by the enemy. Once you pulled out your revolver, you had to shoot. It was a cruel war, one that had created savage, impulsive soldiers that shot first and asked questions afterwards. The brave among the survivors were rewarded with medals. The dead were now mere statistics, war casualties.

Everyone was getting better. The soldiers' wounds were healing. Lodka limped a bit, but otherwise, she was fine. It was such a relief to see her on her feet again, roaming around. We all got stronger and healthier, day by day. But Rauscha was turning into a dangerous place. Almost every day, strangers appeared, looking for whatever they could find to steal, and taking things away from us. When I wouldn't let one take a bicycle and a beautiful doll the tank-driver had brought me, he threatened me with a gun. I stopped resisting. The tank-driver laughed at me for not knowing how to defend myself and when I complained to him that everyone was stronger than me, he said that he would bring me a revolver.

One day, Rosa had a stomach ache. I went downstairs to the pharmacy to get something for her pain and saw a Soviet soldier in there with a rifle. I turned to leave, but he stopped me and asked me what I was looking for. I told him I needed some valerian drops for a friend of mine. In a second, he found the right bottle. Then, much to my amazement, he took another bottle from the shelf and downed its contents. I was astonished. I asked him if he knew what it was he was drinking. "Yes," he answered, "I'm a pharmacist." He must have been, since he'd found the right bottle in no time.

We often had visits from people who came to see us out of curiosity. Once, a colonel from the Red Army came in. He was a Soviet Jew, a huge, very caring person. He asked how we had survived and chatted for a while. Then he told me that he, his wife and two children lived in the Soviet Union with his mother and that she would be glad to take care of me. I had suffered enough, he said.

I was really tempted. I liked the idea better than any of the others I had heard so far because my mother had been born in Russia and my father had served in the Soviet army in the previous war. Perhaps it was my destiny to go to Russia, to discover my mother's family, maybe even stay with them. But once again, the tank-driver had other ideas. "How do you know that what he is saying is the truth?" he said. "Don't trust other people, stay here."

The tank-driver, his blond corporal and David the singer planned to escort us to Poland. The tank-driver managed to get permits from his commander for all three of them to travel in order to find their units, which were dispersed all over the occupied countries. Finally, the tank-driver found out when a train would arrive. We got ready and went to the station to wait for the train.

Back In Poland

The train slowly pulled into the station. It was a long train, mainly freight cars, with a few passenger cars. In the freight section, the tank-driver found an empty boxcar, which we occupied immediately. The train moved incredibly slowly. It took maybe a week or more to arrive in Lodz because it stopped at every imaginable station and stood there for hours. We often got out to walk, to stretch our legs, to wash our faces and hands. At one station, a Soviet officer approached the tank-driver and asked who I was. The tank-driver answered that I was his sister and the officer asked if he could borrow me for a few minutes! Unbelievable things happened at the time. It was dangerous for girls to be alone and we were lucky to have our protectors with us.

We went directly to the address we had been given by the man we had met in Rauscha, the partisan. Indeed, he did live there with his wife and he did remember us. We were welcomed and everything was fine for a few days. However, one morning he asked the tank-driver why he cared so much about me. "Let her go," he said. "She is not for you. There are all kinds of single girls available here. What do you see in her?" He wasn't speaking discreetly; on the contrary, he wanted me to hear what he was saying. I felt vulnerable. He knew nothing about me, not even who I was. The conversation continued, until I heard the tank-driver ask him, "Do you love your wife? I love mine." It was the end of the conversation. Then, the tank-driver turned to me and ordered, "Don't move from here; don't go out. Don't let him touch you. I will be back soon." My friends were also ordered to protect me.

As soon the tank-driver closed the door, the so-called cousin approached me with a disdainful look. "It doesn't matter what the tank-driver said; he will abandon you sooner or later," he smiled sarcastically. It was another blow to my sensitivity. A few hours later, the tank-driver returned and told us to get all our things together, as he had rented a room. "You see now that you can't trust people?" he said pointedly to me. He went on to say that I still had a lot to learn about people and life and that I would be cheated if I trusted people. I retained this lesson for life, even though he had been the one who trusted the cousin.

We arrived at our new lodgings, which was only one room with a stove. We all slept on the floor the first night. The next morning, the tank-driver and the corporal brought two beds, a table and a few chairs. David had already left us when we arrived in Lodz. A few days later, Lodka asked the tank-driver for money to travel to her home. The tank-driver gave her the money and took her to the station. It turned out she had been right to be obsessed with the idea that she would find some member of her family. After a month, a letter came from her brother. He thanked me for taking care of his sister and invited me to stay in their house as long as I wanted. She also reunited with an uncle. That was all I heard from Lodka. Rachel also asked for money and the tank-driver accompanied her, too, to the station. That was the last we knew of her. She disappeared and we never heard from her again. Rosa missed her handsome officer badly and asked the tank-driver if he could take her to see him. He took her to the unit the officer had rejoined. Rosa pretended to be his sister and the captain reluctantly let them see him. It turned out that the handsome officer was in jail for getting involved with the captain's wife! Rosa returned empty-handed and tried to forget him.

As the Jews who survived the camps returned to their homes, they weren't welcomed. Before the war, Jews in Poland were always simply labelled as "the Jews." After the war, however, we entered the statistics as "Polish citizens who perished in the war." In my experience, the older Polish people never talked to the younger generation about what really happened during the war, denying all the barbarous facts. Many Jews who went back home after the war, hoping to reclaim their property or look for family, were killed by antisemitic Polish gangs. Everyone imagined that, when the war ended, they would simply go back to where they had been when it started and get on with life. It seemed reasonable enough, but many of them paid for it with their lives. So when I wanted to go to Pruszków and Warsaw to look for family, I asked the tank-driver to accompany me. He refused to let me go. We had already heard about people getting killed.

In Lodz, a Jewish policeman from Skarżysko-Kamienna, who had heard we were in Lodz, visited me and Rosa. He was one of the good ones and we had called him "Little Apple" there because of his rosy face. He was well-behaved and invited us for a coffee at a nearby café. I'm sure the tank-driver wouldn't have let us go, but he wasn't home at the time. Another surprise visitor was the man who had been in charge of the men's barracks in Plaszów, where Alina and I had been put as dangerous criminals. He came to take me to his brother Henek, who had asked for me. Henek was alive in a hospital, although, as I mentioned, he had been shot through the head shortly before the end of the war. The tank-driver got up and stood between him and me, saying, "She is with me, and she's not going anywhere." This was my last chance to change my destiny.

In the same building in Lodz where we rented the room, on the second floor, lived a father, his son and two daughters. His wife and his older son had been killed at Werk A in Skarżysko-Kamienna. They often had visitors, including survivors and Jewish soldiers who were anxious to enjoy a family life. Neither the tank-driver nor I ever visited them, but Rosa did and met a Polish army officer, Mietek Wolman, whom she brought to meet us. He was handsome, tall, with dark blond hair and sparkling blue eyes. He greeted me in a friendly way and asked who else lived with us. I told him about the tank-driver and his rank as a sergeant-major. "I'm his senior. He'll have to salute me first," he exclaimed proudly.

"I doubt it," I said, "He doesn't salute anyone."

"We'll see," he said.

At that very moment, the tank-driver opened the door. The officer took one look at him, then stood up stiffly and remained that way until the tank-driver told him to take a seat. I felt satisfied, which was perhaps childish. The tank-driver was a rebel. Probably everyone who knew him or had heard about him had been told that he was not easy to approach. So far, I couldn't understand why people feared him. For me, maybe it was enough to have someone to take care of me. He helped out others, too. When someone needed something and he could help, he was happy to do it.

A few months later, Rosa married the proud officer in a simple religious ceremony at the home of another neighbour. The family gave up a room for them to live in. We still formed a group of three: the tank-driver, the corporal and me. The corporal often got my back up. If he bought a bag of cherries, he ate the last one before he entered the room. He never brought anything for the household, although he ate and slept in the same room. Since he was the tank-driver's friend, however, I didn't interfere. Besides, as I learned later, it wouldn't have helped.

Once, the corporal brought a white leather jacket and asked me to try it on. It looked very nice on me, but when I asked him if he would give it to me as a present, he refused. I tried to convince him by telling him that the tank-driver would pay him for it, but he said that he wouldn't accept money from him. I was angry with him and demanded that he not stay with us. He calmly answered, "I will sleep on the floor, near the door, but I will stay where the tank-driver stays." I had to laugh. This was loyalty, indeed. I told the tank-driver about the incident, but he didn't bother to say a word in my favour. I was disappointed. A similar incident occurred at a market, where I saw a pair of red shoes that fit me perfectly. However, Rosa said that red wasn't practical, that I was capricious. I really wanted them, but I had no money and the tank-driver wouldn't buy the shoes for me. I realized that I would never have the last word. His friends always came first. Was it my destiny? I presumed so. To him, I represented home and was all he needed. He had a very strong personality, but was that what I needed?

The tank-driver decided to take me to a photo studio to get our picture taken. We were waiting in the reception room when a Soviet captain came in. He walked right up to the tank-driver and asked him to show his documents because of all the soldiers waiting there, the tank-driver was the only one who didn't immediately get up to salute the captain. The tank-driver showed him his identification, giving his rank and a description of his many medals and where he had won them. When the captain asked him where the medals were and the tank-driver said they were at home, the captain said, "If I see you again without your medals and badges pinned on, I will arrest you. This time, I'm letting you go because you're with this young lady." After scolding him, the captain offered him his parade jacket for the picture, but the tank-driver didn't accept. Many soldiers were no longer proud of their uniforms and had changed to civilian clothes.

We soon heard that the son of the neighbours from the second floor had been to Germany twice and was ready to go again. His name was Isaac and he was approximately our age. Rosa, her husband, the tank-driver and I talked over the idea of leaving Poland. We got ready and set out for Germany with Isaac, who knew the route. The corporal got sick and didn't come with us. So in the fall of 1945, three or four months after living in fear in our native land, we abandoned Poland, never to return again. By then, I knew that my sister was not alive.

Journeys

We had no trouble getting as far as Prague. The whole of Eastern Europe was occupied by the Soviets. We didn't even need passports or identification. In Prague, we had to change to the train going to Munich, which was in the American Zone and meant crossing a border checkpoint. Since we had no travel permits, we lay down on the top of the train, hiding until it had crossed the border. After crossing the border, we easily entered the compartment in the passenger wagon. Finally, we arrived in Munich and went from there to a displaced persons camp in Feldafing, where a few thousand survivors were living under American supervision.

A few months later, on February 16, 1946, the tank-driver and I got married. There were three couples at the same ceremony. We all signed for each other as witnesses. None of us could understand the judge's legal German vocabulary, but we signed anyway. When we left City Hall, we celebrated our marriages by throwing snowballs at each other. There was no hurry to go home, since nobody was waiting for us. The rooms were cold and there was nothing to eat.

~

We stayed in Feldafing for about two years and then decided to go to Israel. We arrived in Haifa in April 1948, shortly before Passover. Some friends met us and took us to their home. After a few days, they heard that there were some empty barracks available behind the hospital – we weren't legally allowed to occupy them but they suggested that we start out there and move somewhere better later.

The place was deplorable. It was Haifa Bat Galim, at the edge of the Mediterranean Sea, behind the British Government Hospital of Haifa, later renamed Rambam. It was literally at the edge of the sea. When there was a storm, the high waves furiously hit the window. From the window, though, the view was beautiful. We could see the sunrise appearing as a ball of fire reflected on the calm sea where the Arab fishermen threw their nets from small boats.

There were a few concrete buildings and the rest of the barracks were made of wooden planks. It was a recreational place for the British soldiers when they had free time for a swim and shower. This was before Israel became an independent state. When the immigrants from Europe arrived in Israel, there were not enough buildings to rent and the money we had wasn't enough to rent a better place. The Soviets we lived with called this place Posolek, settlement.

The entrance to the dwelling was made of stones cast up on the shore by the sea during storms. There was no water, no washrooms and no light. We could only ask the hospital to let us make an outlet pipe and a faucet to supply our daily water. There were no other buildings around. However, at the end of our settlement were a few wires serving as a fence to separate it from the naval base barracks. The soldiers discovered it and jumped over the wire to sneak out without permission from the authorities, crossing into our settlement. Sometimes the soldiers had cigarettes to sell from their daily ration, if they weren't smokers. The soldiers would also sell fish to us that they had stunned with a grenade.

We sent a delegation with a petition to the hospital asking for the indispensable source of life – water. In the beginning, they wouldn't accept our petition because we were illegally occupying the place, which was true. But we touched their emotions in that they knew that without water there is no life and they agreed to let us use water from the hospital. Slowly, everyone began to enlarge their rooms. We made a kitchen, a toilet and a shower. So did a few others. We had arrived very early after the war and there was no money for a civilized life. Soon, the men got whatever jobs were available. Two years later, an Arab engineer who was working for the Palestine Electricity Corporation came and told us that we would have electric light the following week. We were finally recognized.

We understood that Israel wasn't prepared for so many people to come at once. Besides, the government had very little sympathy for us. Not much attention was given to the survivors of the brutal war. We felt rejected, outcasts. It didn't matter that we understood the precarious situation in Israel and we took care of ourselves without government assistance.

Among us were engineers, nurses, musicians, stage artists, social workers, government employees and journalists, all from their various native countries, so language was a barrier. Although we came from different countries with different languages, we could socialize and live in harmony with each other. For example, the majority were Romanian, but there were also Polish, Hungarian, Egyptian and Soviet women married to Polish men, Czechs and one French woman married to a Polish man. The French woman was a social worker during the war, working behind the lines with the French troops. She organized a contest for who had the best-decorated room. I had everything in brown and beige and put yellow flowers on the table and won the first prize.

Time passed and she bought a book as a gift for me – a translation from Russian to German, as I had become fluent in German. It was a novel from the time of the occupation of France by the Germans.

Every morning, the men went to their jobs, leaving the women and children behind. One day, we heard our neighbour Licy yelling so loudly that we all rushed out of our dwellings to see what had happened. She was determinedly calling for attention, yelling that one of our neighbours had fainted and that she needed help. Everyone rushed back inside and then came out running: one with a lemon, one with vinegar, the other with medicinal drops, and one with an aspirin and a cloth with ice. As we reached the neighbour's room, Licy burst into laughter. It was typical Romanian love for theatre. "I wanted to convince myself that we are truly good neighbours," she said. We were. I offered to watch the children when the moms went to the grocery store. They didn't trust me with the errands because I didn't look experienced. My husband and I were the youngest among them. Still, we all respected each other and were sure that we could ask for help for whatever we needed.

Once, a neighbour got so sick that we took her to the hospital, but they wouldn't admit her. We put her on a stretcher, opened the gate and left her there. Running away, we hid behind a building to see what would happen. They took her inside and she was there for two weeks, suffering from a nervous breakdown. I still exchange letters with her. Her husband was working far away, coming home only for the Sabbath and she had two children older than the rest of the children there.

In the 1990s, I went to Israel and visited our neighbours from the time we left four decades ago. A friend drove me to where we had lived and it was unrecognizable. The dwellings had disappeared and it was now a landing area for helicopters. At the edge of the sea there is a reserved place for swimmers and a sandy strand for sunbathing, well maintained and guarded by Israeli soldiers. The soldiers let us in. I took off my sandals and dipped my feet in the Mediterranean Sea.

Argentina

After seven years in Israel, we decided to move to Argentina. My cousin Benjamin had moved there before the war, though I had had no contact with him for years. My husband, our two children, Sonia and Nathan, and I arrived at the shore of Buenos Aires on March 6, 1955. Sonia had been born in 1947 and Nathan four and a half years later. We travelled on a French ship called the *Charles Tellier*. A delegation of four men waited for us to come off the ship. The president of the Jewish immigration organization Soprotimis, Mr. Shindelman, his secretary, a medical doctor and a clerk helped us with the luggage. The community leaders had arranged a reservation for us at the Hotel Castro.

I knew that my cousin Benjamin lived in Buenos Aires. Teresa, the daughter of the hotel owner, found my cousin's number in the telephone book. She phoned him to say that we were in Buenos Aires and she gave him the address of the hotel. Although it wasn't very close to him, he came to visit us immediately. He had left Poland when I was only eight years old, but I recognized him from the photos I used to see. We greeted each other and then I invited him upstairs to introduce him to my family. We chatted for a while and then he asked me to repeat some Spanish words. When I did it correctly, he told me that I would learn Spanish in no time.

Benjamin lived in the Cabildo area with his wife and two children. An older daughter was married. He invited us to his home, explaining how to get there. We had no difficulty finding his house. It was a Saturday afternoon when we knocked on the door and Sofia, his wife, came out saying, "Don't you know that in Argentina we have a siesta?" We apologized, as we hadn't.

Benjamin told me that my father's cousin Zelda lived in the city and that she had two brothers on the outskirts of Buenos Aires. Zelda and her husband invited us for dinner the next week. Her brothers also invited us to various occasions, but peoples' reaction to us was the same as everywhere. No one had much interest in the survivors of the war.

Weeks later, Benjamin and Zelda invited me to a fancy night out at a local tango show. The people were elegantly dressed and the atmosphere was festive. Although I didn't understand one word of Spanish, I fell in love with the tango. Every tango lyric is a story of love, greed or revenge. Some songs have advice, others, a philosophical interpretation of life. Carlos Gardel, the most venerable tango singer in Argentina who died in a plane crash over Medellín, Colombia, in 1935, is remembered as having an unmistakable voice. There are circles of tango fanatics loyal to him and his pictures are still displayed in the buses and some stores.

Under Perón, immigrants were not allowed to live in Buenos Aires until they had resided in another part of the country for a year. Accustomed to respecting the law and because of these visa conditions, we had to move to a city not less than one hundred kilometres from Buenos Aires. Some people we knew suggested we settle in Bahía Blanca, about six hundred kilometres from Buenos Aires. It was a progressive and nice, clean city. We moved into a new house with a big yard. Immediately, I started to grow flowers and small vegetables. My daughter had been accepted into the second grade of the public school in Bahía Blanca. Soon, the teacher chose her for a play to celebrate Argentina's Independence Day on July 9. She had only been at the school for two months. After the presentation, I heard the teacher saying, "The German girl didn't fail us." Because we had lived in Germany before going to Israel, we were considered Germans. My son attended kindergarten. He was only three years old and for some reason he pronounced R the same hard way it is pronounced in Israel, where he was born. The R in Spanish is soft spoken.

I got a job as a negative retoucher, working at home for Foto Garbus, a well-known photography studio. I bought a German-Spanish dictionary and while I was working I listened to the radio and looked up words in the dictionary. This way, I could help the children with their homework. In no time, I spoke and read Spanish. My husband got a job in his trade as a cabinetmaker. The wife of the owner spoke German. We didn't feel isolated. Since my husband was accustomed to reading the newspaper daily, my duty was to translate the news every evening for him. A few months later, I started to buy *Reader's Digest* in Spanish and the children's magazine *Billiken*. The lady from the kiosk used to let me bring the magazines home, indifferent to whether I had the money to pay her or not. The neighbours trusted and respected us. The area we lived in was new, with nice little houses where mostly sailors' families lived. Everything was fine and I liked it there. However, there is always a "but" and that was that the winds were so strong that they picked up dirt from the street, which was always getting into eyes and nostrils. Also, the city was too small, so we eventually returned to Buenos Aires.

We rented a little chalet in Olivos, on the outskirts of Buenos Aires, not far from the villa where the president lives during his mandate. Only twenty minutes from the capital city, the air was better than downtown. The majority of families who lived in the area were English, Dutch and German. Mr. Garbus sent the negatives from Bahía Blanca by mail to retouch at my home. Soon, through the ads in the newspaper, I was working for another four studios. The children continued their schooling and my husband also found a place to work. Naturally, we had to take buses to get downtown. I had to travel, taking many different buses to deliver the negatives to different studios.

One Sunday afternoon, I heard my doorbell ringing. I opened the door and there stood a family of four asking for me. The woman said that her maiden name was Kenigstein and that she was from Pruszków. I invited them into the living room. I was sewing drapes for the windows when they arrived, since it was only a few weeks after we had moved into the house. I folded the material and invited my guests to sit at the table. All of them were chewing gum. (Later I found out from my cousin that because of our last name, Thon, for some reason, they thought that my husband was an American and chewing gum would please him.) The woman said that she had met my cousin Benjamin and that he had given her my address. "I wanted to see you," she said, "because I was very much in love with your father." I could not miss the excitement on her face while she was talking. "Your father was a very good-looking man. All the girls in Pruszków at that time dreamed of being his sweetheart. I knew your mother too."

Her family had a shoe business where we used to shop sometimes. Once a year, in the spring, when my sister and I were little, the shoemaker used to measure our feet and make shoes for us in light beige-coloured leather by hand.

I offered them coffee, cake, some soft drinks; she refused anything I offered, intent on her purpose only. I felt as if the offer interfered with her memories. She was entranced, remembering her youth through me. It lasted only as long as her yearning to revive her past. Then, she abruptly turned to her husband and two daughters and told them it was time to go. I thanked her for the visit and invited her to return whenever she felt nostalgic for the past. I never saw them again.

～

Around 1965, my daughter started university and our son started high school. A few years later she went for a visit to Canada and decided to stay in Toronto. She married and had a daughter, Naomi. We immigrated to Canada in 1980 to be close to our daughter. We were present when she graduated with a Ph.D. at the University of Toronto. In 1986, the Canadian government invited professionals to immigrate to Canada. Our son and daughter-in-law, both architects, had graduated from the University of Buenos Aires and they and their two sons, Jonathan and Joshua, came to join us.

I miss the neighbours in Buenos Aires. They were caring and helpful any time I needed them. I remember that if you met someone who knew you at a bus stop, the person would ask where you were going and buy a ticket for you. I don't know if that is still the custom there.

I'll also always remember the following episode from our time in Buenos Aires. We were on a bus when a woman fell as she tried to get off at her stop. She was drunk. Two men lifted her up and guided her to a restaurant, sat her on a chair and asked the waiter for a glass of water and a strong coffee. The bus driver didn't move the vehicle until he saw the woman was safe.

We didn't really have any difficulties adjusting to life in Argentina. We went back to visit our neighbours in Argentina four times and still exchange letters after many years.

Afterword: Canada

Our life in Canada is one where every dream has come true. After so many problems and grief, Canada was wonderful – a place to breathe. We both could work and our children and grandchildren could thrive, studying and making their own lives. My daughter became a full professor and my son worked as an architect. All of our grandchildren have also become professionals – one a lawyer, one a doctor of science at Harvard, and one a doctor of psychology. Who would have thought from such hard beginnings that our children and grandchildren could do so well? It's a gift.

Poems

At Twelve

With wide-open eyes I perceived the world
As it was then in my naïve mind.
At twelve I saw reflected in the mirror
My happy face and braids on both sides
And inner dreams, where the spirit resides,
Of a girl who grew without a single cloud.
I wore a sailor suit that Mom sewed for me.
And, shining shoes laced up, I see
In the mirror the reflection of that year
Of my innocent life.
I read and wrote, inspired, alone.
Nothing wrong came my way
Jealousy and hate unknown.
At twelve, my loving family together at home
I couldn't wish anything more
Than for my dreams to come true.

In the Fields, Czerniaków

In the beginning, I was mostly happy
Appreciating the beauty of the morning in the fields,
The wondrous brilliance of the dew on the grass,
Breathing in the freshness of the lake.

The coming events cast a shadow on us,
Silencing the songs that purified our minds.
Meanwhile, in the Warsaw ghetto
The weak envied those sick enough to die.
New days were like yesterdays.

From dawn to sunset with bent bodies
Caressing the soil to plant the seedlings,
Later harvesting the fruit of the patient earth
Blood from my open wounds mixed with mud.
I thought of my childhood,
Trying to recapture fading dreams.
The spiritual light wasn't strong enough
To illuminate the deep dark nights.

Youth kept its feelings restrained.
The impotence to rebel tasted bitter.
Heaven have mercy, we prayed
That tomorrow will not be too late.
You will be judged!

Why?

Early spring in a place
Where the flowers forgot to bloom
Where the birds flew away in horror
And the stars lost their shine
The air emits a stench of death.

He left without saying goodbye,
Too painful for him to part,
And for me a shock in the morning
To find an empty chair
Where he had leaned on the table
With his hands supporting his head.

The night before
The train took him far away.
Never to see him again,
Torn whether to stay or go
I decided to stay and not hurt those
He left behind in this place without flowers,
Without birds or freshness of spring,
My source of advice and love
Left this gloomy place
Without a goodbye.

For the Heroes of the Warsaw Uprising

We lower the flag to honour you
Heroes of the uprising.
Fate guided you to sublimity,
You weren't born in vain.

We remember you, and we mourn.
The spark of hope for your ideal
Caught fire and exploded.
You were ready,
To the end you remained.

We remember you, and we mourn.

Like soldiers
You fought for freedom
With a vision of justice
And lost your lives.

We remember you, and we mourn.

Heroes don't rest, even after death,
Since we nourish the memory
And shield the eternal flame

You didn't die in vain.

We remember you, we pay homage, and we mourn.

Vanished Glitter

Rhythmically the waves push the seashell
As Mother's gentle hand rocked my cradle,
Inside the shell is my world now. Sealed,
I choose isolation, having left behind
The glamorous promise of youth,
The beauty of a peaceful world.

Defeated, I walk to find a sign of life.
A starless dark sky confuses my way,
Vague in my memory was the past.

Vanished like the glitter of the stars
As if the earth had swallowed
The happy, pounding hearts,
The sweetness of voices,
The open, smiling lips
Silenced by the roar of the beast.
Grim memories of the outside world.

I am lost, utterly.
Curled in a shell at the edge of the sea,
That is my world now.
Desolate, alone.

Labyrinth of Memory

In the mysterious labyrinth of memory,
I exist, I breathe in spite of the tragedy
That killed my roots, taking them away,
Separated by time and distance,
Far away, until their images
Begin to be erased from the screen in my mind.

In the mysterious labyrinth of memory,
It is a daily effort to recall their dear faces,
They disappear, not all at once, but slowly, painfully.
In spite of my grieving heart,
Life goes on ... I exist.

In the mysterious labyrinth of memory,
It is impossible to reconstruct their shapes.
All of them fading away...
It's hopeless, tiring
To grasp what is left of the past.
Rage and rebellious thoughts don't help.
In my mouth there is an aftertaste of bitterness.
I'm alive. They are in my mind, always.

Guilt

Grief for the dead has turned to guilt.
I stand disturbed and wonder,
A knot tight in my throat
Like a sealed barrel of gunpowder
Ready to explode. Remember!

Memory, like a curse, is moored inside me.
Will this pain stay forever?
Horrified, I see only dust
All that remains of that black thunder.
Reflection – is living a gain?
Hope is swept away, but the past still remains.
My soul howls in despair.
Resentment becomes a heavy stone,
The weight of sorrow hard to carry alone.
There is only the illusion of freedom.

I have remorse for surviving.
It's my fault.
The cruel question I ask, enraged,
Where will be my home?

Memorial

Don't just pass by! Raise your eyes
To the monument erected for us.
You can see our risen arms
In the shape of flames
Imagined by the sculptor
To perpetuate the horror....

You can hear our voices
As, for the last time,
We called for mercy.
We don't rest like the dead
In other places.
There is no silence here.

We claim to remain in your memory
With our faces,
Not tongues of flame,
For our last thoughts
Were of love for you, in our hearts.

We were there, where darkness reigned,
Where the bells tolled, pitying our departure.
Our souls are still in pain
With sorrow like abrasive flames.
We have claimed justice ever since –
We know who to blame.

Listen to our lament,
Don't restrain your tears.
Raise your eyes and pray
That this horror shall not happen again.

With every stroke of the sculptor's hands
Our risen arms appear in the shape of flames.
We also dwell behind the clouds,
Above the monument erected for us.
Restless, we bewail our fate
Until you remember to raise your eyes.
Don't just pass by! Don't look away!

Time

Heal my wounds, Time,
You are the only one
Who can do it.
Make me forget the past
The loss of love,
The anguish of loneliness.

Heal my heart
And my confused mind.
I cry out with the misery I feel.
In my injured pride
Seeking warmth,
I perceive hypocrisy.

Heal me!
I still fear prejudice
That hurts me so much.
Fill me with hope.
Erase my bad memories.

Touch me with magic, Time
That heals all wounds.
Pull the melancholy out of me.
Heal me!
Heal my wounds!
You are the only one who can do it.

For My Mother, Father and Sister

Your souls soar through time and space
To erase my anxiety, to shorten
The distance as I long to see
Your names engraved on the black granite stone.

Only souls moved by love
Can wander over oceans,
Forests and borders to rest where I can touch
Your names engraved on the black granite stone.

Here your souls dwell, relieved of the journey
To be close, to be where I can lay flowers
And glimpse written below
Your names engraved on the black granite stone.

I heard trumpets glorify your descent,
Preannounced by my inner feelings,
With tears in my eyes and a heavy sigh
I have attained my desire to greet you
At this humble home where you now live forever,
The black granite stone.

It was not in vain that my loving memory for you
Endured restless, anxious waiting until
I could honour your names
Engraved on the black granite stone.

Glossary

Adamowicz, Irena (1910–1973) A leader of the Polish Scout movement and member of the Polish underground Home Army, or Armia Krajowa, during World War II. Adamowicz was a devout Roman Catholic who was interested in the Zionist organization Hashomer Hatzair before the war and participated in its educational activities. In 1941, she met with members of Hashomer Hatzair, who would eventually help establish the Jewish Fighting Organization in Warsaw, to discuss how she could help them. In the summer of 1942, Adamowicz undertook dangerous missions to deliver messages and assist Jewish resistance groups in the ghettos of Warsaw, Bialystok, Vilnius and Kovno, acting as a liaison between the various Jewish resistance groups and the Polish Home Army. In 1985, Adamowicz was posthumously honoured with the title of Righteous Among the Nations by Yad Vashem, the Holocaust Martyrs' and Heroes' Remembrance Authority in Jerusalem, which honours non-Jews who risked their lives to help save Jews during the Holocaust. *See also* Hashomer Hatzair; Jewish Fighting Organization; Polish Scout movement.

aliyah (Hebrew; pl. *aliyot*, literally, ascent) A term used by Jews and modern Israelis to refer to Jewish immigration to Israel; the term is also used to refer to "going up" to the altar in a synagogue to read from the Torah.

All Saints' Day An annual Roman Catholic holy and commemorative day to honour saints.

Amchu (Hebrew; abbreviation of Amcha Beis Yisroel; in English, Your nation, the People of Israel) A word used during and immediately after the war that acted as a "code" for Yiddish-speaking Jews in Poland to identify one another. Jews could ask one another "Amchu?" without giving away their Jewish identity. Someone familiar with Jewish prayer terminology would recognize it and answer appropriately, whereas it wouldn't make sense to someone who wasn't Jewish.

American Jewish Joint Distribution Committee (JDC) Also known colloquially as the "Joint." A charitable organization that provided material support for persecuted Jews in Germany and other Nazi-occupied territories and facilitated their emigration to neutral countries such as Portugal, Turkey and China. Between 1939 and 1944, JDC officials helped close to 81,000 European Jews find asylum in various parts of the world. Between 1944 and 1947, the JDC assisted more than 100,000 refugees living in DP camps by offering retraining programs, cultural activities and financial assistance for emigration.

American Zone One of four zones in Germany administered by the Allied powers between 1945 and 1949. The other three zones were administered by Britain, France and the Soviet Union.

Anielewicz, Mordecai (1919–1943) Commander of the Jewish Fighting Organization (JFO) and leader of the Warsaw Ghetto Uprising. Anielewicz, a former youth leader in Hashomer Hatzair, began to organize self-defense groups and armed resistance in the Warsaw ghetto in 1942, after he had learned of the deportations to death camps. On January 18, 1943, Anielewicz led a major resistance action against German soldiers who had come to the ghetto to gather Jews for deportation to Treblinka. Subsequently, he prepared fighters to resist any further deportations, which culminated in the month-long Warsaw Ghetto Uprising that began in April 1943. Anielewicz was killed in the JFO headquarters on May 8, 1943. In 1944 he was posthumously honoured with the Cross of Valour by the Polish government-in-exile and with the Cross of Grunwald by the Polish People's Army in 1945. In Israel, Kibbutz Yad Mordecai was named after him and memorials commemorate him in Warsaw and his hometown of Wyszków. *See also* Hashomer Hatzair; Jewish Fighting Organization; Warsaw Ghetto Uprising.

antisemitism Prejudice, discrimination, persecution and/or hatred against Jewish people, institutions, culture and symbols.

Ave Maria (Latin; also known as the Hail Mary or Angelic Salutation) A traditional Catholic prayer asking Mary, the mother of Jesus, to intercede on behalf of the worshipper. Used in both public liturgy and in private worship as part of the Rosary devotions.

Beth Jacob (in Hebrew, Beit Yaakov; house of Jacob) A movement founded in Poland in 1917 by seamstress Sarah Schenirer (1883–1935) to provide formal Orthodox education for girls.

Blockälteste (German; literally, block elder) Prisoner appointed by the German authorities as barrack supervisor, charged with maintaining order and accorded certain privileges.

Bolsheviks (from the Russian word *bol'shinstvo*, majority) A political party in Russia that originated in 1903 after separating from the Russian Social Democratic Labour Party and that came to power during the second half of the 1917 Russian Revolution. The Bolsheviks, founded by Vladimir Lenin and Alexander Bogdanov, were hailed as a proletariat-focused party and eventually became the Communist Party of the Soviet Union. *See also* Mensheviks; Russian Revolution.

British Mandate Palestine The area of the Middle East under British rule from 1923 to 1948, as established by the League of Nations after World War I. During that time, the United Kingdom restricted Jewish immigration. The area encompassed present-day Israel, Jordan, the West Bank and the Gaza Strip.

chalutzot (Hebrew) Pioneers. Immigrants who moved to pre-state Israel to help clear the land, plant trees and drain marshes to establish settlements and build self-sustaining communities. *Chalutzot* are primarily associated with the wave of immigration known as the Third Aliyah (1919–1923) that followed in the wake of World War I and the establishment of the British Mandate in Palestine. The term *chalutzot* was also used within Zionist youth movements outside of Palestine to refer to its members who hoped to immigrate there.

chavera (Hebrew) A society or communal group. Also, a friend or comrade.

cheder (Hebrew; literally, room) An Orthodox Jewish elementary school that teaches the fundamentals of Jewish religious observance and textual study, as well as the Hebrew language.

Chujowa Górka A hill near the Płaszów forced labour camp that was used as a mass grave for prisoners from the camp. In the spring of 1944, the site was excavated and the exhumed remains were cremated to destroy the evidence of the more than 10,000 bodies buried there. *See also* Płaszów.

Czerniaków A suburb of Warsaw and the site of a privately-owned farm where the Dror Zionist movement made an arrangement for Jewish workers to be housed and fed in exchange for providing labour. Approximately eighty Jews worked eight- to ten-hour days on the farm, after which they were free to spend time as they liked, from mid-1941 until November or December 1942, when the Nazis ordered the Polish estate owner, Mr. Zatwarnicki, to turn over all Jewish labourers to Nazi authorities. The Dror movement also used the Czerniaków farm as a base for underground activities such as storing weapons, training in self-defence and communicating with messengers from other ghettos.

Danzig (German; in Polish, Gdańsk) A city state and seaport situated at the mouth of the Vistula River on the Baltic Sea, located about 340 kilometres north of Lodz and 500 kilometres northeast of Berlin. Danzig, also known as the "Polish Corridor," belonged to Germany prior to World War I but was made an autonomous "Free City" by the peace settlement following it. Under the authority of the League of Nations throughout the interwar period, Danzig/Gdańsk was a major point of contention between Germany and Poland, with the latter maintaining special economic rights in the area and acting as the representative of the city-state abroad. In September 1939 the Germans occupied and immediately re-annexed the city. During the war the city endured heavy Allied and Soviet bombardment by air and during the Soviet capture of the city in March 1945 it was largely destroyed. In the post-war settlement agreed to by the Allies, Gdańsk became part of Poland.

Death's Head Also known as the *Totenkopf* (German; literally, death's head or skull), the Death's Head was one of the first combat divisions of the SS. The skull insignia was displayed on the caps of the SS and the Waffen SS units. *See also* SS; *SS-Totenkopfverbände.*

Dror (Hebrew; freedom) A secular Zionist youth movement that originated in Russia and was founded in Poland in 1915. By the 1930s, Dror was centred in Warsaw, gradually spreading to other communities in Eastern Europe and South America. Dror established a kibbutz training commune in the Warsaw ghetto, and many of its members were involved in underground and resistance work and fought in the Warsaw Ghetto Uprising. Still in existence, the organization merged with Habonim Union in 1982 to create Habonim Dror, a Labour Zionist youth movement. *See also* Czerniaków; kibbutz; Warsaw Ghetto Uprising.

Esperanto An international language created by Dr. Ludwig Zamenhof in the 1870s in Bialystok. Zamenhof's intention was to create a language that would foster communication between people of different ethnicities. Esperanto is currently spoken in 115 countries and estimates of Esperanto speakers range from 10,000 to two million. *See also* Zamenhof, Lidia.

Gestapo (German) Abbreviation of Geheime Staatspolizei, the Secret State Police of Nazi Germany. The Gestapo was the brutal force that dealt with the perceived enemies of the Nazi regime and were responsible for rounding up European Jews for deportation to the death camps. They operated with very few legal constraints and were also responsible for issuing exit visas to the residents of German-occupied areas. A number of Gestapo members also joined the Einsatzgruppen, the mobile killing squads responsible for the roundup and murder of Jews in eastern Poland and the USSR through mass shooting operations.

ghetto A confined residential area for Jews. The term originated in Venice, Italy in 1516 with a law requiring all Jews to live on a segregated, gated island known as Ghetto Nuovo. Throughout the Middle Ages in Europe, Jews were often forcibly confined to gated Jewish neighbourhoods. During the Holocaust, the Nazis forced Jews to live in crowded and unsanitary conditions in rundown districts of cities and towns. Most ghettos in Poland were enclosed by brick walls or wooden fences with barbed wire. *See also* Krakow ghetto; Warsaw ghetto.

Gobelin A style of dyed tapestry invented in fifteenth century Paris by Jehan Gobelin.

gołąbki A traditional Polish food made from minced meat wrapped in cabbage leaves.

Göth, Amon (1908–1946) Austrian Nazi captain and commandant of the Płaszów forced labour and concentration camp. Göth was infamous for his volatile nature and brutality against Jews. He murdered and tortured thousands of Jews and was hanged for his crimes in 1946 under a ruling by the Supreme National Tribunal of Poland. *See also* Płaszów.

Gymnasium (German) A word used throughout Central and Eastern Europe to mean high school.

Gypsy *See* Roma.

hachshara (Hebrew; literally, preparation) A training program to prepare new immigrants for life in the land of Israel.

Haller, Józef (1873–1960) Polish lieutenant-general who led battles in World War I and held prominent positions in the Polish military until 1926 when he opposed Józef Piłsudski's May 1926 coup. Shortly after Piłsudski came into power, Haller was ordered to retire. *See also* Piłsudski, Józef.

Hashomer Hatzair (Hebrew) The Youth Guard. A left-wing Zionist youth movement founded in Central Europe in the early twentieth century to prepare young Jews to become workers and farmers, to establish kibbutzim – collective settlements – in pre-state Israel and work the land as pioneers. Before World War II, there were 70,000 Hashomer Hatzair members worldwide and many of those in Nazi-occupied territories led resistance activities in the ghettos and concentration camps or joined partisan groups in the forests of east-central Europe. In the Warsaw ghetto, Hashomer members established underground education and members fought in the Warsaw Ghetto Uprising. Hashomer Hatzair is the oldest Zionist youth movement still in existence. *See also* Dror; Warsaw Ghetto Uprising.

high holidays (also High Holy Days) The autumn holidays that mark the beginning of the Jewish year and that include Rosh Hashanah (New Year) and Yom Kippur (Day of Atonement). Rosh Hashanah is observed with synagogue services where the leader of the service blows the shofar (ram's horn), and festive meals where sweet foods, such as apples and honey, are eaten to symbolize and celebrate a sweet new year. Yom Kippur, a day of fasting and prayer at synagogue, follows ten days later.

Jewish Fighting Organization (JFO) (in Polish, Żydowska Organizacja Bojowa, ŻOB) A collaborative resistance organization formed in the Warsaw ghetto in 1942 and comprised of members from the youth movements Dror, Hashomer Hatzair, Hechalutz and Bnei Akiva. The group's purpose was to communicate with other underground groups in ghettos in occupied Poland, maintain contact with Polish underground organizations, amass weapons and organize armed resistance against the Nazis. On January 18, 1943, the group's first insurrection disrupted the Nazis' deportation attempts; then, on April 19, 1943, in response to imminent deportation, the J F O instigated the Warsaw Ghetto Uprising, the largest singular act of resistance during the Holocaust. *See also* Warsaw Ghetto Uprising.

kibbutz (Hebrew) A collectively owned farm or settlement in Israel democratically governed by its members. Among some of the Zionist youth movements in Poland, the term was also used to refer to groups whose loyalty was to Palestine, although they did not yet live there. Members were organized into "kibbutz training groups" and some attended preparation training to immigrate to British Mandate Palestine. *See also* Czerniaków; Dror; *hachshara*; Hashomer Hatzair.

kierpce Traditional leather footwear worn by the indigenous Górale, highlanders who live in the Tatras mountain region of southern Poland.

Korczak, Janusz (1878–1942) Pseudonym for Henryk Goldszmit. A Jewish educator, doctor and writer who advocated for respecting children's rights and independence, focusing on understanding their emotions. In 1912, Korczak established a Jewish orphanage in Warsaw called Dom Sierot, and also created a children's newspaper. In 1940 when his orphanage was moved into the Warsaw ghetto, Korczak was given many opportunities to escape but always refused, instead choosing to stay with the children. On August 5, 1942, Korczak steadfastly accompanied "his" children on a deportation to the Treblinka death camp, where he perished. Associations that have been created in his memory in Israel, Poland and Canada were founded to commemorate his heroism and recognize his contribution to children's education. Korczak's works include more than ten fiction and four non-fiction books, including *How to Love A Child* and *The Child's Right to Respect*.

kosher (Hebrew) Fit to eat according to Jewish dietary laws. Observant Jews follow a system of rules known as *kashruth* that regulates what can be eaten, how food is prepared and how meat and poultry are slaughtered. Food is kosher when it has been deemed fit for consumption according to this system of rules. There are several foods that are forbidden, most notably pork products and shellfish.

Krakow ghetto An area established in March 1941 in the Podgórze district of Krakow where more than 15,000 Jews were forced to live in a confined space that had previously housed only 3,000 people. The Nazis dissolved the ghetto on March 13, 1943 and deported 6,000 Jews to the forced labour camp at Płaszów. *See also* Płaszów.

kvutza (Hebrew; pl. *kvutzot*) Group. Also used to refer to pioneers who settled in pre-state Israel.

Leipzig A city in Germany two hundred kilometres south of Berlin that was the site of a forced labour camp between June 1944 and April 1945. Leipzig, the largest of seven auxiliary camps administered by the Buchenwald concentration camp, was classified as a Hugo Schneider Aktiengesellschaft Metalwarenfabrik (HASAG) camp and served as one of Germany's largest munitions plants. The Leipzig barracks, where approximately two hundred men and five thousand women – including 1,200 Jews – from eighteen countries were incarcerated, were set up two kilometres from the armaments factory.

Lord's Prayer (in Latin, Oratio Dominica, also called Pater Noster, "Our Father") A common prayer in Christian liturgy, it appears in the New Testament in two versions (short and long) as part of the teachings of Jesus and as a model of prayer.

madrich (Hebrew) Leader; guide.

Majdanek A concentration camp in Lublin, Poland in operation from October 1941 to July 1944, when it was liberated by the Soviet army. More than 60,000 Jewish prisoners died at the camp.

Mensheviks (from the Russian word *men'shinstvo*, minority) A political party in Russia that split from the Russian Social Democratic Labour Party in 1903. Led by Julis Martov, the Mensheviks supported a revolution but adopted a more liberal platform than the Bolsheviks. *See also* Bolsheviks; Russian Revolution.

Obersturmführer (German; senior storm leader) A Nazi military rank. Within the SS, the role of the *Obersturmführer* could vary from Gestapo officer to concentration camp supervisor. *See also* Gestapo; SS.

Oneg Shabbat (Hebrew; Joy of Sabbath) A Friday evening or Saturday social gathering to celebrate the Sabbath, often with singing or group discussion. *See also* Sabbath.

Organization for Rehabilitation through Training (ORT) A vocational school system founded for Jews by Jews in Russia in 1880. The name ORT derives from the acronym of the Russian organization Obshestvo Remeslenogo Zemledelcheskogo Truda, Society for Trades and Agricultural Labour.

Piłsudski, Józef (1867–1935) Leader of the Second Polish Republic from 1926 to 1935. Piłsudski was largely responsible for achieving Poland's independence in 1918 after more than a century of being partitioned by Russia, Austria and Prussia. Piłsudski's regime was notable for improving the lot of ethnic minorities, including Poland's large Jewish population. He followed a policy of "state assimilation" whereby citizens were judged not by their ethnicity but by their loyalty to the state. Many Polish Jews felt that his regime was key to keeping the antisemitic currents in Poland in check; many voted for him and actively participated in his political bloc. When he died in 1935, the quality of life of Poland's Jews deteriorated once again.

Płaszów A labour camp constructed on two Jewish cemeteries in a suburb of Krakow in 1942 and enlarged to become a concentration camp in January 1944. Płaszów was also used as a transit camp – more than 150,000 people passed through the camp, many en route to Auschwitz. About 80,000 were murdered in the camp itself, either by execution or through hard labour. By mid-1944, Płaszów held more than 20,000 prisoners; inmates were used for slave labour in the quarry or railway construction and were subject to the volatile whims of camp commandant Amon Göth, who was personally responsible for more than 8,000 deaths. *See also* Göth, Amon.

pogrom (Russian; to wreak havoc, to demolish) A violent attack on a distinct ethnic group. The term most commonly refers to nineteenth and twentieth-century attacks on Jews in the Russian Empire.

Polish Scout movement (in Polish, Związek Harcerstwa Polskiego, ZHP) A youth organization that began in 1910 and was officially established in 1918. The Scouts were a social and educational group that taught Polish history and values, and basic military training. During World War II, the Nazis declared the group a criminal organization and killed many of its members and leaders. The Scouts continued to exist underground, collaborating with the Polish Home Army and taking part in resistance activities. The legal status of the Scouts was restored between 1945 and 1949, when it was banned by the Polish Communist government. The organization began operating again in 1953 under government control and is still in existence today.

Purim (Hebrew; literally, lots) The celebration of the Jews' escape from annihilation in Persia. The story revolves around Haman, advisor to the King of Persia, who planned to murder the Jews, but his plot was foiled by Queen Esther and her cousin Mordecai, who convinced the king to save them. Purim, during which people masquerade as one of the figures in the Purim story, is celebrated with parades, costumes and a retelling of the story.

Ravensbrück The largest Nazi concentration camp created almost exclusively for women that was established in May 1939 and located about 90 kilometres north of Berlin. Throughout the war, subcamps were built in the area around Ravensbrück to serve as forced labour camps. From 1942 on, the complex served as one of the main training facilities for female SS guards. Medical experiments were carried out on the women at Ravensbrück and in early 1945 the SS built a gas chamber, where approximately 5,000 to 6,000 prisoners were murdered. More than 100,000 women prisoners from all over Nazi-occupied Europe had passed through Ravensbrück before the Soviets liberated the camp on April 29–30, 1945. Approximately 50,000 women died in the camp.

Red Cross A humanitarian organization founded in 1863 to protect the victims of war. During World War II the Red Cross provided assistance to prisoners of war by distributing food parcels and monitoring the situation in POW camps, and also provided medical attention to wounded civilians and soldiers. Today, in addition to the international body, there are National Red Cross and Red Crescent societies in almost every country in the world.

Roma Also known as Romani. An ethnic group primarily located in central and eastern Europe. The Roma were commonly referred to as Gypsies in the past, a term now generally considered to be derogatory, and they have often lived on the fringes of society and been subject to persecution. During the Holocaust, which the Roma refer to in Romani as the *Porajmos* – the devouring – they were stripped of their citizenship under the Nuremberg Laws and targeted for death under Hitler's race policies. The estimation of how many Roma were killed varies widely and has been difficult to document; estimations generally range between 200,000 and one million.

Rosh Hashanah (Hebrew) New Year. The autumn holiday that marks the beginning of the Jewish year and ushers in the High Holy Days. It is observed by a synagogue service that ends with blowing the *shofar* (ram's horn). The service is usually followed by a family dinner where sweet foods, such as apples and honey, are eaten to symbolize and celebrate a sweet new year. *See also* Yom Kippur.

Russian Revolution The 1917 February and October revolutions that led to the dissolution of the autocratic tsarist regime and the creation of a Communist government, respectively. The provisional government, which was established after the February revolt, was defeated by the Bolsheviks in October. The Bolshevik government – also referred to as the "reds" – was subsequently challenged by the "whites" or anti-Bolsheviks, which resulted in a five-year civil war. *See also* Bolsheviks.

Russo-Japanese War (1904–1905) The war between Russia and Japan that was fought over territory in Manchuria and Korea.

Rydz-Śmigły, Edward (1886–1941) Marshal of Poland and Commander-in-Chief of Poland's armed forces until Poland fell to the Germans in 1939.

Sabbath (in Hebrew, Shabbat; in Yiddish, Shabbes, Shabbos) The weekly day of rest beginning Friday at sunset and ending Saturday at sundown, ushered in by the lighting of candles on Friday night and the recitation of blessings over wine and challah (egg bread); a day of celebration as well as prayer, it is customary to eat three festive meals, attend synagogue services and refrain from doing any work or travelling. *See also* Oneg Shabbat.

Shema Yisrael (Hebrew; "Hear, O Israel") The first two words of a section of the Torah and an extremely important prayer in Judaism. The full verse is "Hear, O Israel: the Lord is our God, the Lord is one" and refers to faith and loyalty in one God, which is the essence of Judaism. The *Shema* prayer comprises three verses in the Torah and observant Jews recite the *Shema* twice daily, morning and evening.

shmirah (Hebrew) Guard duty.

Simchat Torah (Hebrew; literally, rejoicing in the Torah) The holiday that marks the end of the annual cycle of readings from the Torah and the beginning of a new one. The holiday is celebrated in synagogue by singing and dancing with the Torah scrolls.

Skarżysko-Kamienna A town in east-central Poland that also became the site of a Nazi forced labour camp after the town's entire Jewish population was deported to the Treblinka death camp in

1942. Between October 1942 and August 1, 1944, when the camp was dissolved, 25,000 to 30,000 Jews were brought to Skarżysko-Kamienna; 18,000 to 23,000 of them died there.

Soprotimis Abbreviation of Sociedad de Protección a los Immigrantes Israelites (Spanish; in English, Society for Protection of Jewish Immigrants). An organization established in 1922 to help immigrants settle in Argentina by providing them with legal, social and financial aid.

Spanish Civil War (1936–1939) The war in Spain between the military – supported by Conservative, Catholic and fascist elements, together called the Nationalists – and the Republican government. Sparked by an initial coup that failed to win a decisive victory, the country was plunged into a bloody civil war. It ended when the Nationalists, under the leadership of General Francisco Franco, marched into Madrid. During the civil war, the Nationalists received aid from both Fascist Italy and Nazi Germany, and the Republicans received aid from volunteers worldwide.

SS Abbreviation of Schutzstaffel (Defence Corps). The SS was established in 1925 as Adolf Hitler's elite corps of personal bodyguards. Under the direction of Heinrich Himmler, its membership grew from 280 in 1929 to 50,000 when the Nazis came to power in 1933, and to nearly a quarter of a million on the eve of World War II. The SS was comprised of the Allgemeine-SS (General SS) and the Waffen-SS (Armed, or Combat SS). The General SS dealt with policing and the enforcement of Nazi racial policies in Germany and the Nazi-occupied countries. An important unit within the SS was the Reichssicherheitshauptamt (RSHA, the Central Office of Reich Security), whose responsibility included the Gestapo (Geheime Staatspolizei). The SS ran the concentration and death camps, with all their associated economic enterprises, and also fielded its own Waffen-SS military divisions, including some recruited from the occupied countries. *See also* Gestapo.

SS-Totenkopfverbände (German; Death's-Head Units) The Nazi unit responsible for administering the concentration camps in occupied Europe. To distinguish its members from those in the *Totenkopf* unit, the skull insignia was worn on the right collar of the uniform. *See also* Death's Head; SS.

SS *Zug Kommando* (German) Platoon Command in the SS.

Star of David (in Hebrew, *Magen David*) The six-pointed star that is the ancient and most recognizable symbol of Judaism. During World War II, Jews in Nazi-occupied areas were frequently forced to wear a badge or armband with the Star of David on it as an identifying mark of their lesser status and to single them out as targets for persecution.

Starzyński, Stefan (1893–1943) Polish politician and statesman who became mayor of Warsaw in 1934 and improved economic and cultural conditions in the city. During the 1939 siege of Warsaw, Starzyński was provided with many opportunities to escape the city along with other government officials, but chose to stay and both participate in and direct the defense of the city. He was known for his morale-boosting radio broadcasts and for organizing food and shelter for those who had been bombed out. Starzyński was arrested by the Gestapo in October 1939 and, although his fate has never been officially determined, most accounts state that he was killed at the Dachau concentration camp in 1943.

Treaty of Versailles One of the five treaties produced at the 1919 Paris Peace Conference organized by the victors of World War I. The Treaty of Versailles imposed a harsh and punitive peace on Germany, including high reparations, restrictions on German military rearmament and activities, and the redrawing of Germany's borders, which resulted in the loss of territory.

Tsar Alexander III (1845–1894) Also known as Alexander Alexandrovich, he ruled Russia from 1881 until his death. An autocrat and nationalist, Tsar Alexander III persecuted Jewish citizens by barring them from residing in certain rural areas and restricting employment.

Umschlagplatz (German; collection place) The area in the Warsaw ghetto that was connected to a freight train station, where Jews were assembled for deportation. A memorial was built on the site in 1988.

Volksdeutsche The term used by the Nazis to refer to the ethnic Germans living outside Germany in Central and Eastern Europe. Prior to World War II, there were more than ten million ethnic Germans living in these countries, some of whose families had been there for centuries. When the Nazis occupied these territories, they intended to reclaim the *Volksdeutsche* as Germans and strengthen their communities as a central part of creating the Nazis' ideal of a Greater Germany. Ethnic Germans were often given the choice either to sign the *Volksliste*, the list of German people, and be regarded as traitors by their home countries, or not to sign and be treated as traitors to the "Germanic race" by the Nazi occupiers. After the collapse of Nazi Germany most *Volksdeutsche* were persecuted by the post-war authorities in their home countries.

Warsaw ghetto An area designated by the Germans that approximately 400,000 Jews were forced to relocate to in October 1940. The ghetto was enclosed by a ten-foot wall and the conditions inside were horrendous – between 1940 and mid-1942, more than 83,000 people died of starvation and disease. Mass deportations to the Treblinka death camp were carried out between July and September 1942. See also *Umschlagplatz*.

Warsaw Ghetto Uprising The largest rebellion by Jews during the Holocaust, the Warsaw Ghetto Uprising developed in response to the *Gross-Aktion* – the Nazis' deportation of more than 275,000 ghetto inhabitants to slave-labour and death camps and the murder of another 30,000 of them between July and September 1942. When the Germans initiated the dissolution of the ghetto on April 19, 1943, aiming to deport all those remaining to the Treblinka death camp, about 750 organized ghetto fighters launched an insurrection. Despite some support from Jewish and Polish resistance organizations outside the ghetto, the resistance fighters were crushed by the Germans after a month on May 16, 1943. More than 56,000 were captured; about 7,000 were shot and the remainder were deported to death camps and concentration camps. *See also* Anielewicz, Mordecai; Jewish Fighting Organization; Zuckerman, Yitzhak.

Wehrmacht (German) The German army during the Third Reich.

Yiddish A language derived from Middle High German with elements of Hebrew, Aramaic, Romance and Slavic languages, and written in Hebrew characters. Spoken by Jews in east-central Europe for roughly a thousand years from the tenth century to the mid-twentieth century, it was still the most common language among European Jews until the outbreak of World War II. There are similarities between Yiddish and contemporary German.

Yom Kippur (Hebrew; literally, day of atonement) A solemn day of fasting and repentance that comes eight days after Rosh Hashanah, the Jewish New Year, and marks the end of the high holidays. *See also* Rosh Hashanah.

Zamenhof, Lidia (1904–1942) The youngest daughter of Ludwig Zamenhof, creator of Esperanto, she taught the language and also translated many Polish works into Esperanto. Zamenhof taught abroad in the US in 1937, returned to Poland in 1938 and was later incarcerated in the Warsaw ghetto. She helped others in the ghetto by providing food and medicine. Polish Esperantists tried to help her escape the ghetto but she refused, opting to stay with her family and community. She was deported to the Treblinka death camp in 1942, where she was murdered. *See also* Esperanto.

Zuckerman, Yitzhak (1915–1981) Also known by the spelling Icchak Cukierman, Zuckerman was Deputy Commander of the Jewish Fighting Organization (JFO) and leader of the Dror Zionist youth movement in the Warsaw ghetto. Zuckerman, who went by the pseudonym "Antek" during the war, first established underground education in the ghetto and later became involved in organizing armed resistance. As Deputy Commander of the JFO his role was to act as liaison with the Polish underground – the Armia Krajowa (Home Army) and the Armia Ludowa (People's Army) – to amass weapons and cooperate in resistance work. Zuckerman was acting in this role, outside the ghetto, when the Warsaw Ghetto Uprising began. Unable to enter the ghetto to fight, he arranged for some fighters to be evacuated from the ghetto through the sewer system. After the uprising, Zuckerman worked with partisans and helped Jews in hiding. In 1947, he and his wife, Zivia Lubetkin, moved to pre-state Israel and founded the Ghetto Fighters' kibbutz and museum. *See also* Czerniaków; Jewish Fighting Organization; Warsaw Ghetto Uprising.

Zwangsarbeitslager (German) Forced labour camp.

Photographs

1   Elsa Thon (back row, second from the left), age twelve, in a school photo. Pruszków, 1935.

2   Elsa's sister, Regina, in a photo Elsa took while working at the Abramowicz photography studio when she was fourteen. Pruszków, 1937.

3   The Bielec photo studio in Krakow, where Elsa worked between 1942 and 1943. Photo credit: Elwina Pokrywka

Elsa and her husband, Mayer Thon, after the war. Lodz, 1946.

Elsa's aunt Dina (centre) with her children before the war. From left to right are Elsa's cousins Toby, Marysia, Benjamin and Itzhak. Pruszków, circa 1930.

1 Elsa in her mid-twenties. Israel, circa 1948.
2 Elsa and her children, Sonia and Nathan, circa 1954.
3 Elsa's children with their extended family in Argentina. In the back is her cousin Benjamin's son, Sergio; in the middle row, Benjamin's daughter Berta (left), is beside Elsa's daughter, Sonia; and in the front row, Elsa's son, Nathan (left), is beside Benjamin's granddaughter, Diana. Buenos Aires, circa 1956.
4 Benjamin's daughter Susanna Synalewicz.

1 Elsa and her children, Sonia and Nathan, in Argentina. Circa 1965.
2 Mayer, Elsa and Nathan in Argentina in the mid-1970s.

1 Nathan at his graduation from university in Buenos Aires with his wife, Lucia.

2 Elsa with her daughter, Sonia, and her granddaughter, Naomi, after Sonia was awarded her PhD from the University of Toronto.

3 Elsa and Mayer with their family at grandson Joshua's admission to the bar. From left to right: Joshua's wife, Cindy; Joshua; Jonathan's wife, Lauren; Elsa's grandson Jonathan; Sonia; Nathan; and Nathan's wife, Lucia. Toronto, 2012.

1 The Thon family soon after Nathan's arrival in Toronto in the mid-1980s. From left to right: Mayer, Naomi, Sonia, Lucia, Elsa and Nathan. Seated in front are Joshua (left) and Jonathan (right).

2 Elsa's childhood friend Halina with her family in Toronto in the 1980s.

1 Elsa and family at the inauguration of the Canadian Society for Yad Vashem's Wall of Remembrance Holocaust memorial at Earl Bales Park, where her parents' names are engraved. Joshua and Nathan are in the back row; in front, Elsa, Lucia and Mayer. Toronto, 2001.

2 Elsa speaking at Holocaust Remembrance Day, with member of parliament Art Eggleton standing behind her on the far left. Toronto, 2002.

3 Elsa signing the Spanish edition of her memoir. Buenos Aires, 2000.

1 The Thon family in the 1990s.
2 Elsa's great-grandson, Matthew.
3 Elsa's granddaughter, Naomi, celebrating Rosh Hashanah with Mayer and Nathan. Toronto, circa 2005.

1 Mayer, Joshua, Jonathan and Nathan. Toronto, circa 2006.
2 Mayer and Elsa. Toronto, 2007.

Elsa. Toronto, 2007.

Index

The Azrieli Foundation was established in 1989 to realize and extend the philanthropic vision of David J. Azrieli, C.M., C.Q., M.Arch. The Foundation's mission is to support a wide spectrum of initiatives in education and research. The Azrieli Foundation is an active supporter of programs in the fields of Jewish education, the education of architects, scientific and medical research, and education in the arts. The Azrieli Foundation's many well-known initiatives include: the Holocaust Survivor Memoirs Program, which collects, preserves, publishes and distributes the written memoirs of survivors in Canada; the Azrieli Institute for Educational Empowerment, an innovative program successfully working to keep at-risk youth in school; and the Azrieli Fellows Program, which promotes academic excellence and leadership on the graduate level at Israeli universities.